THE IMPACT OF
FEMINIST RESEARCH
IN THE ACADEMY

THE IMPACT OF FEMINIST RESEARCH IN THE ACADEMY

EDITED BY
CHRISTIE FARNHAM

FOR
THE WOMEN'S STUDIES PROGRAM OF INDIANA UNIVERSITY

INDIANA UNIVERSITY PRESS *Bloomington and Indianapolis*

Manufactured in the United States of America

Library of Congress Cataloging-in-Publication Data

The Impact of feminist research in the academy.

1. Women's studies—United States.   2. Women's
studies—Indiana.   3. Feminism—United States.
4. Feminism—Indiana.   I. Farnham, Christie.
II. Indiana University, Bloomington.   Women's
Studies Program.
HQ1181.U5I48   1987   305.4'2'0973   87-45098
ISBN 0-253-32807-1
ISBN 0-253-20448-8 (pbk.)

1 2 3 4 5 91 90 89 88

To the Women's Studies Program of Indiana University

CONTENTS

Paradigmatic Implications

EDITOR'S ACKNOWLEDGMENTS

This collection was initially planned by the Coordinating Committee of Indiana University's Women's Studies Program, whose members, in addition to myself as director, included Kathy Caras, Nancy Demand, Joan Hoff-Wilson, Catherine Hoyser, Cory Krupp, Elyce Rotella, Sylvia Stalker, Gayle Stuebe, and Robyn Wiegman. Numerous other members of the Program's adjunct faculty provided advice, including Susan Gubar, Marjorie Hershey, Margaret Intons-Peterson, Anya Royce, and Mary Jo Weaver. This volume received the financial support of the College of Arts and Sciences, the Women's Studies Program, and private gifts. And finally, the Program wishes to thank the contributors themselves who have agreed to donate all royalties from the collection to the Women's Studies Endowment Fund.

THE IMPACT OF
FEMINIST RESEARCH
IN THE ACADEMY

INTRODUCTION

THE SAME OR DIFFERENT?

Christie Farnham

Women's studies programs, as the academic arm of the feminist movement, are central to the development and elaboration of feminist theory as well as being the locus for much of the research presently being done in the United States on women. But perhaps the single most important function of these programs is that of conservator of feminist learning—a sort of bureaucratic bastion against the suppression of the feminist perspective—so that history will not be forced to repeat itself, the wheel to be reinvented, before future generations come to realize, like those who came of age in the nineteen fifties, that there is more to feminism than gaining the vote.

The first women's studies program was established only as recently as 1970 at San Diego State University (Boxer, 1982); yet, in the short space of a little more than fifteen years an enormous corpus of scholarship has been produced whose importance lies in its paradigmatic implications for almost all the traditional disciplines. Indiana University has been one of the pioneers of this movement, offering its first women's studies course in 1970 and founding its program in 1973 (Dwyer, 1983).

This volume of essays was conceived by the Coordinating Committee of Indiana's Women's Studies Program as a tribute to the program's first decade. The Indiana University Advocates for Women's Studies, a campus group of more than one hundred faculty members who support the program's goals, was solicited for names from which contributors were chosen. The Women's Studies Program commissioned most of the essays that appear in the following pages, several of which were also presented to the campus in a lecture series. The task given to these scholars was not so much one of surveying the literature of their respective fields as providing an interpretive analysis of women's studies scholarship from the vantage point of their years of involvement in the movement. Thus, these essays are not meant to be comprehensive but rather insightful, reflecting their authors' experiences working in this new interdisciplinary field.

1

Several themes emerge from these assessments. Unlike the pessimism expressed in earlier disciplinary analyses (see, for example, Spender, 1981; Langland Gove, 1983; and DuBois et al., 1985) which deplore the ghettoization of feminist research, these authors tend to see the neglect of research findings by the establishment as evidence of the pattern Thomas Kuhn identified in the sciences (Kuhn, 1962), whereby new paradigms fail to convince established researchers and must await the rise of a new generation of scholars before attaining general acceptance. The new paradigms in women's studies are based on a shift in focus from male to female-and-male. Such an inclusive perspective throws into sharp relief the inadequacies of previous theory building and research design, as Carol Gilligan's work demonstrates. Nor is it just a matter of incorporating women into the equation that necessitates a paradigm shift. Such shifts may also occur when a concept considered important to the female experience, as shown by Carol Christ's discussion of the goddess, is inserted into the structure of a discipline, for this insertion calls into question the very nature of that structure.

The essays that follow are grouped under four heads. In "The Articulation of Gender as an Analytical Category" Louise Lamphere and Joan Wallach Scott analyze the different approaches that have been taken to scholarship on women in anthropology and history. Lamphere sees research on the differences among women and Scott the research linking gender to the workings of power as the most promising avenues for future concentration. Research strategies are examined under "Methodological Moves from Margin to Center." Carol P. Christ proposes a model of eros and empathy to replace the false dualism of objective and subjective types of research. Carol Gilligan demonstrates the problems that are raised when females are omitted from the mapping of human development and proposes that the addition of interdependence will not only provide better mapping of women's moral development but will permit us to see how the "parent is nurtured by the child, how the teacher learns from the student, how the therapist is healed by the patient, and how the researcher is informed by the subject." Carol Jacklin describes how including women as both researchers and subjects shifts the prevailing paradigm in psychology away from that of the idealized individual to one including a range of differences. In "The Sticking Power of Stereotypes" Ruth Bleier, Barbara Bergmann, Virginia Sapiro, and Nellie McKay trace the impact of conventional stereotypes of women on their respective disciplines. Ironically, it is the lack of objectivity in science that has permitted an all-too-ready acceptance of what are essentially unproven explanations of unproven gender differences. According to Bergmann, traditional gender ideology still retains a firm grip on economics as well, with the New Home Economics advancing a conventional attempt to support traditional gender roles in the guise of a perspective drawn from analyzing national imports and exports. Virginia Sapiro finds political socialization still framed for the most part in traditional terms. Nevertheless, she shows the ways in which feminist research offers the best hope of moving the field forward. Nellie McKay describes how early black women writers sought to dispel negative stereotypes and compares their work to contemporary black women's fiction in which black women are presented in all of their complexity. Finally, the section on "Paradigmatic Implications" explores the notion of paradigm shifts. Both Jessie Bernard and Carolyn Heilbrun are sanguine about the eventual acceptance of the feminist paradigm.

The Prison of Our Frame of Reference

The nineteenth century witnessed the popularity of what Barbara Welter has termed the cult of true womanhood (Welter, 1966), or what was popularly known as the doctrine of "separate spheres." Man's appropriate sphere was the world, where he ruled by law; woman's sphere was the home, where she reigned by persuasion. A lady was thought to be inherently nurturant, morally superior to man, self-sacrificing, self-abnegating, submissive, pure, and pious. If she were not, she was no lady—indeed, she was unsexed, according to her contemporaries. Carl Degler sees the sharply differentiated functions of spouses as related to the emergence of the modern family (1980, 26), and although controversy continues over whether this cultural ideal was more or less restricting than what had gone before, nevertheless it clearly was society's rationalization for male privilege: Men and women are treated differently because they are inherently different.

Thus, it should come as no surprise to find that early American feminists chose to base their attack upon male privilege on the assertion of the equality of the sexes. Fifteen years before feminists organized at Seneca Falls, Angelina Grimké, rebuked by the Pastoral Letter of the Congregational clergy for speaking in public in the course of her fight against slavery, responded in *Letters on the Equality of the Sexes* that God had created woman as man's equal, not as his dependent. From this position she argued that "whatsoever is morally right for a man to do, it is morally right for a woman to do" (Lerner, 1971, 192–93). In 1848 the convention at Seneca Falls opened its Declaration of Sentiments with the assertion that "we hold these truths to be self-evident: that all men and women are created equal . . ." (Kraditor, 1970, 50). These early feminists focused primarily on public rights denied to women, like married women's property rights. Nevertheless, they still thought of themselves as ladies, and only a few, like Paulina Wright Davis, Elizabeth Cady Stanton, and Lucy Stone, recognized the significance of marriage and sexuality for women's autonomy.

The number of early feminists was small; most women thought that they were not unequal to men—just different. The newer generation of feminists who took their places in 1890 with the merger of the American and National Woman Suffrage Associations was less radical than its predecessors. Discarding the argument for equality, they turned to the notion of separate spheres from which they lifted the claim of woman's moral superiority. By this logic women deserved the vote, for as one suffragist explained, "No longer is home encompassed by four walls. Many of its most important duties lie now involved in the bigger family of the city and state" (Kraditor, 1971, 52). Although such a reinterpretation of the prevailing Victorian cultural ideal undoubtedly hastened the passage of the suffrage amendment (giving pause to feminists who failed to pass the Equal Rights Amendment), it also had the effect of ratifying those differences upon which so many of women's disabilities had been founded.

The second wave of feminism, like the first, grew out out of the struggle for the rights of blacks; and, also like the first, it emphasized equality and traced the oppression of women to false notions of inherent differences between the sexes. Hester Eisenstein argues that feminist thought "concentrated on establishing the distinction between sex and gender, and developed an analysis of sex roles as a mode of social control" which was new and was "explicitly or implicitly" an argument for androgyny (Eisenstein, 1983, xi). Feminist research focused upon the socialization of women, and the combination of media attention, the disjunction between women's educational and work experiences, and the image of the happy homemaker gave the second wave of feminism a mass appeal unknown to their foremothers and, as a consequence, raised expectations. However, women's attempts to enter the world of men were only partially successful, due to the national resurgence of conservatism. American women began to feel that they had exchanged the kitchen sink for a typewriter—not a briefcase.

Once again, feminists are returning to the cult of true womanhood in order to celebrate the feminine-labeled characteristic of nurturance, especially as it relates to peace and caring relationships. A similar phenomenon occurred in the late sixties and seventies within the black community, with the emergence of Black Power. Disillusioned by the pace of change and disgusted by the unrelenting torment of white violence, blacks began to denounce assimilation and to celebrate those aspects of black culture that contrasted with the dominant culture. Black Power has many meanings, ranging from revolution to cultural nationalism. Similarly, feminist thought of the eighties ranges from attempts to discover those aspects of women's experience that have been special sources of strength to arguments for a female essence out of which blossoms a superior subculture (see, for example, discussions in Eisenstein, McFadden, and Jardine). In the latter sense feminist thought is retracing the steps of the suffragists in arguing from innately superior differences.

Both strategies in the struggle for women's autonomy, i.e., the argument for equality and the argument for differences, have produced gains. The argument for equality is most appealing in the heady days of a movement when all things seem possible, the argument for differences when disillusionment sets in. The egalitarian argument encourages the development of analyses of opportunity structures, and it benefits from the cultural consensus that exists around democratic values. But, as other ethnic and racial groups have discovered, something is lost in the process. Not everything about the dominant culture is worthy of emulation, and not everything developed within the confines assigned by the dominant class is thereby worthless, simply because it developed out of victimization or dependency or limited opportunity or by filling the interstices of the system that the dominant class found of too little value to occupy. There is no equality if the standards of the dominant class are the only ones applied and the positive attributes of the victims are ignored. Yet, the celebration of differences increases women's vulnerability to oppression by providing for its rationalization, even as the insistence upon equality obscures what has been forged in the crucible of adversity.

The tension between these two positions is a creative one, as feminist scholarship in this collection makes clear; but as long as questions remain framed in terms of traditional masculine and feminine characteristics that are stereotypical of the Euro-American experience, feminist theory building will be imprisoned in a neo-Victorian frame of limited possibilities. Margaret Mead has been influential among feminists in showing that many characteristics of traditional sex roles are classified differently in other cultures (see, especially, *Sex and Temperament in Three Primitive Societies,* 1935). Nonetheless, the implications of this fact have yet to be fully realized. To celebrate certain characteristics like nurturance as feminine is to limit them to one sex; whereas, to work for androgyny is to stitch together categories of opposites. Both these strategies have the effect of reinforcing the connection between trait and sex. Although this has been highly productive, it has the potential for being culturally bound, universalizing from the experiences of white women in the same way, though not to the same extent, as men have generalized to women.

What happens to theory and analysis when traits thought to be masculine in terms of traditional gender ideology are part of the core identity of one group of American women? Such is the case for black women who see themselves as providers, a key component of white middle-class masculinity. This characteristic of black women has roots in West African traditional societies, where women were generally responsible for feeding their husbands and children. Men and women often had separate incomes and separate obligations. Women's obligation to feed their families was facilitated by the practice of elders in parceling land out to individual women for their own use. Any surplus remaining after the needs of their families were met belonged to the women, since resources were not pooled as is the case in white, middle-class, nuclear families. The existence of surpluses encouraged the development of female entrepreneurship, which often took the form of petty trading. Women formed organizations to regulate the marketplace, and some achieved wealth and status through trade. Thus, providing for their families was not only a primary obligation but a core part of female identity under which a constellation of other characteristics might be subsumed that also have a masculine connotation in America, e.g., strength, competence, leadership, etc. (see Sudarkasa 1981a, 1981b; Robertson and Klein, 1983; Brooks, 1976).

Black Americans have been influenced by this heritage, which was further reinforced under slavery by the use of female agricultural labor. Although some historians like Stanley Elkins see the provisioning of the slave family as a usurpation by the master of the male slave's prerogative (Elkins, 1959, 130), an argument can be made that the slaves saw it differently. They often "took" food from the kitchen and storehouse, but they did not consider this to be stealing, since they grew the food (Genovese, 602). In fact, women were proud of their strength and competence in the field, and there is nothing in the historical record to indicate that black men felt they were any less feminine because of it.

After Emancipation black women realized that death and desertion, the twin evils of segregation and the economic dependence on white males, might leave them the sole providers of their families (Jones, 1985). Despite the buffeting of cultural images of white women, fragile and in need of a man, the realities of life forced black women to retain the identity of the provider as it was embodied and celebrated in the image of the strong woman surviving. This was not necessarily the image of a woman who was physically strong but of one whose strength came from her commitment to her family and to her race, which she demonstrated by her ability to endure and to put food on the table despite the long hours and low pay of menial jobs (Hooks, 83).

Traditional gender ideology demarcates traits along a line of dependency. Yet, black women's gender identity has not been based on dependent relationships with men. Nor has this threatened their femininity. Thus, a larger frame of reference is needed for analyzing sexism. One crucial area that has received inadequate attention in terms of access to power is that of the domestic division of labor. Despite the fact that power is incorporated at the societal level in the public sphere, access to that sphere remains limited so long as women are responsible for the domestic sphere. Cross-culturally, men have been successful to a large degree in resisting domestic labor. In America, both black and white women have been unable to effect an equitable distribution of labor in the home (Blumstein and Schwartz, 1983).

Future analyses that take into account the differences among women and the ways in which gender relates to the workings of power in a given society have the potential for extricating the argument from the equal versus different controversy. Recognizing that femininity and masculinity are myths will open up new frames of reference with the potential for even greater explanatory power in the study of the nature of sexism in human society. The essays in this collection point the way to paradigms of increasing complexity, a complexity that comes closer than the previous dualism to mirroring the human experience.

WORKS CITED

Blumstein, Philip W. and Pepper Schwartz. *American Couples: Money, Work, and Sex.* New York: William Morrow, 1983.

Boxer, Marilyn. "For and About Women: The Theory and Practice of Women's Studies." *Signs* (1982):661–95.

Brooks, George E. "The Signares of Saint-Louis and Gorée: Women Entrepreneurs in Eighteenth-Century Senegal." In Nancy J. Hafkin and Edna G. Bay, eds., *Women in Africa: Studies in Social and Economic Change.* Stanford: Stanford University Press, 1976.

Degler, Carl. *At Odds: Women and the Family in America from the Revolution to the Present.* New York: Oxford University Press, 1980.

DuBois, Ellen Carol et al. *Feminist Scholarship: Kindling in the Groves of Academe.* Urbana and Chicago: University of Illinois Press, 1985.

Dwyer, Ellen. "Women's Studies at the Beginning." *Women's Studies in Indiana* (September 1983): 1–2.

Eisenstein, Hester. *Contemporary Feminist Thought.* Boston: G. K. Hall, 1983.

Elkins, Stanley. *Slavery: A Problem in American Intellectual and Institutional Life.* Chicago: University of Chicago Press, 1959.

Genovese, Eugene D. *Roll, Jordan, Roll: The World the Slaves Made.* New York: Vantage 1972.

Hooks, Bell. *Ain't I a Woman: Black Women and Feminism.* Boston: South End Press, 1981.

Jardine, Alice. "Prelude: The Future of Difference." In Hester Eisenstein and Alice Jardine, eds., *The Future of Difference.* Boston: G. K. Hall, 1980.

Jones, Jacqueline. *Labor of Love, Labor of Sorrow: Black Women, Work, and the Family from Slavery to the Present.* New York: Basic Books, 1985.

Kraditor, Aileen. *The Ideas of the Woman Suffrage Movement, 1890–1920.* New York: Doubleday, 1971.

——, ed. *Up from the Pedestal.* New York: Quadrangle, 1970.

Kuhn, Thomas. *The Structure of Scientific Revolutions.* Chicago: University of Chicago Press, 1962.

Langland, Elizabeth and Walter Gove, eds. *A Feminist Perspective in the Academy: The Difference It Makes.* Chicago: University of Chicago Press, 1983.

Lerner, Gerda. *The Grimké Sisters of South Carolina.* New York: Schocken, 1971.

McFadden, Maggie. "Anatomy of Difference: Toward a Classification of Feminist Theory." *Women's Studies International Forum* (1984): 495–504.

Mead, Margaret. *Sex and Temperament in Three Primitive Societies.* New York: Morrow, 1935.

Robertson, Claire C. and Martin A. Klein, "Women's Importance in African Slave Systems." In Robertson and Klein, eds., *Women and Slavery in Africa.* Madison: University of Wisconsin Press, 1983.

Spender, Dale, ed. *Men's Studies Modified: The Impact of Feminism on the Academic Disciplines.* Oxford: Pergamon, 1981.

Sudarkasa, Niara. "Female Employment and Family Organization in West Africa." In Filomina Chioma Steady, ed., *The Black Woman Cross-Culturally.* Cambridge: Schenkman, 1981.

——. "Interpreting the African Heritage in Afro-American Family Organization." In Harriette Pipes McAdoo, ed., *Black Families.* Beverly Hills, CA: Sage, 1981.

Welter, Barbara. "The Cult of True Womanhood." *American Quarterly* (Winter 1966): 151–69.

*The Articulation of Gender
as an Analytical Category*

FEMINISM AND ANTHROPOLOGY

THE STRUGGLE TO RESHAPE OUR THINKING ABOUT GENDER

Louise Lamphere

More than ten years have passed since women's studies programs like the one at Indiana University were founded. In anthropology, too, it has been more than a decade since the revival of interest in women was marked by the publication of *Woman, Culture, and Society* (Rosaldo and Lamphere, 1974) and *Towards an Anthropology of Women* (Reiter, 1975). Anthropology has been known as a discipline which contained important women (Margaret Mead and Ruth Benedict among the most famous) and as a field where women had been studied as well, (for example, in books by Phyllis Kayberry, 1930, 1952; Landes, 1938, 1947; Leith-Ross, 1965; Underhill, 1936; and Paulme, 1963). However, with these two collections, women scholars, many of whom identified as feminists, began to critique the androcentric bias in anthropology, to explore women's status in a wide variety of societies, and to theorize about women's position in new ways.

Since 1974 there has been a burgeoning interest within anthropology in the study of women, sex roles, and gender. This new "subfield" within anthropology has called into question many of our assumptions as well as the validity of the very categories that anthropologists use in their writing. In some respects this questioning within feminist anthropology parallels rethinking within the discipline as a whole. However, feminist work has yet to have much impact on the teaching of introductory courses and on anthropology as presented in textbooks or other subdisciplines. In order to understand both feminist anthropology and its impact on the field as a whole, it is important to first examine how this subfield has developed and been reshaped (often by the same women as they have grown and rethought the issues). Then an assessment of how this work has been received by others, both nonfeminist anthropologists and feminists in other disciplines, can be undertaken.

The First Phase: Creating a Framework and Defining an Issue

The essays in *Woman, Culture, and Society* emerged from a variety of sources. Jane Collier, Shelly Rosaldo, and a number of graduate students taught a course at Stanford University in the spring of 1971, and several of these same women participated in a symposium given at the American Anthropological Association in November 1971. When Shelly showed me the notes from the course, I felt there was enough material to make the beginnings of a collection of articles. We wrote to twenty-five anthropologists who presented papers at the 1971 American Anthropological Association meetings, which in the end resulted in contributions by Sanday, Hoffer, and Denich. We contacted others through our own personal networks. Shelly brought in a number of contributors from the Stanford community (Margery Wolf, Bridget O'Laughlin, Jane Collier, Lois Paul) as well as Nancy Tanner from nearby Santa Cruz. My contacts included a number of women I had known at Harvard and or met recently through colleagues at Brown (Joan Bamberger, Karen Sacks, Nancy Leis, and Carol Stack.) The theoretical focus of the book took shape through the interaction of Shelly and two of her close friends: Nancy Chodorow and Sherry Ortner.

In Shelly's overview and in the introduction we wrote, we were faced with building a framework where none existed. Margaret Mead's work on sex and temperament was not about women's status, but the quotation we used from her 1950 book, *Male and Female*, pointed to the universality of sexual asymmetry. "Men may cook, or weave, or dress dolls or hunt hummingbirds, but if such activities are appropriate occupations of men, then the whole society, men and women alike, votes them as important. When the same occupations are performed by women, they are regarded as less important." The pervasiveness of sexual asymmetry or the subordination made sense given the range of ethnographic data the Stanford anthropologists had examined in their course and our perusal of the literature. The task, as our quote from Simone de Beauvoir's *Second Sex* suggested, was to develop an explanation.

The essays by Rosaldo, Ortner, and Chodorow offered an integrated set of explanations for sexual asymmetry, each at a different level, that is, in terms of social structure, culture, and socialization. All three note that in every society women bear and raise children and that women's socially and culturally defined role as mother provides the basis for subordination.

Rosaldo argued, for example, that motherhood and the "domestic orienta-tion of women" sets up the opposition between a domestic and a political sphere.

> Put quite simply, men have no single commitment as enduring, time-consuming, and emotionally compelling—as close to seeming necessary and natural—as the relation of a woman to her infant child; and so men are free to form those broader associations that we call "society," universalistic systems of order, meaning and commitment that link particular mother-child groups.
> [Rosaldo, 1974, 24]

Women thus are involved in the "messiness" of daily life; they are always available for interruption by children. Men can be more distant and may actually have separate quarters (such as men's houses) away from women's activities. Men can thus "achieve" authority and create rank, hierarchy, and a political world away from women. The confinement of women to a domestic sphere and men's ability to create and dominate the political sphere thus accounts for men's ability to hold the greater share of power and authority in all known cultures and societies.

In emphasizing cultural evaluations rather than social structure, Ortner began her article with the Lévi-Straussian dichotomy between nature and culture, and argued that every culture sees itself as different from the world of animals, plants, and the natural environment. Ortner built a case that women are universally seen as closer to nature, while men are associated with culture. Since women are seen as closer to nature, they are in a middle status and ambiguous, hence seen as dangerous and polluting. In every culture, Ortner argued, one finds evidence that women's roles are *explicitly* devalued or seen as less prestigious, they are *implicitly* devalued through an ideology of pollution, or women are excluded from participation in some realm in which the highest powers of society are thought to reside. Beliefs that menstrual blood is polluting or the exclusion of women from an important ritual are thus indicators of women's inferior position in a culture, one that can be accounted for by their association with nature rather than culture. Finally, Chodorow showed how a woman's role as mother leads to the creation of different male and female gender person-alities and the reproduction of subordination. In any given society, "femi-nine personality comes to define itself in relation and connection to other people more than masculine personality does" (1974, 44). Women tend to identify more with daughters than sons and push little boys to assume a masculine identity separate and in opposition to them. The boy does this by "repressing whatever he takes to be feminine inside himself, and, importantly, by denigrating and devaluing what he takes to be feminine in the outside world," (1974, 50). Chodorow argued that middle-class women often grow up without firm ego boundaries nor a clear sense of self. In other societies (particularly the Javanese, the Atjeh, and among working-class families in London) women's mothering in a different social context may be characterized by companionship and mutual cooperation and be positively valued rather than characterized by overwhelming guilt and responsibility.

The argument for universal sexual asymmetry followed in a long tradition in anthropology where scholars have sought to look for what is broadly "human" in all cultures. In addition to language, anthropologists have discussed the universality of the incest taboo, marriage, and the family. The notion that women might be universally subordinate to men, thus, made sense as a first attempt at theory building in this newly revived "subfield" within anthropology. Although these three articles argued for universal subordination, they were careful to make clear that there are important variations in women's roles in different cultures. And variation was the theme that was taken up in most of the rest of the articles in the collection. For example, Sanday and Sacks compared women's status in a number of different societies, while Leis examined the structural reasons why women's associations are strong in one Ijaw village in Nigeria, yet absent in another. Finally, in my own article I examined the differences in women's strategies within domestic groups in a number of societies which related to the relative integration or separation of domestic and political spheres.

In sum, *Woman, Culture, and Society* posed an issue, "universal sexual asymmetry," which anthropologists seemed well trained to answer, and the three lead essays provided a related set of explanations for this position. This theme held the volume together and gave it a focus that made it a best-selling collection. On the other hand, it provided a position that could be debated within anthropology, a debate that perhaps overshadowed the emphasis on variability and difference that characterizes the volume as a whole. Ironically, it is this emphasis on variation that, by 1987, at least, has come to be the pervasive theme within the subfield.

Constructing a Counterargument

It is not surprising that others working on women's roles cross-culturally began to challenge the thesis of universal sexual asymmetry, almost simultaneously with the publication of *Woman, Culture, and Society*. In fact, several contributors to the collection, notably Sacks, Sanday, and Tanner, probably did not concur with the analysis of the introductory articles even in 1974. The controversy emerged most sharply over how to characterize foraging or band-level societies, although several authors argued that tribal societies like the Tlingit, Iroquois, and Hopi were egalitarian and that women and men were even in a complementary but equal position in some peasant villages (see Susan Rogers, 1978).

The egalitarian thesis has been put forward by both Marxist and non-Marxist anthropologists. Some non-Marxists, like Jean Briggs (1975) and Alice Schlegel (1977), argued that although there is a sexual division of labor among the Eskimo and the Hopi, roles are "conplementary but equal." Schlegel suggested that the Hopi are an egalitarian society, because, although there are two domains, males' power to control their persons, property, or activities may extend over a different sphere, but is not greater than women's control over their persons, property, and activities (Schlegel, 1974). The male sphere is the community and the female the household, but these spheres are interdependent and balanced (Schlegel, 1977). Likewise, Briggs characterized male and female Eskimo roles as interdependent. Men are first and foremost hunters, while women are responsible for the preparation of hides and meat, sewing, child care, and other household tasks. Women do envy men's ability to travel, hunt, and make political decisions, but they are aware that these activities require endurance and strength in harsh conditions. But women do not feel disadvantaged. In a culture where aggression is devalued and where decision-making is dispersed, their activities are as important and as valued as those of men (Briggs, 1975).

Working primarily from a Marxist perspective, Leacock, Sacks, and others have taken the argument a step further, arguing that colonialism and contact between Europeans and native peoples have transformed and undercut many native economies, in turn creating inequality between the sexes where autonomy had been the norm. Using material from the Naskapi, Leacock argued, for example, that women were autonomous in a society possessing a communal economy with no corporate control of economic resources, dispersed decision making, and interdependence of individuals (both men and women) (Leacock, 1981, 133–40). In the Iroquois case, she argued that women's autonomy became undermined with colonial contact, even as women's power became more formal (1981, 154). Sacks in her early article (1974) described the Mbuti as a communal economy where all production was of the same kind—"production for use." People worked for the communal household rather than for individuals. Decision making, both economic and political, involved the equal participation of all members, men and women. Both sexes were social producers and equal members of the group.

Other Themes

This early period of feminist thinking in anthropology also brought new analyses of the kinds of societies anthropologists study. The most important example was the rethinking of how to examine hunter-gatherer or foraging societies begun with Sally Linton's article "Woman the Gatherer"(1975). Linton's article was passed among feminist anthropologists in the period 1972–74 (as a part of a bibliography by Sue-Ellen Jacobs) before it was reprinted in Reiter's collection. It critiqued the new synthesis posed by Richard B. Lee and Irven DeVore's book *Man the Hunter* and thus had implications for the study of foraging societies in our evolutionary past as well as for the study of contemporary peoples.

Linton challenged the Man the Hunter thesis that hunting played the most crucial role in our evolutionary past, that because of the role of hunting in tool-making, communication, and even complex cognitive skills, it played the "dominant role in transforming a bipedal ape into a tool-using and tool-making man" (Laughlin, 1968, 318). Linton stresses that women's gathering and child-care activities also demanded complex communication, cooperation, and tool-making (slings for carrying children, choppers, grinders, and other tools for gathering). Linton's work was extended by Nancy Tanner and Adrianne Zihlman (Tanner and Zihlman, 1976; Zihlman, 1978; and Tanner, 1981) to re-think gender roles in human evolution. Rather than supposing that hunting was a major activity during the period of *Australopithecus* (2–4 million years ago) or *Homo erectus* (500,000 to 1 million years ago), Tanner and Zihlman proposed a much more flexible model with foraging as the major economic strategy and mother-child units as the important social groups. Big game hunting thus did not emerge as an important strategy until much later in human evolution, after the emergence of *Homo sapiens* 100,000 to 200,000 years ago. In Europe, hunting with hafted projectile points and the celebration of hunting in upper paleolithic cave paintings dates to 30,000 B.C. Even so, other adaptations may have been important in other parts of the world and any hunting-gathering social organization could be presumed to be much more complex and less rigid than current models suggest, with women continuing to take an important role in foraging.

Leila Leibowitz did much to critique and reanalyze the use of data from modern primate populations (e.g., baboons, chimpanzees, gibbons, gorillas, etc.) in the reconstruction of our evolutionary past. Rather than using the model of the male-dominated savannah baboon troop as a prototype for human behavior during the past, Leibowitz argued for the flexibility of primate behavior and its sensitivity to environmental differences. The overall picture is one of a variety of different adaptations within and between species, which leads one to be cautious in choosing one species rather than another as a model (Leibowitz, 1974, 1977).

Other work had the potential of helping us to rethink the traditional way in which other subfields of anthropology had characterized social relationships. Perhaps the best example is the implications of Jane Collier's work on "Women in Politics." Her use of the notion of strategies and her definition of women's activities even in the household as "political" had profound implications for the subfields of political anthropology and kinship and social structure. Political anthropology had tended to be the study of "public political processes," including the relationship between corporate groups and the analysis of male political leaders. By arguing that women had strategies as well as men, Collier was able to show that politics happened "at home" when a woman attempted to influence her husband, brother, or father. Such strategizing had serious implications for the formation and break-up of kin groups such as lineages. Kinship and social structural studies tended to analyze the composition and change within lineages through analysis of male inheritance and authority. Collier showed how continuity and conflict within these groups depended on women's actions as well as those of men. "Women are the worms within the apple of a patrilocal domestic group," she said (1974,92). Since they work to advance the fortunes of their husbands or sons they often create conflict that results in household or lineage fission. Collier's analysis, by placing women squarely at the center of the treatment of kinship and politics, shows how the traditional models needed to be reconceptualized.

The results of this initial period (from 1972–76) were to critique the male bias in anthropology and to reassert an interest in women's roles. The central problem and debate (universal sexual asymmetry) emerged out of an effort to explain women's position cross-culturally, an issue that seemed uniquely suited to the discipline. The positing of a universal was certainly congruent with a long history of analyzing human universals within anthropology. The focus on women opened up new possibilities for reworking and reanalyzing a number of the subfields in anthropology—particularly political anthropology and the study of kinship. It led to rethinking how we viewed hunting-gathering societies, though "bringing women to the fore" provided new analyses of tribal-level and state-level societies as well (see Reiter, 1975; Harding, 1975).

Nevertheless, the conceptual tools that feminists brought to their analyses were those from their traditional training in graduate school. The articles by Rosaldo, Collier, and myself focused on social structure and reflected the training we had received at Harvard in the early and mid-1960s. Ortner's work and its emphasis on cultural analysis and symbols had the stamp of her University of Chicago background, while it is possible to see the Michigan emphasis on history and an emerging Marxism in the work of Rapp and Sacks. As a final example, Peggy Sanday brought the tools of cross-cultural analysis (pioneered by George Peter Murdock) to bear on the issue of women's status.

The Second Phase: Building New Constructions

In a second phase, a number of authors took ideas they had formulated in the initial period and developed them into full-scale analyses that focused on a comparison of a number of societies. The two best examples are the books *Sisters and Wives* by Karen Sacks (1979) and *Female Power and Male Dominance* by Peggy Sanday (1981). Sacks expanded her analysis of four African societies and used notions of mode of production and the changing social relations of production to analyze the transition of women's status from sister to wife. Sanday, while still relying on cross-cultural methodology, examined origin myths and social structure in a large sample of societies to build a theory which accounted for female power in some societies and male dominance in others. Both were still engaged by the debate over universal sexual asymmetry and the possibility of egalitarian societies, a view that challenged the Rosaldo/Ortner/Chodorow thesis.

Other feminists embarked on specific studies of individual societies, bringing into print careful analyses of women in particular social contexts. This period also saw a spate of collections containing articles about women in different parts of the world: women in Africa (Hafkin and Bay, 1976), women in Asia (Wolf and Witke, 1975), women in Latin America (Nash and Safa, 1976), and women in the Middle East (Beck and Keddie, 1978; Fernea, 1977). These collections often included work by anthropologists, but also often included articles by women from the regions being studied. All these contributions were comparative and focused on the variability in women's roles, even if to claim, as Sacks and Sanday did, that such variability meant that in some societies men and women had equal statuses.

Toward the end of this phase, a number of new works had begun to focus on relationships between men and women, rather than on women and women's status alone. Turning away from questions of universality, these authors attempted to build frameworks for looking at diverse women's roles within a particular society and for comparing societies with one another in a more complex way. Three approaches were apparent: (1) Marxist approaches that cast relations between men and women in terms of a model of production and reproduction, (2) models that focused on marriage as the entering point of an analysis of gender relations, and (3) those that emphasized "Prestige Hierarchies" as a focal point for analysis.

One of the first important Marxist analyses of gender for American anthropologists was that of Bridget O'Laughlin (1974). In her article, "Mediation of Contradiction—Why Mbum Women Do Not Eat Chicken," she analyzes relations between men and women in terms of the technical relations of production (how work is organized by a sexual division of labor) and the social relations of production (the allocation of control over resources and products). She locates women's subordination in the contradiction between women's contributions to production and reproduction and their lack of control over their own offspring. Through the system of marriage and patrilocal residence, women are alienated from their own reproduction; they are responsible for the biological reproduction of labor and for socialization, but they have neither the moral nor political authority that this responsibility seems to imply. O'Laughlin sees these contradictions being mediated (or "pasted over) by ideology, particularly the taboo on women eating chicken or other meat (which is reserved for men); breaking the taboo consigns women to sterility. These restrictions are expressions of sexual difference and affirmations of male dominance.

O'Laughlin uses a Marxist model of gender relations to analyze how subordination works, while Janet Siskind uses a similar framework to question the universality of kinship and to suggest that asymmetry or lack of it may be grounded in a particular mode of production (1978). Thus she argues that kinship relations and mode of production are inextricably bound up with one another. Relations of production are actually kin relations in simple societies; it is through kin categories like those of husband and wife, father, mother, and sister or brother that tasks get divided, production gets organized, and one category of individuals is able to appropriate the products of others. Although she does not clearly argue for an egalitarian or hierarchical model, she does point to ways in which gender relations and the sexual division of labor can be analyzed so that one could argue for subordination or "exploitation."

Beginning with the notion that some societies are egalitarian, Karen Sacks's Marxist analysis of four African societies shows how focus on the changing relations of production can illuminate increasing gender inequality. She uses a Marxist model to explore the dynamics and change in relations between the sexes, rather than only the reproduction of gender asymmetry. She examines examples of a communal mode of production (the Pygmies), kin corporate modes of production (the Lovedu and Pondo), and state societies (the Baganda). She assumes that women do not have a single relation to the means of production and divides women into "sisters" and "wives." In the communal political economy sisters, wives, brothers, and husbands all have the same relation to productive means and resources and therefore equal power in relation to the whole. In "kin corporate" systems sisters and wives have different productive relationships. Here sisters and brothers (as in the Lovedu case) hold equal rights in lineage property, but husbands dominate wives; women as sisters have political and economic power, but in their status as wives, they are subordinate. In state societies, not only are there class differences, but women are reduced to subordinate wives and the status of sister does not entail control over productive resources. In examining the transition between the kin corporate mode of production and the state, Sacks isolates the basic contradiction that develops between the forces of production and the relationships of production and creates the dynamic that allows one group of men to come to control the means of production, and reduces other men from clients to peasants from whom wealth is extracted. This process takes place along with the subordination of women through their confinement to a status of wives or wards of their husbands (1979, 117).

These analyses focus on the relationships between men and women using a Marxist model. They neither use dualisms nor assume that women's situation is ahistorical. They neither conflate various forms of reproduction (biological reproduction, the reproduction of labor, and social reproduction) nor do they assume that only women are engaged in reproduction. This tendency toward conflation and dualism was noted in Meillassoux's book, *Maidens, Meal, and Money* (e.g., Edholm et al., 1977) and may be implicit in other Marxist analyses (e.g., see Yanagisako and Collier's critique of Harris and Young, 1985). Marxist models, in some hands, can give interesting and complex interpretations of change and be sensitive to dialectics and history, thus getting us away from more uniform and static approaches.

In contrast, Shelly Rosaldo and Jane Collier begin with marriage, rather than production, as the starting point for their analysis of gender relationships. In their joint article (1981) and in a larger manuscript by Jane Collier (1987), they posit a contrast between bride-service and bridewealth societies. Again, assuming that women and men hold a variety of statuses in any particular society, they focus on the differences between unmarried men, unmarried women, and older men and women in "simple societies" with brideservice. In these societies, including most of the hunter-gatherer examples, marriage is an achievement for men, while it puts women in the position of providing food and shelter for a husband, rather than being relatively free to flirt or eat from someone else's provisions. Marriage establishes men as having something to achieve, e.g., a wife, leaving women without such a cultural goal. Young men, through providing meat for their in-laws, become equal adults, and older men, through egalitarian relations and generosity, become the repositories of wisdom and knowledge. Politics gets focused around the issue of sexuality and around male/ male relationships, which often erupt in conflict and violence. Man the Hunter is celebrated since this ideology gives men a vehicle for establishing their claims over wives in terms of their prowess as hunters or raiders. Women have no such special privileges to justify and hence the roles of Woman the Gatherer or even Woman the Mother do not emerge as cultural themes.

In equal bridewealth and unequal bridewealth societies, marriage relationships are structured in a much different way, so that gender relationships have a much different content, politics are more hierarchical, and ideology plays a different role (see Collier, 1987). Collier argues that such "systematic models" get beyond our own assumptions about males and females, assume that there are a variety of gender roles in any culture, and allow us to understand the complex relationships between cultural interpretations and social structure.

Finally, Ortner and Whitehead in their introduction to *Sexual Meanings* suggest that we examine gender relations in terms of "prestige structures." They, too, are interested in a model that can examine gender relationships in a complex way, with attention to different male and female roles in each case. They, too, wish to combine a cultural and social analysis, though they emphasize the cultural and symbolic more than the social structural. They argue that prestige structures are partially autonomous and not reducible to class relations or the social relations of production. Moreover, gender systems are themselves prestige structures and prestige structures tend toward symbolic consistency. Statuses such as warrior, statesman, Brahmin, or elder get defined as part of a male ranking system, while women get defined as wives and mothers. Thus, there is an elaborate male hierarchy and a kin-marriage hierarchy that includes both men and women. They go on to suggest that some kinship systems emphasize the sister roles, while others emphasize roles of women as wives or mothers. In some ways, this model owes much to Rosaldo and Collier, but in others it is a different attempt to pose models that are comparative, but more complex than earlier models based on universal dichotomies.

By the end of this phase (1981) we see little attention to the issue of universals. Instead feminists have given their attention to the creation of particular models to deal with a much smaller number of comparisons, as well as a number of carefully done monographic analyses. Though feminists often are taking their concepts from other theorists (e.g., Marxist definitions of production and reproduction, Weber's concept of prestige, or Lévi-Strauss's analysis of marriage), the models that result seem more complex because of the effort to include women as part of the model.

The Third Phase: Critiquing Our Concepts

Almost simultaneously with the construction of new frameworks for comparing gender relations, has come a period of critical self-evaluation, one in which the conceptual tools used in early feminist analyses have come under attack. One line of argument came from those who proposed that dichotomies like domestic/public and nature/culture "didn't fit" the realities of other cultures. Thus, the domestic/public split failed to characterize Yoruba lineages where kin relations seemed to be both political and domestic at the same time. And, in Egypt, though there seemed to be a clear dichotomy between the private household and the public arena, women's activities in the domestic sphere had clear political implications (e.g., for marriage arrangements, for the status of men) and men were important actors in the household (Nelson, 1973, 551–64). Likewise, Marilyn Strathern argued that the Hagen conceptions of *romi* and *mbo* are not equivalent to notions of nature and culture and that the dichotomy of *nyim* (prestigious) and *korpa* (rubbish) are associated with male and female respectively. Some aspects of *romi* are associated with male and others with female. Hence, as the title of her article suggests, there is "no nature, no culture" in the Hagen case (Strathern, 1980).

A second line of argument has been to show how these dichotomies are really Western categories that have a specific historical development within our own tradition of thinking. Shelly Rosaldo, in an important critique of her own work, came to view the concepts domestic/public as a revised version of Fortes's notions of a domestic and juro-political domain. Fortes's ideas, in turn, seemed ultimately derived from Victorian notions of public and private spheres, a dichotomy that was rigidly drawn and ideologically one of the most important during the nineteenth century. Likewise, as essays by Jordanova (1980) and the Blochs (1980) show, the dichotomy of nature/culture is not just an analytic tool employed by Lévi-Strauss but a distinction that has historical roots in the Enlightenment. Notions of nature had a complex development during this period, and the association of women and the female body with either nature or civilization is often blurred or contradictory. For example, women were associated with moral virtue on the one hand and with darkness and evil on the other; in addition they were ruled by their emotions and passions, while men were the embodiment of reason and rationality.

Thus notions we intially used that were part of our anthropological "toolkit" in the 1960s turn out to be informed by our own history of gender relations. Where we once thought that to argue against concepts derived from theorists like Lévi-Strauss, Fortes, Evans-Pritchard, or Talcott Parsons was primarily a matter of theoretical preference, in the 1980s, these concepts turn out to have a cultural bias that both informed and distorted our early analysis of gender. Here feminists have begun not just to criticize male anthropologists for androcentric bias or ignoring women, but have begun to question concepts and assumptions that have been at the center of the discipline, particularly in the study of politics, kinship, and social structure.

Perhaps the most extensive questioning of our own concepts and assumptions has come through the conference on "Feminism and Kinship Theory" organized by Jane Collier and Sylvia J. Yanagisako (and Shelly Rosaldo before her death) which was held at Bellagio, Italy in August, 1982. The organizers asked participants to rethink kinship theory in light of feminist analysis, including our assumptions about the domestic and politico-jural domains, descent theory, alliance theory, and property transactions at marriage. It turned out that most participants (who included a number of feminists as well as male and female theorists who were more identified with kinship studies than with feminism) were already engaged in research that was based on premises very different from those implicit in the more traditional kinship theory of the 1940s through 1960s (Yanagisako and Collier, 1985b). Most participants had rejected the notion, for example, that kinship systems are grounded in the assumption that women bear children, men have authority over wives, and the incest taboo prohibits the mating of brothers and sisters. All took a position that gender and kinship is socially created and not just added on to "natural biological facts." Although not all participants would perhaps take the position that Collier and Yanagisako have in their overview article (1987), most seem to have gone beyond notions of domestic and political or even conceptions of what constitutes "patrilineality," to particular analysis that are more historical or argue for the unique social construction of some aspect of kinship or gender from an individual case (see Tsing and Yanagisako, 1983, for a conference summary).

In the meantime, the debate over the universal subordination of women has reached a "dead end." Critiques of concepts like nature/culture and domestic/political (as well as other dichotomies, see Yanagisako and Collier, 1985) have made it clear that such dualisms are too simple to provide an analytical framework. And, we are now well aware that colonialism and Western contact have had a profound impact on women's roles, cautioning us not to compare cultures as if they were static entities untouched by world history.

A number of us see profound problems with the egalitarian hypothesis. First of all, since all early data come through the writing of Western male explorers, military men, or missionaries, it is extremely difficult to evaluate, especially with regard to women's status, and it is woefully incomplete. In some sense, we really will never know what it was like to be an Iroquois woman in the sixteenth century or a Navajo woman in the eighteenth, nor exactly what political power these women had. Second, colonialism could have either enhanced women's roles or undermined them. On the one hand, nineteenth-century trade probably pushed the Tlingit toward a more stratified, male-oriented society, increasing the cultural emphasis on the potlatch. On the other hand, the impact of the fur trade on the Iroquois during the seventeenth and eighteenth centuries probably strengthened women's position, their control over agriculture, and their input into political decision making.

Third, even in societies characterized as having "dispersed" decision making, it is my impression that women have input into decisions, but they are rarely the "articulators" of decisions that involve the entire band or community, such as a decision to move camp, engage in a communal hunt, etc. Usually this role falls to a male, though older women are not entirely excluded. The lack of recognition of this "male bias" in the way decisions are made, even in these dispersed decision-making systems, is, in my opinion, one of the critical deficiencies in the egalitarian thesis.

Finally, none of these analysts take the sexual division of labor as a serious component of inequality. Either the division of tasks is said to be complementary or both men and women are "owners" and producers, each contributing equally. This leaves the sexual division of labor unexplained but, more important, omits the possibility of discovering what the consequences are for status and power of women's focus on gathering and child care or men's control of hunting and ritual. For example, if meat is more widely distributed by men than gathered food is by women, perhaps some men (e.g., younger hunters or aging recipients of a son-in-law's meat) may translate that distribution into enhanced prestige, status, or "say-so" in group decisions. As Yanagisako and Collier point out, the division of labor constrains men and women to participate in certain kinds of activities; rather than being treated as "natural," this division itself needs to be explained (Yanagisako and Collier 1985, 20.)

All this discussion and debate has led us to call for more attention to individual cases, more attention to historical data so that particular cultural configurations can be analyzed as changing and not static, and more effort to construct complicated models that see men and women, not as opposed, unitary categories but as occupying a number of different roles in each society, which in turn have a complex set of interrelationships (see Yanagisako and Collier, 1985, for example). On the other hand, relatively few analysts have changed their minds. Though we are more sensitive to our own concepts, the impact of colonialism and the knotty problem of interpreting the data, most feminists still hold the position on the issue of sexual asymmetry that they did seven to ten years ago. Instead, we have gone on to the more concrete, specific, and historically sensitive studies that we have called for.

The Impact of Feminism on Anthropology

In the last ten years gender studies and feminist analysis has become an important subfield within anthropology. A large number of sessions at each annual American Anthropological Association are devoted to women's roles in education, health, development, and urban settings. The large number of books and monographs about women in other cultures has generated at least one course (if not more) on sex roles or gender in most anthropology departments. Anthropologists are important contributors to women's studies programs and women's research centers. Yet, this new scholarship has had limited impact on the field as a whole.

Perhaps the most clear-cut example is that the research and writing on Woman the Gatherer has failed to make an impact on textbook analyses of human evolution. Textbooks in the late 1960s and early 1970s (e.g., Howell, 1976) discussed human evolution in terms of "Man" (e.g., *Homo erectus*: A True Man at Last), used drawings of males to suggest the evolution of the species, and featured hunting as the main activity throughout human evolution. To his credit, John Pfeiffer changed the overall shape of his textbook between 1972 and 1978, replacing chapters on "The Rise of Big-Game Hunting and the Psychology of the Hunt" and "The Impact of Big-Game Hunting on Human Evolution" with a single chapter on "Food Quest and Big-Game Hunting." The tendency seems to be to quote Sally Linton and Tanner and Zihlman piecemeal rather than laying out a complex analysis of the potential role of gathering and female activities in human evolution. Hunting seems to be playing less of a role, since competing theories about scavenging and food sharing, proposed by male anthropologists, have been increasingly cited in texts. Typical is the new edition of *Humankind Evolving* (1982) which still stresses hunting (along with scavenging) and the increasing dependency of hominid young with increased mothering for *Australopithecus*, but focuses on *Homo erectus* as a full-fledged "Man the Hunter." Zihlman argues that the perspective put forward by those who write about females as active agents in prehistory (both in productive and reproductive roles, as gatherers and mothers) has been ignored, dismissed, and even co-opted (Zihlman, 1985a, 1985b). For example, Owen Lovejoy's theory (Lovejoy, 1981, 341–45) of the importance of food gathering rather than hunting in human prehistory basically posits that men gathered food to bring home to their immobile womenfolk, a sort of "Man the Gatherer" hypothesis.

Margaret Conkey and Janet Spector in their analysis of archaeology and the study of gender (1984) discuss the deep-rooted androcentric bias in archaeology. They discuss the Man the Hunter model as a particularly good example of how feminist work has been ignored. They argue that "the homebase" or "food-sharing" hypotheses are more subtle versions of the previous emphasis on hunting because they involve underlying assumptions about the division of labor, allocating certain tasks to males or to females. They conclude that "the basic features of the Man the Hunter model persist in anthropology and the alternatives have been ignored or dismissed" (1984, 9). Often, in other archaeological studies, tools and activities are sexually assigned, male activities receive more attention, and passive rather than active verb forms are used to describe female activities. Like Yanagisako and Collier within social-cultural anthropology, Conkey and Spector argue that the division of labor needs to be explained rather than assumed.

On the other hand, there has been an outpouring of research on female primates and other mammals, much of it influenced by a reanalysis of Darwinian notions of sexual selection and concepts taken from sociobiology, particularly that of parental investment. (Fedigan, 1982, gives an overview of primate studies.) With new data from a much wider variety of primate species, these researchers examine female reproductive strategies, with an emphasis on female choice, female elicitation of male support, and variation in mothering styles and skills (Hrdy and Williams, 1983). Some of these data are being used to re-evaluate assumptions about female primates (such as presumed attachment to home range, lack of dominance hierarchies, and lack of sexual assertiveness) (Lancaster, 1984). At least in this literature, assumptions about females that are still found in books on hominids and human prehistory are not only under revision but are seen as clearly outmoded.

The impact of feminist theory and research is ambiguous at best in social/cultural anthropology, the largest subdivision within anthropology (one of the four major fields, the others being archaeology, physical anthropology, and linguistics). Gender studies is now a well-developed subfield within social/cultural anthropology, but its impact on other subfields such as political anthropology, economic anthropology, development studies, studies of kinship and social structure, and urban anthropology has been mixed. On the one hand, the increase in articles on women and gender roles in the major anthropology journals has been greater than in education, history, literature, or philosophy. Although anthropology had a tradition of publications on women before 1970, the large number of articles that have appeared since that time have kept the discipline ahead in terms of the overall percentage of articles published on women. Nevertheless, in the period between 1976 and 1980, this was only 8.48% of the total (Dubois 1985, 166–70). Moreover, a number of articles that could have benefitted from the new scholarship on women either overlooked women as a category for analysis or failed to take a feminist perspective into account (Dubois, 1985, 186–88). In other words, feminist anthropologists can be proud of the fact that we have made more of an impact on the major publications in our field than is true of some other disciplines, but we still have a long way to go in terms of making women and analysis of women central to many of the major topics anthropologists study.

At a more basic level, it is also apparent that the feminist literature on women has not been incorporated in general anthropology courses, especially those at the introductory level, which are usually the undergraduate student's only exposure to human prehistory and cross-cultural diversity. In view of this situation, in 1985 a group of feminist anthropologists organized a "Women and the Anthropology Curriculum Project." At the 1985 annual meetings, the Board of Directors of the American Anthropological Association approved the goals of the project, appointed a board of directors for the project, and contributed $500.00 to help raise funds for the curriculum development. Between 1986 and 1988 those working with the project hope to (1) produce a series of bibliographic essays and curriculum guides for incorporating gender studies in introductory anthropology courses, (2) collaborate with the authors of the major textbooks in anthropology in terms of revising the next edition of their texts, and (3) organize a number of special sessions at the annual meetings in 1986, 1987, and 1988, where gender issues unique to each of the world geographic areas and to the subdisciplines within anthropology can be discussed.

The work of the "Women in the Anthropology Curriculum" project may succeed in introducing the scholarship produced in the first two phases of feminist research to a wider audience. The potential impact of the self-questioning begun in the third phase is not yet clear. This phase is perhaps paralleled by a good deal of re-examination in the field as a whole. A good example is the work of David Schneider in kinship studies. His *Critique of the Study of Kinship* (1984) calls into question anthropological studies of kinship that presume that sexual reproduction provides a universal genealogical grid through which kinship systems can be analyzed. Such a framework, Schneider argues, is really our own "folk theory" of kinship, which is based on notions of sexual intercourse, blood and relations "in-law" (Schneider, 1968). Yanagisako and Collier point out these parallels between their critique of gender studies and that of Schneider's vis-à-vis kinship studies. Anthropologists in both cases have implicitly assumed that there were a set of "natural facts" that could be the bedrock for the beginning of an analysis. Sexual reproduction or the difference between men and women could be presumed as universal, rather than the things that need to be explained and examined.

Thus feminism, on the one hand, cannot claim to be solely responsible for the transformation of other subfields like kinship and politics. Nor can we safely say that the work of feminist anthropologists is finding its way into introductory textbooks or into the way in which general anthropology is taught. On the other hand, feminism has certainly transformed the thinking of a number of anthropologists (largely women), and gender studies is a thriving subfield within the discipline. There are now over ten years of evolving and changing theoretical writing on women, sex roles, and gender—scholarship that has expanded and transformed our thinking about human evolution, the uses of language, kinship, and politics, and even archaeological reconstructions of the past. Most recently, feminist theory has questioned our categories of analysis and undermined the very assumptions of earlier work on women.

Conclusions

So where are we? Having undercut all of our conceptual frameworks, can feminists and anthropologists begin to build new models? The questioning and undercutting can easily lead to extreme cultural relativism, i.e., the notion that each culture has its own set of categories and must be understood on its own terms, essentially blocking comparison with any other culture. Or it can lead to extreme cultural constructionism—the notion that there are no biological "facts" or differences between men and women and that all is constructed in each cultural situation. Extreme relativism and extreme constructionism can be paralyzing.

On the other hand, anthropologists, in wrestling with these issues, are coming to terms with problems of interest to feminists in other fields. For example, feminists have become interested in developing a feminist epistemology, one that takes seriously a feminist, rather than a universalist, standpoint. The disadvantage of this view is that it comes to an epistemological relativism that most theorists want to avoid. Anthropologists, since Sapir and Whorf at least, have worried about a parallel problem, extreme cultural relativism or the impossibility of translating one culture into the terms of another (or even one language or world view into another). Yet, the anthropological project is just this—the "tacking back and forth" between one culture or social structure and our own, attempting to make sense of another way of life using our own language and concepts— but stretching them to better make the translation. Thus, the anthropological example has much to offer feminists who wish to build a more complex theory about women, not WOMAN. Often contemporary feminists may be reluctant to see any relevance in an analysis of male cults in New Guinea, or female exchange networks among the Navajo, yet the models anthropologists are now attempting to build are much more complex than our earlier ones.

Shelly Rosaldo warned us of the "abuses of anthropology," i.e., the tendency of feminists to wish that anthropology would help us to discover what women (including, and most particularly, ourselves) are really like. Now that feminist anthropologists have begun to question their own concepts and categories and to build models that are more historically sensitive and culture-specific, anthropology has much to offer feminism in suggesting that women are really different, not the same. It is attempting to understand and compare those differences that has become the project of feminist anthropology—a project that can perhaps enrich the work of feminists in other disciplines.

BIBLIOGRAPHY

Beck, Lois and Nikki Keddie, eds.
    1978   *Women in the Muslim World.* Cambridge: Harvard University Press.

Bloch, Maurice and Jean H. Bloch
    1980   "Women and the Dialectics of Nature in Eighteenth-Century Thought." In Carol MacCormack and Marilyn Strathern, eds., *Nature, Culture and Gender.* Cambridge: Cambridge University Press.

Briggs, Jean
    1975   "Eskimo Women: Makers of Men." In Carolyn J. Matthiasson, ed., *Many Sisters.* New York: Free Press.

Campbell, Bernard
    1982   *Humankind Emerging.* Boston: Little, Brown and Company.

Chodorow, Nancy
    1974   "Family Structure and Feminine Personality." In Michelle Rosaldo and Louise Lamphere, eds., *Woman, Culture and Society.* Stanford: Stanford University Press.

Collier, Jane
    1974   "Women in Politics." In Michelle Rosaldo and Louise Lamphere, eds., *Woman, Culture and Society.* Stanford: Stanford University Press.
    1987   *Marriage and Inequality in Classless Societies.* Stanford: Stanford University Press.

Collier, Jane and Michelle Z. Rosaldo
    1981   "Politics and Gender in Simple Societies." In Sherry Ortner and Harriet Whitehead, eds., *Sexual Meanings.* New York: Cambridge University Press.

Collier, Jane and Sylvia Yanagisako
    1987   "Introduction." *Gender and Kinship: Essays toward a Unified Analysis.* Stanford: Stanford University Press.

Conkey, Margaret and Janet Spector
    1984   "Archaeology and the Study of Gender." In Michael Schiffer, ed., *Advances in Archaeological Method and Theory*, Vol. 7. New York: Academic Press.

Dubois, Ellen et al.
    1985   *Feminist Scholarship: Kindling in the Groves of Academe*. Urbana: University of Illinois Press.

Edholm, Felicity, Olivia Harris and Kate Young
    1977   "Conceptualizing Women," *Critique of Anthropology* 9 and 10, 101–131.

Fedigan, Linda Marie
    1982   *Primate Paradigms: Sex Roles and Social Bonds*. Montreal: Eden Press.

Fernea, Elizabeth Warnock and Basina Quatta Beziran
    1977   *Middle Eastern Muslim Women Speak*. Cambridge: Harvard University Press.

Hafkin, Nancy J. and Edna G. Bay
    1976   *Women in Africa*. Stanford: Stanford University Press.

Harding, Susan
    1975   "Women and Words in a Spanish Village." In Rayna Reiter, ed., *Toward an Anthropology of Women*. New York: Monthly Review Press.

Harris, Olivia and Kate Young
    1981   "Engendered Structures: Some Problems in the Analysis of Reproduction." In Joel S. Kahn and Joseph R. Llobera, eds., *The Anthropology of Pre-Capitalist Societies*. London: Macmillan.

Howell, F. Clark
    1976   *Early Man*. New York: Time-Life Books.

Hrdy, Sarah Blaffer and George C. Williams
    1983   "Behavioral Biology and the Double Standard." In Samuel K. Wasser, ed., *Social Behavior of Female Vertebrates*. New York: Academic Press.

Jordanova, L. J.
    1980   "Natural Facts: A Historical Perspective on Science and Sexuality." In Carol MacCormack and Marilyn Strathern, eds., *Nature, Culture and Gender*. Cambridge: Cambridge University Press.

Kaberry, Phyllis M.
    1939   *Aboriginal Women, Sacred and Profane*. London: G. Routledge.
    1952   *Women of the Grassfields*. London: H.M. Stationery Office.

Lancaster, Jane
    1984   "Introduction." In Meredith F. Small, ed., *Female Primates: Studies by Women Primatologists*. New York: Alan R. Liss.

Landes, Ruth
    1938   *The Ojibaw Woman, Part I: Youth.* New York, Columbia University, Contributions to Anthropology, Vol. 31.
    1947   *The City of Women: Negro Women Cult Leaders of Bahia, Brazil.* New York: Macmillan.

Laughlin, William S.
    1968   "Hunting: An Integrating Biobehavior System and Its Evolutionary Importance." In Richard B. Lee and Irven DeVore, eds., *Man the Hunter.* Chicago: Aldine Press.

Leacock, Eleanor
    1981   *Myths of Male Dominance.* New York: Monthly Review Press.

Leibowitz, Lila
    1975   "Perspectives on the Evolution of Sex Differences." In Rayna Reiter, ed., *Toward an Anthropology of Women.* New York: Monthly Review Press.
    1978   *Females, Males, Families: A Biosocial Approach.* North Scituate, Mass.: Duxbury Press.

Leith-Ross, Sylvia
    1939   *African Women: Study of the Ibo of Nigeria.* London: Faber and Faber.

Linton, Sally
    1974   "Woman the Gatherer." In Rayna Reiter, ed., *Toward an Anthropology of Women.* New York: Monthly Review Press.

Lovejoy, Owen
    1981   "The Origin of Man—Review." *Science* 211, 341–50.

MacCormack, Carol and Marilyn Strathern
    1980   *Nature, Culture and Gender.* Cambridge: Cambridge University Press.

Mead, Margaret
    1979   *Male and Female: A Study of the Sexes in a Changing World.* New York: W. Morrow.

Meillassoux, Claude
    1981   *Maidens, Meal and Money.* Cambridge: Cambridge University Press.

Nash, June and Helen Icken Safa
    1976   *Sex and Class in Latin America.* New York: Praeger.

Nelson, Cynthia
    1973   "Public and Private Politics: Women in the Middle Eastern World." *American Ethnologist* 1, no. 3, 552–64.

O'Laughlin, Bridget
    1974   "Mediation of Contradiction: Why Mbum Women Do Not Eat Chicken." In Michelle Rosaldo and Louise Lamphere, eds., *Woman, Culture and Society.* Stanford: Stanford University Press.

Ortner, Sherry B.
    1974   "Is Female to Male as Nature to Culture?" In Michelle Rosaldo and
            Louise Lamphere, eds., *Woman, Culture and Society*. Stanford: Stan-
            ford University Press.

Ortner, Sherry and Harriet Whitehead
    1981   "Introduction" to *Sexual Meanings*. Cambridge: Cambridge Univer-
            sity Press.

Paulme, Denise, ed.
    1963   *Women of Tropical Africa*. Berkeley: University of California Press.

Pfeiffer, John
    1972   *The Emergence of Man*. New York: Harper and Row.
    1978   Second and Third Editions.

Reiter, Rayna
    1975   *Toward an Anthropology of Women*. New York: Monthly Review Press.
    1975   "Men and Women in the South of France: Public and Private Do-
            mains." In Rayna Reiter, ed., *Toward an Anthropology of Women*. New
            York: Monthly Review Press.

Rogers, Susan
    1978   "Female Forms of Power and the Myth of Male Dominance: A Model
            of Female/Male Interaction in Peasant Society." *American Ethnologist*
            2, no. 4, 727–56.

Rosaldo, Michelle
    1974   "Woman, Culture and Society: A Theoretical Overview." In Michelle
            Rosaldo and Louise Lamphere eds., *Woman, Culture and Society*.
            Stanford: Stanford University Press.

Rosaldo, Michelle
    1980   "The Uses and Abuses of Anthropology." *Signs* 5, no. 3, 389–417.

Rosaldo, Michelle and Louise Lamphere, eds.
    1974   *Woman, Culture and Society*. Stanford: Stanford University Press.

Sacks, Karen
    1974   "Engels Revisited: Women, the Organization of Production and Pri-
            vate Property." In Michelle Rosaldo and Louise Lamphere, eds.,
            Woman, Culture and Society. Stanford: Stanford University Press.
    1979   *Sisters and Wives: The Past and the Future of Sexual Equality*. Westport,
            Conn.: Greenwood Press.

Sanday, Peggy
    1981   *Female Power and Male Dominance*. Cambridge: Cambridge University
            Press.

Schlegel, Alice
    1974   "Women Anthropologists Look at Women." *Reviews in Anthropology*
            1, no. 6 (November/December 1974), 553–60.
    1977   *Sexual Stratification*. New York: Columbia University Press.

Schneider, David
   1968   *American Kinship: A Cultural Account.* Englewood Cliffs, NJ: Prentice-Hall.
   1984   *A Critique of the Study of Kinship.* Ann Arbor: University of Michigan Press.

Siskind, Janet
   1978   "Kinship and Mode of Production." *American Anthropologist* 80, no. 4, 860–72.

Strathern, Marilyn
   1980   "No Nature, No Culture: The Hagen Case." In Carol MacCormack and Marilyn Strathern, eds., *Nature, Culture and Gender.* Cambridge: Cambridge University Press.

Tanner, Nancy and Adrienne Zihlman
   1976   "Women in Evolution. Part I: Innovation and Selection in Human Origins." *Signs* 2, no. 3, 585–608.

Tanner, Nancy
   1981   *On Becoming Human.* Cambridge: Cambridge University Press.

Tsing, Anna and Sylvia Yanagisako
   1983   "Feminism and Kinship Theory." *Current Anthropology* 24, no. 4, 511–16.

Underhill, Ruth
   1936   *Autobiography of a Papago Woman. Memoirs of the American Anthropological Association,* No. 46.

Wolf, Margery and Roxanne Witke, eds.
   1975   *Women in China.* Stanford: Stanford University Press.

Yanagisako, Sylvia and Jane Collier
   1985   "Feminism, Gender, and Kinship." Paper prepared for the volume resulting from Conference on Feminism and Kinship Theory, Bellagio, Italy, August 1982. To be published as "Toward a Unified Analysis of Gender and Kinship" in Collier and Yanagisako, 1987.

Zihlman, Adrienne
   1978   "Women in Evolution, Part II: Subsistence and Social Organization among Early Hominids." *Signs* 4, no. 1, 4–20.
   1982   "Whatever Happened to Woman-the-Gatherer." Paper presented at the American Anthropological Association Meetings, Washington, D.C.
   1985a   "Gathering Stores for Hunting Human Nature: A Review Essay." *Feminist Studies* 11, 2.
   1985b   "Sex, Sexes and Sexism in Human Origins." Invited Keynote Address, American Association of Physical Anthropologists, Knoxville, April 12.

WOMEN'S HISTORY AND THE REWRITING OF HISTORY

Joan Wallach Scott

What one wants, I thought—and why does not some brilliant student at Newnham or Girton supply it?—is a mass of information; at what age did she marry; how many children had she as a rule; what was her house like; had she a room to herself; did she do the cooking; would she be likely to have a servant? All these facts lie somewhere, presumably, in parish registers and account books; the life of the average Elizabethan woman must be scattered about somewhere, could one collect it and make a book of it. It would be ambitious beyond my daring, I thought, looking about the shelves for books that were not there, to suggest to the students of those famous colleges that they should rewrite history, though I own that it often seems a little queer as it is, unreal, lop-sided; but why should they not add a supplement to history? calling it, of course, by some inconspicuous name so that women might figure there without impropriety?[1]

During the last decade, Virginia Woolf's call for a history of women—written more than fifty years ago—has been answered. Inspired directly or indirectly by the political agenda of the women's movement, historians have documented not only the lives of the average woman in various historical periods, but they have charted as well changes in the economic, educational, and political positions of women of various classes in city and country and in nation-states. Bookshelves are now being filled with biographies of forgotten prominent women, chronicles of feminist movements,

This article first appeared in *Past and Present: A Journal of Historical Studies*, no. 101 (November 1983), pp. 142–57, under the title "Women in History: The Modern Period." It is reprinted here with some changes by permission of The Past and Present Society, 175 Banbury Road, Oxford, England, which holds the world copyright.

and the collected letters of female authors; the book titles treat subjects as disparate as suffrage and birth control. Journals have appeared which are devoted exclusively to women's studies and to the even more specialized area of women's history.[2] And, at least in the United States, there are major conferences each year devoted entirely to the presentation of scholarly papers on the history of women.[3]

The production of materials is marked by extraordinary diversity in topic, method, and interpretation. Indeed, it is foolish to attempt, as some historians have recently done, to reduce the field to a single interpretive or theoretical stance. Reductionism of that sort creates an illusion that the reviewer commands, indeed that he dominates, a profusion of disparate texts. At the same time, the illusion obscures the professed end of such reviews: an accurate account of the "state of the art," and of the meaning and importance of its diversity and complexity. It is precisely in the ac-knowledgment of its complexity and confusions that one finds both an understanding of women's history and also the basis for critical evaluation of it.[4]

Some of the complexity comes from the sheer variety of topics studied. The confusion results from the proliferation of case studies and large interpretive attempts that address neither one another nor a similar set of questions and from the absence of a definable historiographic tradition within which interpretations are debated and revised. Instead, woman as subject has been grafted on to other traditions or studied in isolation from any of them. While some histories of women's work, for example, address contemporary feminist questions about the relationship between wage-earning and status, others frame their studies within the context of debates among Marxists and between Marxists and modernization theorists about the impact of industrial capitalism.[5] Reproduction covers a vast terrain in which fertility and contraception are sometimes treated within the confines of historical demography as aspects of the "demographic transition." Alter-nately they are viewed within the context of discussions of the conflicting political analyses of Malthusian political economists and socialist labor leaders, or within the very different framework of evaluations of the impact of the nineteenth-century "ideology of domesticity" on the power of women in their families. Yet another approach stresses feminist debates about sexuality and the history of women's demands for the right to control their own bodies. Additionally, some Marxist-feminists have redefined reproduction as the functional equivalent of production in an effort to incorporate women into the corpus of Marxist theory.[6] Investigations of politics have sought either to demonstrate simply that women were to be found "in public," or to illustrate the historical incompatibility between feminist claims and the structure and ideology of organized trade unions and political parties (the "failure" of socialism, for example, to accommodate feminism). Another, quite different approach to politics examines the interior organization of women's political movements as a way of documenting the existence of a distinctively female culture.[7]

Still, there is a common dimension to the enterprise of these scholars of different schools and that is to make women a focus of inquiry, a subject of the story, an agent of the narrative—whether that narrative is the familiar chronicle of political events (the French Revolution, the Swing riots, World War I or II) and political movements (Chartism, utopian socialism, feminism, women's suffrage), or the newer, more analytically cast account of the workings or unfoldings of large-scale processes of social change (industrialization, capitalism, modernization, urbanization, the building of nation states). The titles of some of the books that launched the "women's history movement" in the early 1970s explicitly conveyed their authors' intentions: Those who had been *Hidden from History* were *Becoming Visible*.[8] Although book titles are now more circumspect (in part in order to legitimate claims to serious academic consideration), the mission of their authors remains to construct women as historical subjects. That effort goes far beyond the naive search for the heroic ancestors of the contemporary women's movement to a re-evaluation of established standards of historical significance. It culminates in a debate whose terms are contained in Woolf's phrases: Can a focus on women "add a supplement to history" without also "rewriting history"? Beyond that, what does the feminist rewriting of history entail?

There are several positions in the debate, which is less a debate than a different set of approaches to the "rewriting of history." Most scholars working in women's history assume their work will transform history as it has been written and understood; they differ on the question of how that will be accomplished. Some see the recovery of information and the focus on female subjects as sufficient to the task. Others use their research to challenge received interpretations of progress and regress. In this regard, for example, an impressive mass of evidence has been compiled to show that the Renaissance was not a renaissance for women,[9] that technology did not lead to women's liberation either in the workplace or at home,[10] that the "Age of Democratic Revolutions" excluded women from political participation,[11] that the "affective nuclear family" constrained women's emotional and personal development,[12] and that the rise of medical science deprived women of autonomy and a sense of feminine community.[13] Still others—a much smaller number at this point—attempt to join their evidence more directly to "mainstream" social and political history. Evidence about women becomes a way into examining social, economic, and political relationships and the conclusions are less about women themselves than about the organization of societies, the dynamics of power, the content and meaning of historically specific politics. For this approach, a focus on women leads to the articulation of gender (or sexual difference) as a category of historical analysis, to the incorporation of gender into the historian's analytical tool box, and to a conceptual perspective that makes possible a genuine "rewriting of history."

In this essay I will examine these various approaches less in terms of their conclusions than in terms of their assumptions and methods. I will draw most heavily on North American scholarship not only because I am most familiar with it, but because in the United States there has been produced during the past ten or twelve years the largest volume of, the most varied examples of subject and interpretation in, and the fullest elaboration of theoretical debates about, women's history.[14]

The first approach writes women's history as "her-story," a narrative of women's experience either alongside or entirely outside conventional historical frameworks. The assumption here is that women have had different experiences from men and that those differences matter in the writing of history. The aim of this approach is to give value as history to an experience that has been ignored and thus devalued and to insist on female agency in the "making of history." Investigations that seek to uncover women's participation in major political events and to write a women's political history attempt to fit a new subject—women—into received historical categories, interpreting their actions in terms recognizable to political and social historians. A book on the history of the French women's suffrage movement by Steven Hause nicely exemplifies this approach. The author interprets the weakness and small size of the movement (in comparison with its English and American counterparts) as the result of the ideologies and institutions of French Catholicism, the legacy of Roman law, the conservatism of French society, and the peculiar political history of French republicanism, especially the Radical Party during the Third Republic. Hause also analyzes divisions among feminists and he tells the entire story in terms of the ideas and organizations of the women leaders.[15] Another example of this kind of approach examines a women's political movement from the perspective of its rank-and-file members rather than its leaders. In the best traditions of the social histories of labor (which were inspired by the work of E. P. Thompson) Jill Liddington and Jill Norris offer a sensitive and illuminating account of working-class women's participation in the English suffrage movement. Their material, drawn largely from Manchester records and from oral histories they collected, documents the involvement of working-class women in the campaign to win the vote (previous histories described it as almost entirely a middle-class movement) and links demands by these women for suffrage to their work and family lives and to the activities of trade union and Labour Party organizers. The predominance and wisdom of the Pankhurst wing of the movement is called into question for its elitism and its insistence on female separatism (a position rejected by the majority of suffragettes).[16]

A different sort of investigation, still within the "her-story" position, departs from the framework of conventional history and offers a new narrative, different periodization, and different causes. It seeks to illuminate the structures of ordinary women's lives as well as those of notable women, and to discover the nature of the feminist or female consciousness which motivated their behavior. Patriarchy and class are usually assumed to be the contexts within which nineteenth- and twentieth-century women defined their experience, but these are rarely specified or examined concretely. Since these are the given contexts, however, a number of histories tend to emphasize moments of cross-class collaboration among women and those actions that directly addressed women's oppression, but such topics are not the defining characteristic of this approach. Rather the central aspect of this approach is the exclusive focus on female agency, on the causal role played by women in their history, and on the gender determinants of that role. Evidence consists of women's expressions, ideas, and actions. Explanation and interpretation are framed within the terms of the female sphere: by examinations of personal experience, familial and domestic structures, collective (female) reinterpretations of social definitions of women's role, and networks of female friendship that provided emotional as well as physical sustenance. The exploration of the women's world has led to the brilliant insights of Carroll Smith-Rosenberg about the "female world of love and ritual" in nineteenth-century America,[17] to an insistence on the positive aspects of the domestic ideology of the same period,[18] to a dialectical reading of the relationship between middle-class women's political action and the ideas of womanhood that confined them to domestic realms,[19] and to an analysis of the "reproductive ideology" that constructed the world of the *bourgeoises* of northern France in the mid-nineteenth century.[20] It has also led Carl Degler to argue that American women themselves created the ideology of their separate sphere in order to enhance their autonomy and status. In his rendering of the story, women create a world neither within nor in opposition to oppressive structures or ideas that others have imposed, but to further a set of group interests, defined and articulated from within the group itself.[21] Although Degler has been accused of misreading the histories upon which he draws for his account, his conceptualization follows from the causality implied in "her-story's" construction of the woman as historical subject and from its frequent failure to distinguish between the valuation of women's experience (considering it worthy of study) and the positive assessment of everything women said or did.

This approach to women's history substitutes women for men, but it does not rewrite conventional history. To be sure, it raises questions that call for answers by offering documentation about women's activities—public and private—that happened, but were not included in conventional accounts. It insists as well that "personal, subjective experience" matters as much as "public and political activities," indeed that the former influences the latter.[22] It demonstrates that sex and gender need to be conceptualized in historical terms, at least if some of the motives for women's actions are to be understood. Yet it does not then move on to challenge conventional history directly. Although women are substituted for men as the subject of historical accounts, their story remains separate—whether different questions are asked, different categories of analysis offered, or only different documents examined. For those interested there is now a growing and important history of women to supplement and enrich conventional political and social histories, but it remains embedded in the "separate sphere" that has long been associated exclusively with the female sex.

The second approach to the "rewriting of history" is most closely associated with social history. Social history offered important support for a women's history in several ways. First, it provided methodologies in quantification, in the use of details from everyday life, and in interdisciplinary borrowings from sociology, demography, and ethnography. Second, it conceptualized as historical phenomena family relationships, fertility, and sexuality. Third, social history challenged the narrative line of political history ("male leaders make history") by taking as its subject large-scale social processes as they were realized in many dimensions of human experience. This led to the fourth influence, the legitimation of a focus on groups customarily excluded from political history. Social history's story is ultimately about processes or systems (such as capitalism or modernization, depending on the theoretical stance of the historian), but it is told through the lives of various groups of people who are the ostensible, though not always the actual, subjects of the narrative. Since social experience or relations of power are embodied everywhere in a society, one can choose among a variety of topics, and it is relatively easy to extend the list from workers, peasants, slaves, elites, and diverse occupational or social groups to include women. Thus, for example, studies of women's work were undertaken, much as studies of workers had been, to assess capitalism's impact or to understand its operation.

These studies have led to a proliferation of that "mass of information" Virginia Woolf asked for. We know what kinds of jobs women did, what their patterns of labor force participation were, what stage of the life cycle coincided with work away from home, under what conditions they formed labor unions or went on strike, what their wages were and how all of that has changed during the past hundred and fifty years.[23] The mass of information has, furthermore, suggested the importance of including questions about family organization and sex-segregated labor markets in analyses of working-class history, but it has stopped short of meeting the challenge to "rewrite history." That is because most of the social history of women's work has been contained within the terms of social theories based on analytic categories that are primarily economic. There are many arguments advanced about women and work. Some insist that wage-earning enhanced women's sexual identity. Others that women were exploited as a cheap labor supply and that, as a result, men perceived women as a threat to the value of their own labor. Still others point out that sex-segregation undermined women's job control and hence their ability to organize and strike. Some historians have insisted that family divisions of labor attributed economic value to a wife's domestic role, others that family conflict centered around control of wages. One recent article suggests that when women commanded sufficient resources they engaged in collective action identical to men's. In all these studies the explanation ultimately has to do with economic variables not gender.[24] Sexual divisions, their definition and elaboration are explained as the result of economic forces when, in fact, it is equally plausible and probably more accurate to suggest that cultural definitions of gender differences permitted the implementation of economic practices such as sex-segregated labor markets or the use of women to undercut the wages of skilled craftsmen.[25]

Some historians of women's work have used a notion of patriarchy as a way of including gender in their analyses, but the term seems insufficiently theorized. Most often political, class, and family systems are described as forms of male dominance which either transcend particular historical situations and social relations *or* follow directly from economic causes.[26]

If social history has freed historians to write about women and given them some methods by which to document the experience and agency of women in the past, it has also limited the potential of women's history to "rewrite history." Few studies of social processes or social movements have yet been fundamentally altered as a result of studies focused on women. Women are a department of social history; they are one of the groups mobilizing resources, being modernized or exploited, contending for power or being excluded from a polity; they are explained, in other words, within the terms of behaviorist or Marxist or modernizationist models. The history of women enriches and adds new perspectives, but it has not yet been central to social history's largely successful effort to reconceptualize political history. That is because the issue of gender—implicit in the materials studied—has not been sufficiently singled out as either providing qualitatively different insights or as raising different kinds of analytic questions. Sexual difference, in the social history approach, is not an issue requiring study in itself. In a sense, if "her-story" tends to too separatist a position, much of the social history of women has been too integrationist, subsuming women within received categories of analysis. Put in other terms, the "her-story" approach assumes that sexual difference creates different histories for women and men, but it does not problematize the construction of sexual difference, it does not ask how the terms of gender difference work. The social history approach, in contrast, assumes that sexual difference is a by-product of other factors. Both approaches offer supplements to history, but they have not found a way to convince or demonstrate to other historians that it is essential to take their findings into account. They have not, in other words, "rewritten history." That rewriting is the project of the third position in the "debate" I have constructed, and it builds on, indeed it is made possible by, the work of both "her-story" and the social history of women.

The third position was articulated in prescriptions for women's history by some of its most important American representatives, but it has proved difficult to put into practice. Usually beginning with a focus on women, its subject is nonetheless gender. The late Joan Kelly set as the goal for this women's history making sex "as fundamental to our analysis of the social order as other classifications such as class and race."[27] For Natalie Zemon Davis the aim is: "to understand the significance of the sexes, of gender groups in the historical past. Our goal is to discover the range in sex roles and in sexual symbolism in different societies and periods, to find out what meaning they had and how they functioned to maintain the social order or to promote its change."[28] The point is to examine social definitions of gender as they are developed by men and women; constructed in and affected by economic and political institutions, expressive of a range of relationships which included not only sex, but class and power. The results throw new light not only on women's experience, but on social and political practice as well. In addition, inquiries into gender permit historians to raise critical questions that lead to the "rewriting of history."

Studying gender consists of examining women and men in relation to one another, of asking what the definitions or laws that apply to one imply about the other, what the comparative location and activities of men and women reveal about each, and what representations of sexual difference suggest about the structure of social, economic, and political authority. The point is not to assume we know what gender is, but to ask how the meanings of sexual difference are constructed. Thus Temma

Kaplan's *Anarchists of Andalusia* analyzed the different appeals of that political movement to men and women and the different but complementary ways in which male and female peasants and workers were organized to revolutionary struggle. Her parallel treatment of men and women within anarchism illuminates gender relationships in Andalusian society in relation to the nature and meaning of this particular political·movement's attack on capitalism and the state.[29] Tim Mason developed important insight about the "reconciliatory function of the family" in Nazi Germany as a result of an inquiry into the position of women and policies towards women. The factual materials he gathered about women, who were largely "non-actors" in the politics of the period, "provided an exceptionally fruitful new vantage point from which the behavior of the actors could be—indeed, had to be—reinterpreted."[30] Taking Foucault's suggestions in the *History of Sexuality* as her starting-point, Judith Walkowitz delved into Josephine Butler's campaign against the Contagious Diseases Acts in late Victorian England. Avoiding what might have been the temptation to write a simple heroic account of the success of a woman's movement aimed at combating the double standard of sexual morality, Walkowitz used her material for an investigation into economic, social, religious, and political divisions in English society.[31] Although she did not directly offer criticism of conventional historical accounts of the period, her book implies such criticism. The study establishes that a debate about sexual conduct took place openly, within parliament as well as outside, that it was instigated by women (and supported by men) within the terms of their moral and religious preoccupations and carried on "in public," that it resulted in institutional and legal change, in short that sex was an explicit political issue for at least several decades. These findings not only question the conventional characterization of the period as "repressed," but suggest the need for rewriting a political history that has focused largely on the contests between Disraeli and Gladstone and on issues such as Irish Home Rule. How can the debate on prostitution and sexual standards be written into that political history? What critical perspective do we gain from the fact that it has, until now, been left out? At points of contact such as these the history of gender establishes a critique of political history and the means for rewriting it.

It seems no accident that many of the best efforts at joining women's history with established history take place in studies of politics broadly defined. Political structures and political ideas—structures and ideas that create and enforce relationships of power—shape and set the boundaries of public discourse and of all aspects of life. Even those excluded from participation in the discourse and activities of politics are defined by them; "non-actors," to use Mason's term, are acting according to rules established in political realms; the private sphere is a public creation; those absent from official accounts partook nonetheless in the making of history; those who are silent speak eloquently about the meanings of power and the uses of political authority. Feminist desires to make woman a historical subject cannot be realized simply by making her the agent or principal character of a historical narrative. To discover where women have been throughout history it is necessary to examine what gender and sexual difference have had to do with the workings of power. By doing so historians will both find women and transform political history.

At this point the approach I am suggesting is best undertaken by specific studies of discrete periods, movements, or events. One could, for example, recast studies of suffrage campaigns to uncover relationships between gender and power in late nineteenth-century America or England. Brian Harrison has described the opposition to suffrage and others have analyzed the ideas and supporters of the movement.[32] But there has as yet been no study which brings together in a context larger than the issues of the vote itself all the participants—militants, moderates, antis, government ministers, and members of parliament. What did the debate over the vote for women signify about conceptions of authority and political rights? How are patriarchal ideas articulated and in what terms? Where do conflicts about women (really about sexual difference) fit in the distribution of social, economic, and political power in a nation? What is at stake and for which groups in a society when questions of gender difference become the focus of dispute, legislative consideration, and ideological conflict?

Another example stems from work on the French Revolution. Studies of women in that revolution have moved from documentation of female participation to considerations of iconography and of the question of when and why sexual difference became an issue for dispute. Darlene Levy and Harriet Applewhite have focused on the debates in 1793 which outlawed women's clubs in the name of protecting femininity and domesticity.[33] Why did gender become a means of drawing political lines? What issues beyond those having literally to do with women's rights were being addressed in prohibitions of female political organization? What was the significance of the revolutionaries' choice of a female figure to represent liberty and the republic? Was there any connection between iconographic representations and political rights for women? How did men and women differ in their discussions of women's political role? What do the political debates about sexual difference add to our understanding of the legitimation of authority and the protection of power during the French Revolution? These questions cannot be answered without information about women, but they are not limited to woman as subject or agent. Instead they include gender as a way of gaining a new appreciation of the politics and of the social and political impact of the French Revolution.

Studies of politics in the sense in which I employ the term need not deal only with issues of power at the level of nation states, for my use of the term extends to contests (expressed in language as well as institutional arrangements) about power and authority in all aspects of social life. Indeed the work of Deborah Valenze on women preachers in English popular "cottage" religion demonstrates the interconnectedness between religious ideas and gender in expressions of opposition to change in community and household economies.[34] Leonore Davidoff explores the ways in which individuals played with culturally defined categories of gender and class in her article on Arthur J. Munby; she reminds us of the complicated ways in which personal relationships are variations on social themes of power, status, and authority.[35] Some recent considerations of the labor and socialist movements have used questions about gender to advance discussion beyond documentation of misogyny or condemnation of male leaders and beyond reductionist economic interpretations of the ideas and actions of workers. Parallel considerations of the discourses and experiences of working men and women have led to new interpretations, in one instance emphasizing the relative openness of utopian socialism to feminism, as compared to Marxian socialism's marginalization of women.[36] Inquiries about the significance of sexual difference have led, in addition, to readings of representations of work which include sexual, familial, and religious dimensions. Work then has meaning beyond the literal description of productive activity, and studies about the place of women in the work-force and the labor movement offer insight both about women and the sexual politics of male and female workers *and* about the nature, meaning, and purpose of their organizations and collective actions.[37] The analysis must include women's actions and experiences, ideas and policies which define their rights, and metaphoric and symbolic representations of feminine and masculine. The problem for empirical historical investigation is to select moments when all of these are somehow at issue and to ask how they illuminate not only women's experience but politics as well.

To ignore politics in the recovery of the female subject is to accept the reality of public/private distinctions and the separate or distinctive qualities of women's character and experience. It misses the chance not only to challenge the accuracy of binary distinctions between men and women in the past and present, but to expose the very political nature of a history written in those terms. Simply to assert, however, that gender is a political issue is not enough. The realization of the radical potential of women's history comes in the writing of narratives that focus on women's experience *and* analyze the ways in which politics construct gender and gender constructs politics. Female agency then becomes not the recounting of great deeds performed by women, but the exposure of the often silent and hidden operations of gender, which are nonetheless present and defining forces of politics and political life. With this approach women's history enters the terrain of political history and inevitably begins the rewriting of history.[38]

NOTES

I would like to thank for their assistance and suggestions Ellen Furlough, Sherri Broder, and Donald M. Scott. Discussions with members of the research seminar at Brown University's Pembroke Center for Teaching and Research on Women, and especially with Elizabeth Weed, have been invaluable for the conceptualization of this article.

1. Virginia Woolf, *A Room of One's Own* (London, 1929), p. 68.

2. The American journals are *Signs, Feminist Studies, The Women's Studies Quarterly,* and *Women and History.* In France *Pénélope* published scholarly work in women's history from 1979–1986. In Britain historical studies are published in the *Feminist Review,* and *History Workshop* is now a journal of socialist and feminist historians. *RFD/DRF (Resources for Feminist Research/Documentation sur la Recherche Feministe)* is the Canadian journal.

3. The largest of these is the Berkshire Conference on the History of Women.

4. Richard Evans, "Modernization Theory and Women's History," *Archiv für Sozialgeschichte,* xx (1980), 492–514, applies the same reductionism that Tony Judt did in his review of American social history scholarship, forcing all practitioners into a single "deviation," the common denominator of which is ultimately not theory, method or subject, but national character. See also Richard Evans, "Women's History: The Limits of Reclamation," *Social Hist.,* v (1980), 273–81, which concludes with a sweeping generalization about "so many American historians of women" as compared to their British counterparts.

5. An overview is presented in Alice Amsden (ed.), *The Economics of Women and Work* (London, 1980). For specific interpretations of the relationship of economic development and women's work, see Patricia Branca, *Women in Europe since 1750* (London, 1978); Louise A. Tilly and Joan W. Scott, *Women, Work and Family* (New York, 1978); Eric Richards, "Women in the British Economy since about 1700: An Interpretation," *History,* lix (1974), 337–57; Neil McKendrick, "Home Demand and Economic Growth: A New View of the Role of Women and Children in the Industrial Revolution," in Neil McKendrick (ed.), *Historical Perspectives: Studies in English Thought and Society in Honour of J. H. Plumb* (London, 1974); Ann Oakley, *Women's Work: The Housewife Past and Present* (New York, 1974). On working women in America, see Gerda Lerner, "The Lady and the Mill Girl: Changes in the Status of Women in the Age of Jackson," in her *The Majority Finds its Past* (New York, 1979); Barbara Mayer Wertheimer, *We Were There: The Story of Working Women in America* (New York, 1977); Alice Kessler-Harris, *Out to Work: A History of Wage-Earning Women in the United States* (New York, 1982); the essays in Milton Cantor and Bruce Laurie (eds.), *Class, Sex and the Woman Worker* (Westport, Conn., 1977). On early textile factories in the United States, see Thomas Dublin, *Women at Work: The Transformation of Work and Community in Lowell, Massachusetts, 1826–1860* (New York, 1979). On domestic service, see David Katzman, *Seven Days a Week: Women and Domestic Service in Industrializing America* (New York, 1978); Theresa McBride, *The Domestic Revolution: The Modernization of Household Service in England and France, 1820–1920* (New York, 1976); Leonore Davidoff, "Mastered for Life: Servant and Wife in Victorian and Edwardian England," *Jl. Social Hist.,* vii (1973–74), 406–28. On white-collar workers, see Lee Holcombe, *Victorian Ladies at Work: Middle-Class Working Women in England and Wales, 1850–1914* (Hamden, Conn., 1973). On England,

see Sally Alexander, "Women's Work in Nineteenth-Century London: A Study of the Years 1820–50," in Juliet Mitchell and Ann Oakley (eds.), *The Rights and Wrongs of Women* (London, 1976), 59–111; Sally Alexander et al., "Labouring Women: A Reply to Eric Hobsbawm," *History Workshop,* no. 8 (1979), 174–82; Anna Davin, "Feminism and Labour History," in R. Samuel (ed.), *People's History and Socialist Theory* (London, 1981), 176–81; Barbara Taylor, " 'The Men Are as Bad as their Masters. . .': Socialism, Feminism and Sexual Antagonism in the London Tailoring Trade in the Early 1830s," *Feminist Studies,* v (1979), 7–40. For France, see Madeleine Guilbert, *Les fonctions des femmes dans l'industrie* (Paris, 1966); "Travaux de femmes dans la France du XIXᵉ siècle," special issue of *Le mouvement social,* no. 105 (1978). Madeleine Guilbert et al. (eds.), *Travail et condition féminine: bibliographie commentée* (Paris, 1977) is an extraordinarily thorough and comprehensive source for France.

6. Work on the demographic transition includes Robert V. Wells, "Family History and Demographic Transition," *Jl. Social Hist.,* ix (1975–76), 1–19; Daniel Scott Smith, "Parental Power and Marriage Patterns: An Analysis of Historical Trends in Hingham, Massachusetts," *Jl. Marriage and the Family,* xxxv (1973), 419–28; James A. and Olive Banks, *Prosperity and Parenthood* (London, 1954); James A. and Olive Banks, *Feminism and Family Planning in Victorian England* (Liverpool, 1964); Edward Shorter, "Female Emancipation, Birth Control and Fertility in European History," *Amer. Hist. Rev.,* lxxviii (1973), 605–40. On ideology, see Angus McLaren, "Contraception and the Working Classes: The Social Ideology of the English Birth Control Movement in its Early Years," *Comparative Studies in Society and Hist.,* xviii (1976), 236–51; Angus McLaren, "Sex and Socialism: The Opposition of the French Left to Birth Control in the Nineteenth Century," *Jl. Hist. Ideas,* xxxvii (1976), 475–92; R. P. Neuman, "Working Class Birth Control in Wilhelmine Germany," *Comparative Studies in Society and Hist.,* xx (1978), 408–28. An analysis of the role of the state is in Anna Davin, "Imperialism and Motherhood," *History Workshop,* no. 5 (1978), 9–66. The relationship of feminism and reproduction in the political discourse of the period is analyzed in Atina Grossman, "Abortion and Economic Crisis: The 1931 Campaign against #218 in Germany," *New German Critique,* xvi (1978), 119–37. On "domestic feminism," see Daniel Scott Smith, "Family Limitation, Sexual Control and Domestic Feminism in Victorian America," in M. Hartman and L. Banner (eds.), *Clio's Consciousness Raised* (New York, 1974), 119–36. On women's sexual autonomy, see Linda Gordon, *Woman's Body, Woman's Right: A Social History of Birth Control in America* (New York, 1976); Patricia Knight, "Women and Abortion in Victorian and Edwardian England," *History Workshop,* no. 4 (1977), 57–69; Angus McLaren, "Abortion in England, 1890–1914," *Victorian Studies,* xx (1976–77), 379–400; Angus McLaren, "Abortion in France: Women and the Regulation of Family Size, 1800–1914," *French Hist. Studies,* no. 10 (1977–78), 461–85. On reproduction, see Renate Bridenthal, "The Dialectics of Production and Reproduction in History," *Radical America,* x, no. 2 (1976), 3–11; Nancy Folbre, "Of Patriarchy Born: The Political Economy of Fertility Decisions," *Feminist Studies,* ix (1983), 261–84.

7. Examples of histories of "women in public" are Jane Abray, "Feminism in the French Revolution," *Amer. Hist. Rev.,* lxxx (1975), 43–62; the invaluable document collection by Patricia Hollis, *Women in Public* (London, 1979); and the many studies of women's movements including Ellen Dubois, *Feminism and Suffrage: The Emergence of an Independent Women's Movement in America, 1848–69* (Ithaca, N.Y., 1978); Andrew Rosen, *Rise Up Women! The Militant Campaign of the Women's Social and Political Union* (London, 1974); Richard Evans, *The Feminist Movement in Germany, 1894–1933* (London, 1976); Richard Stites, *The Women's Liberation Movement in Russia* (Princeton, 1978). On working-class movements, unions, and socialism, see Mari Jo Buhle, *Women and American Socialism, 1870–1920* (Urbana, Ill., 1981); Dorothy Thompson, "Women and Nineteenth-Century Radical Politics: A Lost Dimension," in Mitchell and Oakley (eds.), *Rights and Wrongs of Women,* 112–38; Jean H. Quataert,

Reluctant Feminists in German Social Democracy, 1885–1917 (Princeton, 1979); Marilyn Boxer and Jean H. Quataert, *Socialist Women* (New York, 1978); Charles Sowerwine, *Sisters or Citizens? Women and Socialism in France since 1876* (Cambridge, 1982); Alice Kessler-Harris, "Where are the Organized Women Workers?," *Feminist Studies*, iii, nos. 1–2 (1975), 92–110; Sheila Lewenhak, *Women and Trade Unions* (London, 1977); Meredith Tax, *The Rising of the Women: Feminist Solidarity and Class Conflict, 1880–1912* (New York, 1980). On women's culture in political movements, see Blanche Wiesen Cook, "Female Support Networks and Political Activism: Lillian Wald, Crystal Eastman, Emma Goldman," *Chrysalis*, iii (1977), 43–61; Estelle Freedman, *Their Sisters' Keepers: Women's Prison Reform in America, 1830–1930* (Ann Arbor, Mich., 1981); Mary Ryan, "A Woman's Awakening: Evangelical Religion and the Families of Utica, New York, 1800–1840," *Amer. Quart.*, xxx (1978), 602–33; Nancy Cott, *The Bonds of Womanhood: Women's Sphere in New England, 1780–1835* (New Haven, Conn., 1977); Temma Kaplan, "Female Consciousness and Collective Action: The Case of Barcelona, 1910–1918," *Signs*, vii (1981–82), 545–66; Ellen DuBois et al., "Symposium: Politics and Culture in Women's History," *Feminist Studies*, vi (1980), 26–64.

8. Sheila Rowbotham, *Hidden from History* (London, 1973); Renate Bridenthal and Claudia Koonz (eds.), *Becoming Visible: Women in European History* (Boston, 1977); Hartman and Banner (eds.), *Clio's Consciousness Raised;* Berenice Carroll (ed.), *Liberating Women's History* (Urbana, Ill., 1976); Mitchell and Oakley (eds.), *Rights and Wrongs of Women*. The two superb collections edited by Martha Vicinus, *Suffer and Be Still* (Bloomington, Ind., 1972) and *A Widening Sphere* (Bloomington, Ind., 1977) have titles more descriptive of their subject than of their mission, but the introductory essays deal with the same theme.

9. Joan Kelly-Gadol, "Did Women Have a Renaissance?", in Bridenthal and Koonz (eds.), *Becoming Visible*, 137–64.

10. See my summary of this research in "The Mechanization of Women's Work," *Scientific American*, ccxlvii, no. 3 (1982), 167–87. See also Lerner, "The Lady and the Mill Girl"; Susan J. Kleinberg, "Technology and Women's Work: The Lives of Working-Class Women in Pittsburgh, 1870–1900," *Labor Hist.*, xvii (1976), 58–72; Ruth Schwartz Cowan, "The 'Industrial Revolution' in the Home: Household Technology and Social Change in the Twentieth Century," *Technology and Culture*, xvii (1976), 1–26; Joann Vanek, "Time Spent in Housework," *Scientific American*, ccxxxi, no. 5 (1974), 116–20; Susan Strasser, *Never Done: A History of American Housework* (New York, 1982).

11. Joan Hoff-Wilson, "The Illusion of Change: Women and the American Revolution," in Alfred Young (ed.), *The American Revolution: Explorations in the History of American Radicalism* (DeKalb, Ill., 1976), 383–446; Albie Sachs and Joan Hoff-Wilson, *Sexism and the Law: A Study of Male Beliefs and Judicial Bias* (Oxford, 1978); Darlene Gay Levy, Harriet Branson Applewhite, and Mary Durham Johnson, *Women in Revolutionary Paris, 1789–95* (Urbana, Ill., 1979). See also Lee Holcombe, "Victorian Wives and Property: Reform of the Married Women's Property Law, 1857–82," in Vicinus (ed.), *Widening Sphere*, 3–28; Elizabeth Fox-Genovese, "Property and Patriarchy in Classical Bourgeois Political Theory," *Radical Hist. Rev.*, iv, nos. 2–3 (1977), 36–59; Susan Miller Okin, *Women in Western Political Thought* (Princeton, 1979); Linda Kerber, *Women of the Republic* (Chapel Hill, N.C., 1980); Mary Beth Norton, *Liberty's Daughters: The Revolutionary Experience of American Women, 1750–1800* (Boston, 1980).

12. Barbara Ehrenreich and Deirdre English, *For Her Own Good: 150 Years of the Experts' Advice to Women* (New York, 1978); Barbara Welter, "The Cult of True Womanhood, 1820–60," *Amer. Quart.*, xviii (1966), 151–74; Peter T. Cominos, "Innocent Femina Sensualis in Unconscious Conflict," in Vicinus (ed.), *Suffer and Be Still*, 155–72; Blanche Glassman Hersh, *The Slavery of Sex: Feminist Abolitionists in America* (Urbana, Ill., 1978); William Leach, *True Love and Perfect Union: The Feminist Critique of*

Sex and Society (New York, 1980). A different sort of interpretation has emerged among a group of American scholars, who argue that there was an improvement in women's social and family status with the adoption of the ideology of domesticity. See nn. 17, 18, 19 below.

13. Catherine M. Scholten, " 'On the Importance of the Obstetrick Art': Changing Customs of Childbirth in America, 1760–1825," *William and Mary Quart.*, xxxiv (1977), 426–45; Mary Roth Walsh, *Doctors Wanted, No Women Need Apply: Sexual Barriers in the Medical Profession, 1835–1975* (New Haven, Conn., 1977); James Mohr, *Abortion in America: The Origins and Evolution of National Policy* (New York, 1978); Frances E. Kobrin, "The American Midwife Controversy: A Crisis of Professionalization," *Bull. Hist. Medicine*, xl (1966), 350–63; Judy Barrett Litoff, *American Midwives, 1860 to the Present* (Westport, Conn., 1978); Jane B. Donegan, *Women and Men Midwives: Medicine, Morality and Misogyny in Early America* (Westport, Conn., 1978); Barbara Ehrenreich and Deirdre English, *Witches, Midwives and Nurses: A History of Women Healers* (Old Westbury, N.Y., 1973); Jacques Gelis, "La formation des accoucheurs et des sages-femmes aux XVIIe et XVIIIe siècles," *Annales de démographie historique* (1977): "Médecins, médecine et société en France, aux XVIIIe et XIXe siècles," special issue of *Annales. E.S.C.*, xxxii, no. 5 (1977); "La femme soignante," special issue of *Pénélope*, no. 5 (Autumn 1981). On the complicated history of wet-nursing in France, see George D. Sussman, *Selling Mother's Milk: The Wet-Nursing Business in France, 1715–1914* (Urbana, Ill., 1982); Fanny Fay-Sallois, *Les nourrices à Paris au XIXeme siècle* (Paris, 1980). On the relationship between the professionalization of science and the position of women scientists, see Margaret Rossiter, *Women Scientists in America: Struggles and Strategies to 1914* (Baltimore, 1982). On the contributions of women scientists to debate about sexual equality, see Rosalind Rosenberg, *Beyond Separate Spheres: Intellectual Roots of Modern Feminism* (New Haven, Conn., 1982).

14. Extensive bibliographical treatment can be found in Barbara Sicherman, E. William Monter, Joan W. Scott, and Kathryn K. Sklar, *Recent United States Scholarship on the History of Women* (Washington, D.C., 1980); Elizabeth Fox-Genovese, "Placing Women's History in History," *New Left Rev.*, no. 133 (1982), 5–29. For England, see Barbara Kanner, *The Women of England from Anglo-Saxon Times to the Present* (Hamden, Conn., 1979), and her essays in Vicinus (ed.), *Suffer and Be Still* and Vicinus (ed.), *Widening Sphere*. For a review of scholarship on France, see Karen M. Offen, " 'First Wave' Feminism in France: New Work and Resources," *Women's Studies Internat. Forum*, v (1982), 685–9.

15. Steven Hause (with Anne R. Kenney), *The Political Rights of French Women: Feminism, Social Politics and Women's Suffrage in the Third Republic* (Princeton, 1984). An extraordinarily sensitive account which locates the origins of one wing of the American feminist movement in a broad political and social context is Sara Evans, *Personal Politics: The Roots of Women's Liberation in the Civil Rights Movement and the New Left* (London, 1978).

16. Jill Liddington and Jill Norris, *One Hand Tied Behind Us: The Rise of the Women's Suffrage Movement* (London, 1978).

17. Carroll Smith-Rosenberg, "The Female World of Love and Ritual: Relations between Women in Nineteenth-Century America," *Signs*, i (1975–76), 1–29.

18. Cott, *Bonds of Womanhood*; Nancy Cott, "Passionlessness: An Interpretation of Victorian Sexual Ideology, 1790–1850," *Signs*, iv (1978–79), 219–36; Linda Gordon, "Voluntary Motherhood: The Beginnings of Feminist Birth Control Ideas in the United States," in Hartman and Banner (eds.), *Clio's Consciousness Raised*, 54–71; Linda K. Kerber, "Daughters of Columbia: Educating Women for the Republic, 1787–1805," in S. Elkins and E. McKitrick (eds.), *The Hofstadter Aegis: A Memorial* (New York, 1974), 36–59.

19. See for example Anne Firor Scott, *The Southern Lady: From Pedestal to Politics, 1830–1930* (Chicago, 1970); Jacqueline Dowd Hall, *Revolt against Chivalry: Jessie*

Daniel Ames and the Women's Campaign against Lynching (New York, 1979); Mary P. Ryan, "The Power of Women's Networks: A Case Study of Female Moral Reform in Antebellum America," *Feminists Studies*, v (1979), 66–85. A critical perspective on the argument is found in Jill Conway, "Women Reformers and American Culture, 1870–1930," *Jl. Social Hist.*, v. (1971–72), 164–77; and Barbara Leslie Epstein, *The Politics of Domesticity: Women, Evangelism and Temperance in Nineteenth-Century America* (Middletown, Conn., 1981).

20. Bonnie Smith, *Ladies of the Leisure Class: The Bourgeoises of Northern France in the Nineteenth Century* (Princeton, 1981).

21. Carl Degler, *At Odds: Women and the Family in America from the Revolution to the Present* (New York, 1980).

22. Ann D. Gordon, Mari Jo Buhle, and Nancy Schrom Dye, "The Problem of Women's History," in Carroll (ed.), *Liberating Women's History*, 89.

23. In addition to the studies listed in n.5 above, see Tamara K. Hareven, "Family Time and Industrial Time: Family and Work in a Planned Corporation Town, 1900–1924," *Jl. Urban Hist.*, i (1974–75), 365–89; Karen O. Mason et al., "Women's Work and the Life Course in Essex County, Mass., 1880," in Tamara K. Haraven (ed.), *Transitions: The Family and Life Course in Historical Perspective* (New York, 1978); Elizabeth H. Pleck, "A Mother's Wages: Income Earning among Married Italian and Black Women, 1896–1911," in Michael Gordon (ed.), *The American Family in Social-Historical Perspective*, 2nd ed. (New York, 1978), 490–510; Elizabeth H. Pleck, "Two Worlds in One: Work and Family", *Jl. Social Hist.*, x (1976–77), 178–95; Carole Turbin, "And We Are Nothing but Women: Irish Working Women in Troy," in Carol R. Berkin and Mary Beth Norton (eds.), *Women of America: A History* (Boston, 1979); "Immigrant Women and the City", special issue of *Jl. Urban Hist.*, iv, no. 3 (1977–78); Dee Garrison, "The Tender Technicians: The Feminization of Public Librarianship, 1876–1905," in Hartman and Banner (eds.), *Clio's Consciousness Raised*, 158–78; Margery Davies, "Women's Place is at the Typewriter: The Feminization of the Clerical Labor Force," *Radical America*, xviii, no. 4 (1974), 1–28; Claudia Goldin, "Female Labour Force Participation: The Origin of Black and White Differences, 1870 and 1880," *Jl. Econ. Hist.*, xxxvii (1977), 87–108; Linda Nochlin, "Why Have There Been No Great Women Artists?", *Art News*, lxix, no. 1 (1971), 22–39, 67–71.

24. See for example Martha Blaxall and Barbara Reagan (eds.), *Women and the Workplace: The Implications of Occupational Segregation* (Chicago, 1976); Valerie Kincaide Oppenheimer, *Female Labor Force Participation in the United States* (Berkeley, 1970); Tilly and Scott, *Women, Work and Family;* Jane Humphries, "Class Struggle and the Persistence of the Working Class Family," *Cambridge Jl. Econ.*, i, no. 3 (1977), 241–58; Jane Humphries, "Working Class Family, Women's Liberation and Class Struggle: The Case of Nineteenth-Century British History," *Rev. Radical Polit. Econ.*, ix, no. 3 (1977), 25–41; Louise A. Tilly, "Paths of Proletarianization: Organization of Production, Sexual Division of Labor and Women's Collective Action," *Signs*, vii (1981–2), 400–17. An attempt to look at the economic and gender aspects is Ellen Ross, "Fierce Questions and Taunts: Married Life in Working-Class London, 1870–1914," *Feminist Studies*, viii (1982), 575–602.

25. An interesting attempt to describe the interactions of cultural categories and the sex-typing of jobs is Julie Matthaei, *An Economic History of American Women* (New York, 1982).

26. Zillah Eisenstein, "Developing a Theory of Capitalist Patriarchy," and Heidi Hartman, "Capitalist Patriarchy and Job Segregation by Sex," in Zillah Eisenstein (ed.), *Capitalist Patriarchy and the Case for Socialist Feminism* (New York, 1979), 211–30; Heidi Hartman, "The Family as the Locus of Gender, Class, and Political Struggle," *Signs*, vi (Spring 1981), 366–94; Annette Kuhn, "Structures of Patriarchy and Capital in the Family," in A. Kuhn and A. Wolpe (eds.), *Feminism and Materialism* (London, 1978). The exchange in Samuel (ed.), *People's History and Socialist Theory*, 364–73, between Sheila Rowbotham and Sally Alexander and Barbara Taylor airs the debate,

with Rowbotham pointing up the dilemmas for historians of a static conception of the structures of patriarchy. See also Rosalind Coward, *Patriarchal Precedents* (London, 1983).

27. Joan Kelly-Gadol, "The Social Relations of the Sexes: Methodological Implications of Women's History," *Signs*, i (1975–76), 816. See also her "The Doubled Vision of Feminist Theory: A Postscript to the 'Women and Power' Conference," *Feminist Studies*, v (1979), 216–27.

28. Natalie Zemon Davis, "'Women's History' in Transition: The European Case," *Feminist Studies*, iii, nos. 3–4 (1976), 90.

29. Temma Kaplan, *Anarchists of Andalusia, 1868–1903* (Princeton, N.J., 1977).

30. Tim Mason, "Women in Nazi Germany," *History Workshop*, no. 1 (1976), 74–113, and no. 2 (1976), 5–32.

31. Judith Walkowitz, *Prostitution and Victorian Society: Women, Class and the State* (Cambridge, 1980).

32. Brian Harrison, *Separate Spheres: The Opposition to Women's Suffrage in Britain* (New York, 1978). For studies of suffrage movements, see nn. 7, 16 above.

33. Darlene Gay Levy and Harriet Applewhite, "Male Responses to the Political Activism of the Women of the People in Paris, 1789–93" (unpublished paper). See also their discussion in Levy, Applewhite and Johnson (eds.), *Women in Revolutionary Paris, 1789–95*. On iconographic representations, see Maurice Agulhon, *Marianne au combat: l'imagerie et la symbolique républicaines de 1789 à 1880* (Paris, 1979) and Lynn Hunt, "Hercules and the Radical Image in the French Revolution," *Representations*, 2 (Spring 1983), 95–117.

34. Deborah Valenze, "Pilgrims and Progress in Nineteenth-Century England," in R. Samuel and G. Stedman Jones (eds.), *Culture, Ideology, and Politics* (London, 1983), pp. 113–25; and her *Prophetic Sons and Daughters: Female Preaching and Popular Religion in Industrial England* (Princeton, 1985).

35. Leonore Davidoff, "Class and Gender in Victorian England: The Diaries of Arthur J. Munby and Hannah Cullwick," *Feminist Studies*, v (1979), 87–141.

36. Gareth Stedman Jones, "Utopian Socialism Reconsidered," and Barbara Taylor, "Socialist Feminism: Utopian or Scientific?", in Samuel (ed.), *People's History and Socialist Theory*, 138–44, 158–63. See also Barbara Taylor, *Eve and the New Jerusalem: Socialism and Feminism in the Nineteenth Century* (London, 1983).

37. Michelle Perrot, "La femme populaire rebelle," and Christiane Dufrancatel, "La femme imaginaire des hommes: politique idéologie et imaginaire dans le mouvement ouvrier," in C. Dufrancatel, Arlette Farge, and Christiane Faure, *L'histoire sans qualités* (Paris, 1979), 123–56, 157–86. See also essays in Michelle Perrot (ed.), *Une Histoire des femmes est-elle possible?* (Paris, 1984).

38. The same could be said of other topics of social history, which in uncovering information about hitherto "invisible" groups, introduce questions about the reasons for their invisibility, the economic and social conflicts that have been masked and so on. In the same way that much of the so-called apolitical social history provided the documentation, conceptualization, and questions to challenge conventional political accounts, so the various approaches to women's history—those I have called "her-story" and those subsumed within certain branches of social history—prepare the ground for the kind of political women's history I have been advocating. The point, it seems to me, is not to reject and condemn various approaches as incorrect—in the manner of proponents of a narrowly defined political social history, among them Tony Judt, "A Clown in Regal Purple: Social History and the Historians," *History Workshop*, no. 7 (1979), 66–94, and Eugene D. Genovese and Elizabeth Fox-Genovese, "The Political Crisis of Social History: A Marxian Perspective," *Jl. Social Hist.*, x (1976–77), 205–20—but to use them all to advance the enterprise. The rewritten narrative is then a collaborative effort, not the triumph of one school over another.

Methodological Moves from Margin to Center

TOWARD A PARADIGM SHIFT IN THE ACADEMY AND IN RELIGIOUS STUDIES

Carol P. Christ

> When you are criticizing the philosophy of
> an epoch, do not chiefly direct your
> attention to the intellectual positions
> which its exponents feel it necessary
> explicitly to defend. There will be some
> fundamental assumptions which adherents
> of all the varied systems within the epoch
> unconsciously presuppose. Such
> assumptions appear so obvious that
> people do not know what they are
> assuming because no other way of putting
> things has occurred to them.[1]

This quote from Alfred North Whitehead expresses the notion implicit in
the idea of a paradigm shift as defined by Thomas Kuhn in his well-known
book *The Structure of Scientific Revolutions*.[2] Feminist scholarship, as most of
us who practice it are aware, requires a paradigm shift, a questioning of
fundamental and unquestioned assumptions about canon, ideas, value,
authority, and method that operate in the academy and in the disciplines.
Feminist scholars have begun to name the implicit androcentric perspective
that operates in every field to highlight the achievements and accomplishments of elite men and to screen out or obscure the achievements of all
women and non-elite men. We have pointed out that the androcentric
perspective functions to legitimate a patriarchal society, to make it seem
"obvious," as Whitehead puts it, that elite men have always held the power
in the world and always will.[3] In order to see through the androcentric veil,
we must shift to another paradigm, a paradigm that begins with the
assumption that all women (and non-elite men) are as intelligent and
valuable as elite men and that our contributions to history must have been
as significant as those of elite men.

Mary Daly has written that feminist scholarship requires asking "non-questions about non-data."[4] By this she means that questions such as "what have women contributed to history?" and "how has culture functioned to oppress women?" are not considered significant questions from within the androcentric perspective. Similarly, the data that would be necessary to answer such questions have not been preserved or have been purposely destroyed, or where they exist, have not been considered significant. (How many of us have had the experience of finding the book we needed to answer our questions in the library, only to discover that it had not been checked out for twenty or fifty years?)

Lifting the Androcentric Veil

Feminist research in all fields, including religious studies, begins with a paradigm shift that lifts the androcentric veil. The feminist paradigm assumes the importance and value of women, and thus finds it necessary to criticize the implicit androcentric assumptions that have labeled us as "non-data" and our questions as "non-questions." The paradigm shift implicit in making us both questioner and data is profound. We challenge unquestioned notions of *canon:* Was Homer a better poet than Sappho? and of *ideas:* Is war a more important human endeavor than love? and *value:* Does the literary tradition from Homer to Dostoyevsky, from which the works of Sappho were excluded, in fact embody the highest ideals of humankind? and *authority:* Can we trust the values and judgments of the men who created a literary and scholarly tradition from which the works of Sappho were excluded, and in which the fact and the reasons for the burning of Sappho's works (as well as the preservation of Homer) by the Church have rarely been discussed even by the greatest of male scholars? If our critique of our disciplines stopped here, the changes we would make in them would be profound.

But the paradigm shift implicit in feminist scholarship applies not only to the content, but also to the *form* of our disciplines. We not only ask "non-questions" about "non-data," but we also use a "non-method" as Mary Daly has noted. We question the most unquestioned scholarly assumption of all, namely, the assumption that scholarship is objective.

Our work reveals that scholarship which has been presented to us as "objective," "rational," "analytical," "dispassionate," "disinterested," and *"true"* is in fact rooted in an irrational and distorted androcentric vision, and that its implicit passion and interest is the preservation of patriarchy, of elite male power. As feminists we know that the ethos of scholarly objectivity is in fact mythos. We know that there is no dispassionate, disinterested scholarship. We know that our scholarship is passionate, is interested, is aimed at transforming the world we have inherited. There-fore our first task as scholars is to deconstruct the *ethos of objectivity* that operates in the academy as a whole, and to offer a new construction or model of scholarship. This act of deconstruction and construction of schol-arly *method* is one that concerns all feminist scholars, especially those of us who work in the humanities and humanistic social sciences.[5]

Deconstructing the Ethos of Objectivity

I begin this section with three stories which shed light on the problem of deconstruction and reconstruction of scholarly method.

As the sun sets over the Aegean, three women, an Israeli psychologist, an American writer and thealogian, and a Greek-American poet, talk about our work. The Greek-American poet speaks of how she began to translate the work of Greek women poets of the resistance and moved from there to historical work on Greek women in resistance. She speaks of the conflict she feels in trying to present historical research in a style that is not dryly objective. The Israeli women confesses that her work in psychology is based in storytelling, though she is quite capable of doing "controlled" experi-ments. She also reveals that she writes short stories under a pseudonym. I speak of the poetry I write and of my struggle to combine the methods of rational analysis in which I have been trained with personal insight and experience in my current writing. We all feel validated as we discover that we are engaged in similar struggles to include personal experience in our schol-arship.

Later in the summer I visit a colleague who tells me that she has broken through a major writing block when she begins to incorporate her personal story into the fieldwork study she is writing. We confirm each other in our vision of a form of scholarly writing that moves beyond so-called objectivity.

A friend tells me of a long-standing argument she has been having with a friend about his insistence on the need to find a "rational basis" for ethics. Finally after years of discussion, he breaks out of his rational mode briefly to stammer, "But, but . . . if we don't have a rational basis for ethics . . . we'll have . . . irrationality . . . Nazi Germany." "Now at least," my friend says, "I understand the stake he has in the argument. Isn't it amazing that in all these years he never before revealed the feelings which are the basis of his posi-tions?"

For me these stories illustrate the passionate desire many women scholars have to integrate the personal and the political into our scholarship, as well as the fear men have of abandoning the scholarly method which they view as rational, objective, dispassionate, and their defense against chaos.

It is difficult for feminist scholars to deconstruct and disavow the ethos of objectivity for two reasons. One is economic and political, and has to do with the power structure in the university. The other has to do with the distortions of subjectivity and objectivity, reason and emotion, that are rooted in the structure of our thought and language.

As feminist scholars we seek employment in the university. The first and easiest way to discredit our work is to call it personal or political, therefore not objective, therefore not scholarly, therefore no tenure. Because of the very real economic pressures we face, many of us have chosen to hide the personal and social relevance and meaning of our work behind the mask of a dispassionate, objective voice. "I'm not interested in finding the meaning of my life through my work, or in changing the world through it," we say. "I'm only interested in analyzing the meter and form of Sappho's poetry." Even as we adopt this strategy, we know that our work has the capacity to give meaning to our lives and to transform the world, but we hope that the powers of the academy will not notice this, or at least will not think us unscholarly because our work has this capacity. (Of course they do notice, and they do find our work threatening.)

The second reason many of us have used the forms of objective scholarship has to do with the way in which the ethos of objectivity has distorted both itself and the alternatives to it. If the alternative to objective scholarship is "non-scholarship" (to continue Daly's word game), then not all of us who have been trained as scholars will be comfortable embracing it. If the alternative is "irrationality . . . Nazi Germany," then we will call our scholarship objective. We need to deconstruct the ethos of objectivity in order to expose the distortions of thought and feeling, intellect and life which it enshrines, before we can construct alternative notions of scholarship.

The false dualism implicit in the notion of the ethos of objectivity is a dualism that posits rationality, objectivity, dispassion, and analysis on one side, and irrationality, subjectivity, passion, and chaos on the other. The origins of this sort of dualism can be traced back as far as the myths of the slaying of the primordial Goddesses such as Tiamat, Python, and Gorgon, by male Gods and heroes such as Marduk, Apollo, and Hercules in stories which define primordial female power as chaos.[6] Such thinking is also found in the philosophy of Plato, who identified the rational and the good with that which transcends the changeable, the personal, the finite, and the so-called "animal" passions.[7] It can also be seen to be rooted in the Enlightenment notion that Reason is the key that will enable mankind [sic] to rise out of the chaos of Ignorance and Superstition.[8] The ethos of objectivity is of course found in the Scientific Method, in which the researcher aspires to dispassionate, disinterested, "scientific" analysis and control of data.[9]

Continental critical theory and hermeneutical theory have challenged the ethos of objectivity, pointing out that there is no thought which can be divorced from the body and history of the thinker.[10] We all view the world from the perspectives of our own personal experiences, our history, our sex, our nationality, our ethnicity, etc. Even when we attempt to be objective, our own perspectives enter into the way we phrase the questions (and non-questions) and into the choice of data (and non-data) we observe (or do not observe). This of course is the point made by Kuhn in *The Structure of Scientific Revolutions*. Even scientific discoveries come about only when the presuppositions, the paradigms, exist through which data can be noticed, connections made, theory developed.

Though continental critical and hermeneutical theory is widely understood and accepted, it has not displaced the still prevalent ethos of objectivity that enshrouds patriarchal scholarship. The reasons for this are complex, and probably have to do with the unexpressed and unexamined fear that ways of thinking not firmly rooted in so-called rational principles lead directly back to the chaos monster, to Nazi Germany.

The failure to be clear about and to name the fear that lurks underneath the ethos of objectivity means that the emotional basis of the ethos of objectivity cannot be discussed, criticized, or deconstructed. When exposed to the light of day, the fear that an ethic or an ethos not based upon rational principles leads to genocide can be challenged. From the perspective of an ethics of caring, as described by Carol Gilligan in her book *In a Different Voice*,[11] the argument could just as easily be made that the policy of genocide in Nazi Germany was based upon an excess of rationality combined with an insufficient grounding in an ethic of caring and empathy. On the basis of an ethic of caring the Germans would have viewed the Jews as sister and fellow human beings, rather than as abstractions of evil. The Nazis were not overly passionate, it could be argued, but rather too dispassionate in their lack of concern for the human beings they murdered and tortured. It is not my purpose here to explain the origins of evil in Nazi Germany. It is sufficient here to show that the belief that rationality and objectivity can end evil is by no means self-evident. Further, it is important to bear in mind that, if my paradigmatic story has in fact captured the dynamics of the commitment to rationality and objectivity in scholarship, then it becomes evident that the ethos of objectivity is rooted in passionate personal feeling and conviction which is rooted in time and history. And thus that the ethos of objectivity has an other than objective and rational basis.

If we continue to deconstruct the ethos of objectivity, we can see that it is rooted in what "object" relations theorists[12] (this terminology also needs to be deconstructed) would view as a masculine psychology that emphasizes the separation of subject and object rather than their connection. According to object relations theorists, our experiences as babies shape our habitual ways of perceiving the world. For the baby the first experience is one of connection to the mother. For the boy baby, the experience of separation is intensified as he realizes that he is not "like" his mother. For females, on the other hand, the experience of separation is softened as they realize that they are "like" their mothers. According to this theory, though we all continue to experience both separation and connection, males tend to focus more on and be more comfortable with a self that is clearly marked off from others, while females tend to be more comfortable when they can identify with and connect with others. The ethos of objectivity can be related to the male experience of separation and distance, while the ethos of eros and empathy that I will discuss below, and that I propose as an alternative model for scholarship, can be related to the female experience of connection. The ethos of eros and empathy can also be correlated with the ethic of caring which Carol Gilligan has named a distinctively (though not necessarily exclusively) female ethical style, while the ethos of objectivity can be related to the normative male ethics of principle, also discussed by Gilligan. My proposals concerning the ethos of eros and empathy as a model for scholarship do not depend upon object relations theory for their validity. But if object relations theory is correct, it helps us understand one of the reasons women scholars are challenging the ethos of objectivity in scholarship.

Constructing the Ethos of Eros and Empathy
as a Model for Scholarship

The experience of connection suggests the ethos of eros and empathy as a model for scholarship. The ethos of eros and empathy reminds us that the root of our scholarship and research is eros, a passion to connect, the desire to understand the experience of another, the desire to deepen our understanding of ourselves and our world, the passion to transform or preserve the world as we understand it more deeply. At its best, scholarship becomes a way of loving ourselves, others, and our world more deeply. The ethos of eros and empathy reminds us that one of the goals of our scholarship is empathy, a form of understanding that reaches out to the otherness of the other, rooted in a desire to understand the world from a different point of view. Empathy is the ability to put ourselves in the other's place, to feel, to know, to experience the world from a standpoint other than our own. Empathy is possible because we have the capacity to make connections between our own experience and the experiences of others.

Empathy means not simply recognizing the connections, but also the differences between persons, texts, cultures, whatever is being studied.

My discussion of the ethos of eros and empathy[13] is influenced, but not constituted, by the early work of Michael Novak, especially his discussion of the concept of "intelligent subjectivity" in *Belief and Unbelief* and in *Ascent of the Mountain, Flight of the Dove*,[14] by the work of Martin Buber, especially his discussion of the relationship between I and You in his classic work *I and Thou*,[15] and by the work of Audre Lorde, especially her discussion of the power of the erotic in her book *Sister Outsider.*[16] From Novak I adopt the notion of "intelligent subjectivity," which names a way of understanding that transcends the traditional dichotomies of subjectivity and objectivity. I am indebted as well to Novak for his description of intelligent subjectivity as a process beginning in conscious awareness of one's own experience and standpoint, then passing over to the experience of another in order to understand the world from a different point of view, then returning to the now expanded standpoint of the self in an act of judgment that incorporates the insights learned from passing over into the standpoint of another into the standpoint of the self, though I understand this process in a somewhat different way than he does. From Buber I have taken the concept of an I-You relationship (which may exist with other people, with plants or animals, or with what he calls "spiritual forms") in which there is both distance and connection. In the I-You relationship, the integrity of the other as other is preserved, while at the same time, the solipsistic shell of the isolated ego is broken down as "the other side," the You, is understood, in Buber's terms, "bodily." According to Buber, I become I only in relation to You. Thus the act of entering into the consciousness, the world of another is at the same time constitutive of the self. From Audre Lorde, I have taken the word "erotic" as the name for one of the powers that drives us to seek to understand, that imbues our scholarship with pleasure. I am indebted to Lorde, black, American lesbian, poet, mother of a son, sister, and outsider to almost every other woman and man, for her insistence that feminist theory must affirm connection without denying difference. (It is interesting that the three theorists whose work I draw on are all outsiders in the scholarly world. Buber was Jewish, Novak is Catholic. Perhaps the experience of being an outsider, of doing scholarship from a point of view that was different from that of many of the Protestant men whose work they studied, led each of them, as it led me, to reflect upon how we come to know.)

Within the ethos of eros and empathy, the scholar remains firmly rooted in her or his own body, life experience, history, values, judgments, and interests. Rather than presuming to speak universally, objectively, or dispassionately, the scholar speaks out of a standpoint that is acknowledged to be finite and limited. In the first moment of scholarship, she or he names the eros, the passion, the desire—to understand, to connect, to preserve or change the world—that inspired her or his research. This does not mean that the scholar's work is narrowly personal, solipsistic, or self-indulgent, terms taken from the ethos of objectivity. But it does mean that she or he names the interests that inspired and to some extent shape her research.

The second moment of scholarship is directed toward enlarging the scholar's perspective through understanding the experience presented in a text, in the lives of a group of people, in a historical time, etc. The ethos of eros and empathy posits that empathy, the ability to put oneself in another's place (in Novak's terms to "pass over" to the experience of another; in Buber's terms, to experience the other side "bodily"; in Lorde's terms to make an erotic connection through difference), is possible, and is the basis of understanding. Empathy flows from eros, the drive to connect, and is aided by imagination, which enables us to make connections between our own experiences and those of others. Imagination also enables us to see and understand difference, the otherness of the other. All the standard tools of scholarly research, including criticism, historical research, analysis, careful attention to data, statistical research, theory, concern for truth, etc., are brought to bear upon the task of understanding the subject matter in this second moment of disciplined research. In this second moment our work will not differ dramatically from what we have been trained to do under the standards of the ethos of objectivity. What will differ is that we keep in mind the limits of our ability to be objective, while at the same time keeping in mind that we can be far more than simply subjective. Moreover, in this second moment, the scholar does not lose sight of the eros and empathy, the drive to understand and connect that impelled the research in the first place. But in this moment, the goal remains to get as close to the intrinsic meaning of the text, group, historical time, etc., studied, and to a communally verifiable point of view, or truth, as possible.

The third moment of scholarship is judgment. After completing research and analysis, the scholar returns to her or his now expanded standpoint. In an act of judgment, she or he incorporates the insights gained from research and analysis into her or his expanded standpoint or perspective. The scholar acknowledges that the judgments she or he makes are finite, limited by the body, history, life experiences, values, and judgments of their author. But again this does not mean that judgments are narrowly personal, or merely polemical, as the ethos of objectivity would label them. Nor hopefully are they uncritically ethnocentric or imperialistic. Rather, the scholar recognizes that her or his standpoint has been enlarged by her or his research, by entering into the disciplined analysis of a text or historical period, etc. The scholar also recognizes her or his grounding in the community of scholars, a community of discourse, within which she or he shares and receives criticism on both the research and analysis and the judgments made. The scholar avoids solipsism and polemic not by attempting to become objective, but by ever expanding the range of her or his empathy, her or his grounding in an ever expanding community of knowledge and scholarship, which in turn expands her or his standpoint.

Though the ethos of eros and empathy contrasts sharply with the ethos of objectivity as a model for scholarship, it seems to me that the best scholarship has always derived from the ethos of eros and empathy. The best education, study, and research has always been erotic and empathetic because it enables us to see and feel the world differently, because it transforms us through enlarging our vision. It seems to me that not only feminists, but all scholars, would be much more true to the real aims and visions of scholarship if we framed our scholarship explicitly within an ethos that includes eros and empathy rather than within the ethos of objectivity as narrowly defined.

Toward a Paradigm Shift in Religious Studies

Religious studies is a relatively new academic discipline. Before the 1960s, religion was taught primarily from denominational perspectives. In the liberal arts colleges, most of which were founded by members of Protestant denominations, such as Methodists, Presbyterians, Baptists, Quakers, etc., or by Roman Catholics, required courses in scripture and theology, as well as required chapel attendance were the norm. Most of the large private universities in the North, South, and Midwest, such as Yale, Harvard, Princeton, Chicago, Vanderbilt, Duke, etc. had affiliated seminaries or divinity schools, professional schools for the training of Protestant clergy; there were as well denominational seminiaries for the training of Protestant, Roman Catholic, and Jewish clergy. Many seminaries and divinity schools also offered additional programs leading to Masters or Doctor of Theology degrees. Because of the doctrine of the separation of Church and State, departments of religious studies were not established at publicly funded colleges and universities.

During the past twenty-five years, religious studies as an academic discipline has separated itself from the denominational context. The argument was made that teaching "about" religion could be separated from the teaching "of" religion. Religious history could be studied as history; the Bible and other scriptures could be studied as history and literature; even theology and ethics could be studied as the history of ideas and values. The argument for the establishment of religious studies departments was stated in the language of the prevailing ethos of the university, the ethos of objectivity. In order to insure objectivity, it was argued that the study of religions other than Protestant Christianity, including Catholicism, Judaism, Hinduism, Buddhism, etc., would become integral parts of religious studies curricula. In practice, religious studies departments were usually formed around a core of scholars trained at seminaries in Protestant Christian theological and Biblical studies. Gradually specialists in Catholicism, Judaism, and non-Western religions (usually Hinduism or Buddhism, more rarely Islam or nonliterary religious traditions) were added to the departments. In the late 1960s and early 1970s religious studies departments burgeoned as the baby boom generation, an expanding economy, and abundant federal funding allowed the growth of universities. When this expansion came to a halt in the mid-1970s, religious studies departments were firmly entrenched in the universities, but their proposed (and needed) growth was curtailed.

Though there have been many attempts to forge a single methodology for religious studies, in practice the field is multi-disciplinary; some scholars focus on texts and translation; others employ historical, philosophical, literary, anthropological, psychological, sociological, and other methods. The American Academy of Religion, the scholarly and professional association in the field of religious studies, recognizes twelve sections that reflect major areas of interest of members of the academy: Academic Study of Religion; Arts, Literature, and Religion; Comparative Studies in Religion; Ethics; History of Christianity; History of Judaism; North American Religions; Philosophy of Religion; Religion and the Social Sciences; Religion in South Asia; Theology and Religious Reflection; and Women and Religion.[17] In addition, the Society of Biblical Literature, a large professional association (Biblical studies is still the largest single area within religious studies) meets with the American Academy of Religion; and there are a number of other related professional societies, such as the Society for the Scientific Study of Religion, the Society of Christian Ethics, the Catholic Theological Society of America, the American Oriental Society, the Association for Jewish Studies, etc., which attract scholars in the field.

Though women scholars are a small minority in the field of religious studies, and feminist scholars an even smaller group, we have been very visible in recent years.[18] Feminist studies in religion is flourishing and firmly established in the academy, if not in the hiring priorities of major religious studies departments. Feminist scholarship in religion is as diverse as the field itself. Feminist scholars in religion attempt to uncover the religious lives and experiences of women in all times and places, to reconstruct theology on the basis of women's experience, to construct theory with which to understand women's religious lives in patriarchal contexts, to discover whether women have ever named our own religious experience. We study history and prehistory; we study the texts of so-called "higher" religions; we study tribal and nonliterary traditions; we study women religious leaders; we study the effects of patriarchal religious symbolism on culture. Feminist scholarship in religion began with the naming and analyzing of obvious instances of sexism within religious traditions, such as the attribution of evil to Eve, the admonition that women keep silent in church, the symbol of God as Father. As we deepened our analysis, we began to understand that sexism is not peripheral but central in most religious traditions, that the so-called "higher" religions express deeply androcentric visions of God, humanity, and the cosmos. We also discovered that the academic study of religion is based upon implicitly androcentric presuppositions; that what we generally studied was the religious lives and visions of men. We began to insist that the religious lives and visions of women also be studied. Some of us wrote openly about the need to transform or move beyond Judaism and Christianity, while others began to search for times and places before, within, or in reaction to patriarchal religion where women may have been able to express our own religious insights.

Behind all this research, which was expressed in more or less traditional scholarly form and language, there was an enormous longing on the part of most feminist scholars in religion not only to learn about women's religious lives, but to find models for authentic female religious experience. At the same time women in the churches and synagogues began to question women's religious roles, while other women who sought to define spiritual paths outside of traditional religious structures began to create the women's spirituality and Goddess movements. This ferment has produced among other things, many conferences, workshops, and groups on nontraditional forms of women's spirituality, openings to the ordination of women and efforts to retranslate or revise the Bible and liturgy in more liberal Protestant and Jewish groups, as well as a hardening of traditional opposition to women's religious leadership and a hardening of traditional views about women's sexual freedom and social roles in more conservative religious groups. Roman Catholic groups have spearheaded the anti-choice movement, Mormons and fundamentalist Protestant groups have actively worked against ERA, and fundamentalist preachers have made the image of God as Father and the patriarchal family and state the rallying cry for their right-wing political agendas. In the Moslem world as well, fundamentalists have made opposition to female social and sexual freedom central in their opposition to Western imperialism and values. In such a social and political context, it is very difficult to maintain that feminist scholarship in religious studies is objective, impartial, unbiased, that it has no political purpose. Thus the critique of the ethos of objectivity is especially critical in religious studies. However, because the battle to legitimate religious studies within the universities, by construing scholarship in the field according to the ethos of objectivity, has so recently been fought, the feminist critique of the ethos of objectivity touches nerves that are extremely sensitive. This sensitivity may also explain why major departments of religious studies have been slow to hire feminist scholars whose work challenges the ethos of objectivity. (Divinity schools, on the other hand, which do not have a commitment of the same kind to the ethos of objectivity, have been more willing to hire Christian feminist scholars.)

If religious studies, like other disciplines, is guided by implicit andro-centric biases and prejudices, then not only the form, but also the content of what is researched and studied must change. To discuss all the various ways a field as diverse as religious studies will be transformed by feminist scholarship would require far more space than is available here. Therefore, I will limit my discussion of the paradigm shift in religious studies to a single area, which, however, has broad implications for the field as a whole. This area is the study of the prehistoric Goddesses of Old Europe and the Near East. Many of the points I will make with regard to the study of the prehistoric Goddesses of Old Europe and the Near East may also apply to the study of prehistoric Goddesses in other cultures, and to the study of prehistoric and preliterate cultures more generally.

Prehistoric Goddesses and the Paradigm Shift in Religious Studies

The study of prehistoric religions of Old Europe and the Near East in which Goddess symbolism is prominent and in which there is no evidence of female subordination in religion and society, presents a profound challenge to the field of religious studies. The prehistoric Goddesses threaten the alleged truth of patriarchal religion that "in the beginning God created the heavens and the earth" (Gen. 1:1). They also challenge the implicit, unstated, and unexamined principle of patriarchal societies that men have always held the power in religion and society. Finally, they reveal how much the supposedly value-free discipline of religious studies remains shaped by implicit and largely uncriticized androcentric assumptions about God, time, and text which are derived from Biblical religion, and which are implicitly supportive of both patriarchal religions and patriarchal societies. A paradigm shift is required in relation to these assumptions.

Eros and Empathy in Feminist Scholarship on
the Prehistoric Goddesses

Feminist scholar Anne L. Barstow has powerfully stated the eros which has led feminist scholars to research prehistoric religions:

> I became interested in the prehistoric goddess when I first asked myself, "What would a religion created, at least in part, by women be like? What values did it express? What needs would it meet?" I knew that the Western religious tradition in which I had been raised, with its narrow patriarchalism, did not meet my spiritual needs, but I had no knowledge of alternative religious ideas.[19]

Besides deriving from a desire to find a religion created at least in part by women, Barstow's research on Neolithic religion at Çatal Hüyük was also funded by an experience of empathy, a felt connection between her own experience and the symbols at Çatal Hüyük:

> I know what I felt when I first saw the ruins of the shrine at Çatal Hüyük: the goddess figure above the rows of breasts and bulls' horns, her legs stretched wide, giving birth, was a symbol of life and creativity such as I had not seen in a Western church.[20]

Barstow felt a profound sense of validation of her femaleness at Çatal Hüyük. Merlin Stone evoked similar feelings when she wrote, "In the beginning . . . God was a woman. Do you remember?"[21] As Christine Downing points out in *The Goddess*, to learn about the Goddesses is in a profound sense a remembering, a recollection of something we know deeply within about our own power, and a re-membering, an act which gives us back the power of our bodies, the power of our female sexuality.[22]

In discussing feminists' interests in the prehistoric Goddesses, classicist Sarah B. Pomeroy notes that:

> the roles of females both divine and mortal in prehistory has become an *emotional issue with political implications* as well as a topic of scholarly debate.[23] (emphasis added)

Pomeroy seems dismayed that feminists deviate from the ethos of objectivity by having an emotional and political stake in scholarly issues. Because she accepts the ethos of objectivity in scholarship, and attempts to situate her own work within it, she fails to notice that the work of male scholars, or her own, may also be affected by emotional and political interests. For example, she notes that historian Moses Finley dismisses "the primacy of the mother goddess [as] only a 'remarkable fable' and unequivocally attacks the notion of female dominance in prehistory."[24] But she fails to question whether his scholarship on this issue is "objective" or whether it reflects an attempt to justify the patriarchal notion that male power always has been and always will be.

Feminist Scholarship on the Prehistoric Goddesses

The religious life of humankind may go back as far as 70,000–50,000 B.C.E. or earlier. There is archaeological evidence that Paleolithic women and men buried their dead with ceremonies thought to have been the first religious rituals. From the Upper Paleolithic (Old Stone Age, c. 32,000–10,000 B.C.E) come the great cave paintings of bison and deer as well as the so-called Paleolithic "Venuses," small carved stone statues and reliefs, which are among the first religious symbols.[25] According to G. Rachel Levy, the cave was the symbol of the womb of the Creatrix, the Mother, the Earth. The rituals performed in her center reflected Paleolithic people's desire to participate in the creativity of the Mother and in the power of the animals that emerged from her womb.[26] While there is no clear evidence about the role and status of women in what must have been small Paleolithic groups or tribes, it seems likely that women and men shared relative equality in Paleolithic gathering and hunting societies, that everyone's work was valued, that elders of both sexes were valued for their wisdom, and that women knew themselves to be manifestations of the cosmic power of birth, death, and transformation, while men were valued as hunters.

Between 10,000 and 8,000 B.C.E., the last ice age ended. As the ice caps receded from Europe and the Near East, the conditions were ripe for the Neolithic (New Stone Age) revolution (began c. 9000 B.C.E. in the Near East) in which farming was introduced.[27] As Ruby Rohrlich has noted, anthropologists now generally "concede" that women were the inventors of agriculture.[28] The agricultural revolution has long been celebrated as one of the great revolutions in human history, because it enabled human beings to settle down in one place and to begin to develop society and culture as we know them today. But the role of women in the invention of agriculture, in the rapid, almost miraculous, hybridization of grain and in the creation of pottery and weaving in the Neolithic period is generally given little more than cursory acknowledgement by scholars.[29] Some of the most important evidence about Neolithic religion comes from the work of archaeologist Marija Gimbutas. Gimbutas coined the term "Old Europe" to refer to the Neolithic and Chalcolithic (Copper Age) culture of Southern and Eastern Europe and the Greek islands from 6500–3500 B.C.E. In Old Europe Goddess symbolism was prominent, and there is no evidence that women were subordinate in religion or society. Gimbutas describes the society of Old Europe as prosperous, artistic, peaceful, matrifocal, and sedentary. She believes that women played central roles in the religion and society of Old Europe and favors the theory that the towns of Old Europe were theo[sic]centric and were ruled by the priestess queen, in conjunction with her brother or husband.[30] James Mellaart, who excavated the Neolithic town of Çatal Hüyük (6500–5700 B.C.E.) in central Turkey, found a culture similar to that of Old Europe. Goddess symbolism was pre-eminent and he found evidence of matrilinear and matrilocal customs. He believed that women played central roles in the agricultural and religious life of the village. As in Old Europe, there was no evidence of warfare or the kind of centralized authority associated with patriarchal kingship. But though Mellaart theorized that women were not subordinate at Çatal Hüyük, this astonishing possibility is not given central focus in his work.[31] But in the work of feminist scholars such as Barstow and Rohrlich, the role of women at Çatal Hüyük becomes central. A picture begins to emerge of prosperous settled agricultural villages and towns where women played central roles in farming, weaving, and the making of pots, where women's role as birth-giver was connected to her awesome power as transformer of seed to grain to bread, of clay to pot, of wool or flax to thread to cloth. Given the important social roles of women and the predominance of female religious symbolism in this period, there is no reason not to believe that women created or played central roles in Neolithic religion, and in the creation of its symbolism, its ceremonies.

The more familiar Goddesses of classical Greek and later Near Eastern mythology, such as Athene, Aphrodite, Artemis, Ishtar, and Inanna come from later bronze age and iron age societies, which as Rohrlich has theorized began to become patriarchal, militaristic, and centralized beginning about 3500–3000 B.C.E. Rohrlich's study of the transition to patriarchy (which involved the asking of a "non-question", since it had been assumed that patriarchy was not in need of explanation) in Sumer after 3500 B.C.E. indicates that as warfare became widespread in the Near East, the warrior king replaced the priestess queen as the central authority in society, that societies became economically and militarily centralized, that slavery and class stratification became normative, and that the status of women declined.[32] In this situation the Goddesses of the Neolithic and earlier periods were slain or made subordinate to the new Gods of the patriarchal warriors, such as Zeus and Marduk. The primordial Creatrix in Sumer, Tiamat, is named chaos monster and slain by Marduk in the Babylonian epic *The Enuma Elish*. Athene, once an autonomous Goddess, perhaps from Crete, is reborn from the head of Zeus after he swallows (murders) her mother. Forever after Athene becomes the Goddess of the warrior. The Goddesses of patriarchy must be understood to be the creations of patriarchal ideology. They but dimly reflect the power of women and Goddesses in pre-patriarchal societies. They give rise to the myth that Goddesses are the creations of men and that their images everywhere support male power. On the islands such as Crete and Thera (Santorini) which were less vulnerable to military attack than the land-based cities, the Neolithic towns developed into prosperous cities, where it is theorized the status of women and Goddesses remained high for a much longer time, perhaps until c. 1500 B.C.E.[33]

God, Time, and Text
The Prehistoric Goddesses and the Paradigm Shift
in Religious Studies

The prehistory of the Goddesses provides one lens through which we may deconstruct assumptions about God, time, and text which continue to structure the field of religious studies. The notions of God, time, and text which shape the field of religious studies are very much intertwined, and all three can be shown to be related to Biblical and Christian theological categories. Feminist scholars are by no means the first to question the use of Biblical and theological categories to raise questions about and to interpret data from non-Biblical religions. Historians and anthropologists of religion have been raising similar sorts of questions for a long time. However, because of the origin of the field in Biblical and theological studies, and because habits of mind are very hard to break, Biblical and theological notions of God, time, and text continue to exert a very powerful influence on the field. Thus, for example, scholars of non-Western religions remain very much wedded to the analysis of text, and the prehistory of non-Western religions (where Goddesses were also more powerful and more prominent than in their patriarchal texts) is not studied sufficiently. And the scholarly study of the religions of nonliterary peoples remains peripheral in the field of religious studies. Thus it remains important to outline some of the ways in which feminist scholarship about the prehistoric Goddesses challenges the field of religious studies to change its central paradigms.

Time

For those working in Western religions, and these are still the vast majority of scholars in religious studies, time generally begins with the time of the Hebrew patriarchs, with Abraham (c. 1800 B.C.E.) or with Moses (c. 1300–1200 B.C.E.). Time proceeds from Abraham and Moses, through the Davidic kingship (c. 1000 B.C.E.), to the time of the prophets, to the time of the origins of Christianity and Rabbinic Judaism in the first century C.E. If time before Abraham is mentioned, it is usually discussed within the framework provided by Samuel Noah Kramer's book, *History Begins at Sumer* as Anne Barstow has noted. The Babylonian creation epic, *The Enuma Elish*, which depicts the slaying of the primordial Goddess Tiamat and the *Epic of Gilgamesh* in which the Goddess Ishtar is called an "old fat whore" may be discussed as providing evidence about the origins of religion in the Near East. Frequently even this material is discussed primarily as the backdrop which enables us to understand the distinctive (and superior) contributions of Hebrew religion.

From a feminist perspective on the prehistory of the Goddesses, it is clear that these texts derive from a time when patriarchy is already well established. If history begins with Sumer or with Israel, then history is patriarchal history. We may discover the roles of women within patriarchal history (and these may be substantial), but we do not have the history of a time when women's roles in religion and culture were central and unquestioned.[34]

Feminist research on the prehistory of the Goddesses challenges the field of religious studies dramatically to expand its concept of time. The time of the Neolithic revolution (began c. 9000 B.C.E. in the Near East) is nearly 8000 years before the time of Moses and David, more than 5000 years before history was said to have begun at Sumer. The Paleolithic period in which religion originated is tens of thousands of years before the Neolithic revolution. Feminist research on the prehistoric Goddesses challenges the field of religious studies to do more than pay lip service to the time before Moses and Abraham, to the time before Sumer.

Anyone who studies prehistory (or any non-Christian religion, including Judaism), rapidly becomes aware that the Christian naming of time as "before" and "after" Christ distorts their research, making it difficult to grasp the relationships of time "before Christ" (it is counterintuitive to think of 457 B.C.E. as being after 579 B.C.E.), difficult to grasp the relationships of times before and after Christ (there was in fact no major break in history between 50 B.C.E. and 50 C.E.), and even more difficult to grasp the scope of history (the time of Moses is little more than 3000 years ago, while the time of the Neolithic revolution is more than 11,000 years ago). The naming we give to time is not a trivial or arbitrary matter, as Christian rulers recognized when they took control of it. It will be difficult for us to fully grasp and understand ancient prehistory as long as we are rooted by language and conceptuality in the Christian naming of time. (Anthropologists have recognized this and devised their own naming of time as "before present," or b.p.) From this point of view the suggestion made by Merlin Stone that we rename time from a feminist perspective—she suggested that we begin from the time when women invented agriculture—is by no means trivial.[35]

Text

To do more than pay lip service to the origins of religion in prehistory, the field of religious studies will also have to re-examine its *logos* orientation, its commitment to the written word, its commitment to text. "And God spoke, and said, 'Let there be light' " (Gen. 1:1). "In the beginning was the Word, and the Word was with God, and the Word was God" (John 1:1). Scholars of course consider the complex meanings embedded in the notion of speech and in the word *logos* and recognize these two accounts of creation as myth, as historically and culturally grounded. But most scholars in the field of religious studies implicitly accept the deep message of these texts: their reverence for Word, for text. Though they know that nonliterary religions exist, most scholars in the field of religious studies focus on the interpretation of texts—whether those texts be the Hebrew and Christian or other scriptures, the writings of Jewish and Christian or other theologians or interpreters of scriptural texts, or the works of philosophers. The commitment to texts is also found in the field of history. One of the reasons history is said to have begun at Sumer is because writing was invented there in the fourth millennium. The field of history, like the field of religious studies, is deeply committed to the written word. The written word is said to provide the only reliable, "scientific" "evidence" about the past. The terms "history" and "prehistory" themselves reflect the bias in favor of the written word. Where there is no text, we have not history, it is said, but a prelude to history, and history is where everything important happened. This naming serves to diminish the importance of prehistory, almost to render it non-data. New names must be developed. I suggest we abandon the term prehistory, and speak rather of early or ancient history, though I will continue to use the term "prehistory" in quotes in the last part of this article. The texts about Goddesses come from the times of "history" when patriarchy is already established. If texts provide the only reliable evidence, then we would perhaps be forced to conclude that Goddesses do not reflect autonomous female power. Almost all of these texts are written by men and almost all of them implicitly or explicitly support patriarchy. However if we expand our notion of history to include the study of cultures which left no written records, then we can begin to allow the data of "prehistory" and anthropology of religion to transform not only our understandings of Goddesses and women in religion, but also our notions about religious origins and our theories about the nature of religion.

The great historian of religion Mircea Eliade has been influential in the attempt to expand the parameters of the field of religious studies into the study of myth and ritual, including the study of nonliterary traditions. But ritual studies, which by some accounts of the nature of religion, might even form the core of the field, are still relegated to the periphery. More is at stake here than simple inherited prejudice toward the study of texts. Ritual embodies in a fuller way than text, the nonrational, the physical side of religion. Ritual puts us in the presence of body and blood, milk and honey and wine, song and dance, sexuality and ecstasy. Underlying the preference for texts in religious studies lies the fear of the nonrational and the physical, the fear of chaos, a fear which I discussed earlier in relation to the ethos of objectivity in scholarship.

Feminist scholarship on the "prehistoric" Goddesses, then, challenges the field of religious studies to abandon its nearly exclusive commitment to text. Feminist scholarship on the Goddesses requires us to accept physical evidence: paintings, sculptures, bones, pots, weavings, etc., as reliable data upon which to base theory. To do this religious studies would need to strengthen its connections with the fields of archaeology, art history, and anthropology. In a larger sense it means that not only do Neolithic and Paleolithic history need to become more central in shaping our conceptions of religious origins, but also that we need to devote more attention to the religious lives of nonliterary peoples in general, to tribal and folk religions, and to nonliterary expressions within the so-called "higher" religions.

God

Feminist study of the history of the Goddesses also challenges prevailing ideas about divinity. Most of us in the field of religious studies are far more influenced by Biblical notions of God than we care to reflect upon. The Goddesses are presented in the Bible as "abomination," and it is hard to shake the mindset that has encouraged us to think of Goddesses in relation to terms such as "idolatry," "fertility fetish," "nature religion," "orgiastic," "bloodthirsty," "cult prostitution."[36] All of these prejudices can be countered. An idol is another person's religious symbol. The Goddesses represented fertility and sexuality as cosmic power of transformation, not in a limited, certainly not in a negative sense. Sexual rituals associated with Goddess religions celebrated sexuality as transformative power.[37] Prostitution for money is the product of a patriarchal class-stratified society.[38]

Underlying scholars' prejudices about Goddess religion are several deeper issues that bear reflection. One is the notion that divinity represents rationality, order, and transcendence, as opposed to the alleged irrationality and chaos of the finite changeable world, the world we call nature. This notion is the basis of the (usually negative) comparison made between the gods [sic] of nature and the God of history and law, the God of Sinai. As discussed earlier, ancient Near Eastern and Greek mythology also records man's (here the generic seems appropriate) attempts to separate himself and his Gods from the forces of finitude and death (but in so doing also from life and renewal) which he labels chaotic and irrational. The attempt to sever divinity from the forces of so-called "chaos" is vividly depicted in the stories of the slaying of Tiamat by Marduk, Medusa by Perseus, and Python by Apollo, mentioned earlier. The deep structure of these and similar myths depicts female power (for each of these monsters is female) as chaos, as destructive, as associated with darkness and death. Each of these myths tells us that it is the task of the male hero or God to slay and dismember, to banish the forces of "chaos" from his world. By the time of the Genesis 1 creation story, the power of the female forces of chaos had been so diminished that God could subdue *tohu wabohu*, the formless and the void, and *tehom*, the great deep, simply by the power of his word, though the struggle with the chaos monster is reflected in Psalm 89 and in Job 9:8–13. The Hebrew God of the Genesis 1 creation story is identified with the powers of order and goodness; he declares everything he orders and separates "very good." "Chaos" remains to be projected upon the "abominations" worshipped by the indigenous Canaanites and many of the people of Israel and Judah.

Once again we come face to face with dualisms of thought and expression that are deeply embedded in the structure of our thought and language. If we are to grasp the meaning of the prepatriarchal Goddesses, then we must attempt to conceptualize divinity as embodying neither exclusively order, nor exclusively chaos, but as inclusive of both. For me the easiest way to think about this is to think of the prepatriarchal Goddesses as embodying the forces of life, death, and regeneration that occur in all natural and creative processes in the universe. The Goddesses embody the "chaos" of death and disintegration equally as they embody the forces of growth and renewal. These processes are chaotic when viewed from the standpoint of rational control, but they are not essentially chaotic. They have their own inner logic, they follow rhythmical patterns which are regular, though not entirely predictable or controllable. Everything changes, everything that is born will surely die, everything that is will transform. And as Margaret Atwood has written, "nothing has died, everything is alive, everything is waiting to become alive."[39] The "prehistoric"

Goddesses are not difficult to understand, they are not chaos, but their relation to individual finite life and will remains a mystery. We can understand them only if we shed deeply held prejudices that divinity, and especially "higher" divinity, is associated with a rational order which is transcendent of change.

The "prehistoric" Goddesses also challenge us to transcend the philosophical tradition which tells us that divinity, humanity, and nature are three completely distinct categories. The categorical distinction between divinity, humanity, and nature (or as it is more commonly put, God, man, and nature—the status of women is sometimes a non-question, sometimes women are viewed as having the same rational essence as "man," sometimes women are viewed as defective "men"), is embedded in the structure of our language and thinking and is reflected in philosophies and theologies. These categories reflect man's continuing attempt to ally himself with a principle, a transcendent and rational deity, that will enable him to escape finitude and mortality, which he then consigns to the realm of nature. According to most Western philosophies and theologies since Plato, God is identified with a timeless rational principle which transcends the changeable world of nature. Man is situated half-way between God and nature. With his rational mind man communes with timeless principles, while with his body he participates in a world of changeable nature. In this scheme, sexuality which is of the body is viewed as being of a "lower" order and in some sense threatening to man's "higher" nature.

In the absence of written language, we cannot know how Paleolithic and Neolithic peoples understood the images they created which we call "Goddesses." But we do know that in many American Indian and African groups, for example, the categorical distinctions we make between God, man, and nature are unknown. In many American Indian groups "divinity" is called "Grandmother" or "Grandfather" and it does not seem that a clear distinction is being made (as it is in Genesis 2–3) between the ancestors of the clan and the divinity.[40] In thinking about the Goddesses of the Neolithic it seems to me that we are probably dealing with images which incorporate concepts of "awesome female sexual and lifegiving power," "ancestress," "powers of nature," "powers of transformation," "powers of birth, death, and renewal." The "prehistoric" Goddesses were probably not understood to be categorically distinct or separate from the powers of women who give birth, nurture, plant, weave, create pots, and enact roles in ritual, not distinct from the awesome powers of growth, death, and regeneration in nature. To understand them, then, we must develop different understandings of the relation of God, humanity, and nature than those we have inherited.

One aspect of the "prehistoric" Goddesses that has troubled many scholars is their awesome sexuality. Whether full or thin of body, they are often depicted unclothed, with prominent breasts and pubic triangles, to which they often point. Some are giving birth, or holding children, but many simply stand alone, self-confidently affirming their sexual power. Such images of "divinity" are quite alien to recent Western consciousness, because Western thinkers have considered the body and sexuality as "lower" than the rational mind which they associate with the divinity and with man's "higher" nature. Thus the "prehistoric" Goddesses are called mere "fertility fetishes," or "orgiastic images," and are said to reflect a "more primitive" or "lower" stage of consciousness. Only if we dispense with the Western preference for a rational divinity who is transcendent of this life and of change, can we begin to understand the "prehistoric" Goddesses as more than "fertility fetishes."

The "prehistoric" Goddesses, then, challenge us to rethink our concept of God. In order to understand the "prehistoric" Goddesses we must move beyond the notions of divinity as categorically distinct from humanity and nature, as asexual, and as set apart from change, from finitude, from that which has been called chaos.

Conclusion

This paper, which I originally had conceptualized as having two distinct parts, has come full circle. Now we can see that both the ethos of objectivity and the notions of God, time, and text, which continue to influence the field of religious studies are very much connected. The critical issue in both cases, it seems to me, is the erection of a rational structure against powers that are defined as chaos. But as we deconstruct the ethos of objectivity and the concepts of God, time, and text, we begin to see that the chaos feared by many is not chaos at all, but finitude, limitation, body, feeling, change, and death. I believe that feminist thought calls us to embrace this finitude, rather than defend against it. But this takes us into the realm of feminist theology, which is not, strictly speaking, the subject of this paper.[41]

NOTES

1. Alfred North Whitehead, *Science and the Modern World* (New York: The Free Press, 1925), 48.

2. Thomas S. Kuhn, *The Structure of Scientific Revolutions* (Chicago: University of Chicago Press, 1962).

3. For a recent alternative view, see Marilyn French, *Beyond Power* (New York: Summit Books, 1985).

4. Mary Daly, *Beyond God the Father* (Boston: Beacon Press, 1973), 11–12.

5. Also see Evelyn Fox Keller, *Reflections on Gender and Science* (New Haven: Yale University Press, 1985).

6. For the story of Marduk's slaying of Tiamat, see the Babylonian Creation Epic, "The Enuma Elish," in *Primal Myths*, Barbara C. Sproul, ed. (New York: Harper and Row, 1979), 91–113; for the story of Apollo's slaying of Python, see "To Pythian Apollo," in *Hesoid. The Homeric Hymns and Homerica*, Hugh G. Evelyn-White, ed. (Cambridge, Mass.: Harvard University Press, 1950), 337–63.

7. The locus classicus for this view is the vision of the Good in Plato's *Symposium*; see *The Collected Dialogues of Plato including the Letters*, Edith Hamilton and Huntington Cairns, eds. (New York: Bollingen Series LXXI, Pantheon Books, 1966), 562.

8. See Zillah Eisenstein, *The Radical Future of Liberal Feminism* (New York: Longman, 1981).

9. See Fox Keller, chapter 3.

10. See Elisabeth Schüssler Fiorenza, *In Memory of Her* (New York: Crossroad, 1983), especially chapters 1 and 2, for a discussion of continental critical and hermeneutical theory as it applies to New Testament studies.

11. Carol Gilligan, *In a Different Voice* (Cambridge, Mass.: Harvard University Press, 1982).

12. See Nancy Chodorow, *The Reproduction of Mothering* (Berkeley: University of California Press, 1978).

13. I wish to thank Marcia Keller for thoughtful criticism which helped to clarify my ideas in this section.

14. Michael Novak, *Belief and Unbelief* (New York: New American Library, 1965), and *Ascent of the Mountain, Flight of the Dove* (New York: Harper and Row, 1971).

15. Martin Buber, *I and Thou*, Walter Kaufmann, trans. (New York: Charles Scribner's Sons, 1970).

16. Audre Lorde, *Sister Outsider* (Trumansburg, NY: The Crossing Press, 1984), especially "The Uses of the Erotic: The Erotic as Power," 53–69.

17. This information is taken from the program of the *Annual Meeting 1984, American Academy of Religion, Society of Biblical Literature* (Chico, CA: Scholars' Press, 1984), 16. Women and Religion was established in 1971.

18. For overviews on research on women and religion studies and on feminist theology, see Gail Graham Yates, "Spirituality and the American Feminist Experience," *Signs* 9, 1 (1983), 59–72; Anne Barstow Driver, "Review Essay: Religion," *Signs* 2, 2 (1976), 434–42; Carol P. Christ, "The New Feminist Theology: A Review of the Literature," *Religious Studies Review* 3 (1977), 203–12; Carol P. Christ, "Women's Studies in Religion," *Bulletin/Council on the Study of Religion* 10 (1979), 3–5; Rosemary Radford Ruether, "The Feminist Critique in Religious Studies," in *The Feminist Perspective in the Academy*, Elizabeth Langland and Walter Gove, eds. (Chicago: University of Chicago Press, 1981); Rosemary Ruether, "Feminist Theology in the Academy," *Christianity and Crisis* 45, 3 (March 4, 1985), 55–62. Also see *Womanspirit Rising*, Carol P. Christ and Judith Plaskow, eds. (New York: Harper and Row, 1979); *Unspoken Worlds*, Nancy Auer Falk and Rita Gross, eds. (New York: Harper and Row, 1980); and *The Politics of Women's Spirituality*, Charlene Spretnak, ed. (New York: Doubleday, 1982).

19. Anne L. Barstow, "The Prehistoric Goddess," *The Book of the Goddess*, Carl Olson, ed. (New York: Crossroad, 1983), 8.

20. Anne Barstow, "The Uses of Archaeology for Women's History: James Mellaart's Work on the Neolithic Goddess at Çatal Hüyük," *Feminist Studies* 4, 3 (October 1978), 16.

21. Merlin Stone, *When God Was a Woman* (New York: Dial Press, 1976), 1.

22. Christine Downing, *The Goddess* (New York: Crossroad, 1984), 4.

23. Sarah B. Pomeroy, *Goddesses, Whores, Wives, and Slaves* (New York: Schocken Books, 1975), 15.

24. Pomeroy, 14. But see Pomeroy, "Selected Bibliography on Women in Classical Antiquity," in *Women in the Ancient World*, John Peradotto and J. P. Sullivan, eds. (Albany: State University of New York Press, 1984), esp. 325—"The virulence with which the theory of Bronze Age matriarchy has been attacked is remarkable. The theory may have attracted hostility due to its association with Marxism and militant feminism."

25. See Mircea Eliade, *A History of Religious Ideas*, Vol. I, Willard Trask, trans. (Chicago: University of Chicago Press, 1978), chapter 1.

26. G. Rachel Levy, *Religious Conceptions of the Stone Age* (New York: Harper and Row, 1963); first published as *The Gate of Horn* (London: Faber and Faber, Ltd., 1948).

27. See Eliade, *A History*, Vol. I, chapter 2.

28. Ruby Rohrlich-Leavitt, "Women in Transition: Crete and Sumer," in *Becoming Visible*, Renate Bridenthal and Claudia Koonz, eds. (Boston: Houghton Mifflin, 1977), 38. Also see Eliade, *A History*, Vol. I., 40.

29. See Autumn Stanley, *Mothers of Invention*, forthcoming.

30. See Marija Gimbutas, *The Goddesses and Gods of Old Europe 6500-3500 BC* (Berkeley and Los Angeles: University of California Press, 1982), and "Women and Politics in Goddess-Oriented Old Europe," in *The Politics of Women's Spirituality*, 22–31.

31. See James Mellaart, *Çatal Hüyük* (New York: McGraw Hill, 1967), and *Earliest Civilizations of the Near East* (New York: McGraw Hill, 1965).

32. See Ruby Rohrlich, "State Formation and the Subjugation of Women," *Feminist Studies* 6, 1 (Spring 1980), 78–102.

33. See Gimbutas and Rohrlich.

34. See Barstow, "The Uses," I; Elisabeth Schüssler Fiorenza argues that women played central leadership and communal roles in the early Christian movement in *In Memory of Her*, but she does not argue that such roles were normative for women in religion or society in the early Christian period.

35. Merlin Stone, "9978: Repairing the Time Warp and Other Related Realities," *Heresies* 5 (September 1978), 124–26.

36. See Barstow, "The Uses," 10, and Stone, *When God Was a Woman*, xvii–xviv, for citation and discussion of scholarly prejudice against Goddesses.

37. See Eliade, *History*, Vol. I, 283.

38. See Rohrlich, "State Formation," 91–92.

39. Margaret Atwood, *Surfacing* (New York: Simon and Schuster, 1972), 182.

40. See for example, *The Sacred Pipe*, Joseph Epes Brown, ed. (Norman: University of Oklahoma Press, 1953), and the discussion of related issues in Stone, 10–14.

41. See my essay "Finitude, Death and Reverence for Life," in my *Laughter of Aphrodite* (New York: Harper and Row, 1987), chapter 12; also to be published in *Semeia*, and in *Embodied Love*, Paula Cooey, Sharon Farmer, and Mary Ellen Ross, eds. (New York: Harper and Row, 1987).

REMAPPING DEVELOPMENT

THE POWER OF DIVERGENT DATA

Carol Gilligan

The search for a moral beacon to illuminate the path of human life is an eternal quest. The wish for a right answer to the ultimate questions of how to live and what to do arises again in each generation, drawing sustenance in the Western tradition from Socrates' claim that virtue is one as well as from the Biblical injunction of only one God. But with the taking on of this quest in this secular age by psychologists of human development, and with the transposition of the divine order of a "great chain of being" into the secular order of a developmental stage sequence, the question arises: From what perspective or in whose terms are these claims being made? Who frames the values presupposed in theories of human development? Who defines the ideal of maturity that welds judgments of progress to observations of change?

I begin by noting the human construction of theories of human development, not to arrive at the familiar debate between moral monotheism and value relativism or moral nihilism but to lay the groundwork for an alternative formulation. By asking the psychologist's question, how do we come to hold moral values, and by tracing the ontogenesis of values to the experience of human relationships, I will claim that two moral predispositions inhere in the structure of human connection, given the inequality and the attachment of child and parent. Thus in contrast to unitary theories of moral growth or the counterposition of an endless variation, I will distinguish two primary moral orientations that evolve through different dimensions of relationships and identify these two dimensions of relationship as the coordinates for a new map of development. This remapping reveals the perspective toward relationships embedded in current

This paper was delivered in June 1983 at the Heinz Werner Symposium at Clark University and published in *Value Presuppositions in Theories of Human Development*, S. Wapner and L. Cirillo (eds.), Hillsdale, NJ: Lawrence Erlbaum Associates, 1986. Reprinted by permission of Lawrence Erlbaum Associates.

stage theories by expanding the angle of vision. But it also explains why the adoption of a single perspective creates a persistent problem of discrepant data.

My approach in this paper is historical. I retrace a process of discovery that began with the observation of a discrepancy between theory and data in research on moral judgment. As the research extended through a series of studies conducted over a period of ten years, the observation of discrepancy led me to explore its dimensions and to consider its implications for the psychology of human development. In demonstrating the power of divergent data to illuminate current theories and inform new models of growth, I hope not only to identify the value presuppositions that have colored developmental theories but also to explain how different value positions reflect different ways of experiencing and understanding relationships.

I. The Observation of Discrepancy

In the early 1970s I began to study the relationship between moral judgment and action and the role of experience in moral development. I was interested at the time in discovering how people thought about actual rather than hypothetical moral conflicts, how their thinking affected their actions, and how their actions affected their conceptions of morality and of themselves. The awareness of a discrepancy between theory and data grew out of an observation made in the course of selecting a sample for a longitudinal study of moral and ego development. The sample was to be randomly chosen from a list of college seniors who as sophomores had taken a course with Lawrence Kohlberg on moral and political choice. Reviewing the list, I noticed that of the seventy students who enrolled, twenty subsequently dropped the course. This fact, although not remarkable in itself, was striking to me because of the twenty students, sixteen were women and only ten women remained in the class. When the women who left were contacted and interviewed, their responses to questions about moral conflict were at first hard to understand. Their descriptions of moral problems they faced did not fit the prevailing categories of moral thought but seemed rather to confirm the opinion that women confuse moral problems with problems of interpersonal relationships.

The recurrence of this observation of difference between women's moral thinking and theories of moral development was prepared although not intended by the decision to base a study of judgment and action on a sample of pregnant women who were considering abortion. The study was designed to discover how the women thought about this decision, whether they construed it in moral terms and, if so, what the nature of that construal was. Since females had been excluded from the research samples upon which both Piaget and Kohlberg had based their descriptions of moral judgment, the abortion decision study was the first to draw moral categories from the analysis of women's language and thought. This analysis revealed a reiterative use of the words *selfish* and *responsible* to define the moral parameters of choice, and this language called attention to a construction of the moral problem as a problem of responsibility in relationships. In this relational construction, responsibility connoted not an obligation to fulfill an abstract duty but an ability to respond with care and avoid hurt. The word *selfish* conversely denoted a morally problematic separation associated with a failure of response.

The abortion dilemma, thus construed, was a dilemma of relationships, premised on the recognition of self and other as connected and therefore interdependent. This premise conflicted with the view of self and other as separate that underlies the understanding of moral problems as problems of conflicting rights. Assuming relationship, the women identified the moral problem as a problem of care. Seeing no way not to act and no way of acting that would not affect the connection between others and self, they asked whether it was responsible or irresponsible, moral or immoral, to have a child or to end a pregnancy in circumstances where caring for the child was for various reasons problematic. Consequently, the question was not whether to act or whether action could be justified but rather how to act responsibly in a situation where hurt seemed inescapable. Rather than appealing primarily to principles of fairness and rights, the women centered their consideration on their understanding of responsibility and care and their knowledge of human relationships.

This formulation of morality as a problem of care and responsibility in relationships, premised on an assumption of connection and associated with a view of self and other as interdependent, challenged the opposition between self and other and thus the distinction between egoism and altruism that traditionally has been central to the construction of the moral domain. The abortion dilemma, by highlighting the fact of connection, illuminated the assumption of interdependence that previously had rendered the moral judgments of women opaque. Seen in this light, the focus on relationships in women's moral thinking, rather than signalling a failure to differentiate the moral from the interpersonal domain, signified a different understanding of relationships and a different way of thinking about oneself as a moral agent.

Key to this work was a shift in methodology that removed definitional categories from the instruments of measurement. By asking people to describe moral conflicts in their lives and to discuss choices they faced rather than presenting them with dilemmas for resolution, it was possible to identify ways of constructing moral problems that differed from those represented in the prevailing instruments of psychological assessment. Since women's thinking had not been considered in defining the moral domain, theirs was a different voice. Although this difference had repeatedly been noted in the psychological literature on moral development and was cited by Piaget as the reason for excluding girls from his study of children's games, this difference had previously been interpreted as indicative of a problem in women's development, variously explained but seen as having no theoretical significance. Yet the analysis of the differences observed in girls' and women's moral thinking pointed instead to a problem in theory—a failure to imagine or represent a different conception of morality and self.

The values of justice and autonomy that are presupposed in current theories of human growth and embedded in the definitions of morality and of the self imply a view of the individual as separate and of relationships as either hierarchical or contractual, bound by the alternatives of constraint and cooperation. In contrast, the values of care and connection that emerge saliently in women's thinking imply a view of self and other as interdependent and of relationships as networks sustained by activities of care-giving and response. The two moral voices that articulate these visions thus denote different ways of viewing the world. Within each perspective, all the key terms of social understanding appear to take on different meanings, reflecting a change in the imagery of relationships and signifying a shift in orientation. Like the shifting perception of the vase and the faces in the illustration of the ambiguous figure, there appear to be two ways of perceiving self in relation to others, both grounded in reality but imposing on that reality a different organization. Since moral judgments, as Piaget notes, reflect the logic of social understanding, these different forms of organization emerge most clearly as different ways of defining and resolving moral problems.

The nature of these differences and their implications are clarified by an example. Two four-year-olds were playing together and wanted to play different games. In this particular version of this common dilemma, one said, "Let's play next-door neighbors." "I want to play pirates," the other replied. "Okay," said the first, "then you can be the pirate who lives next door." By comparing this inclusive solution of combining the games with the fair solution of taking turns and playing each game for an equal period, it is possible to see not only how these two approaches yield different ways of solving a problem in relationships but also how each solution differentially affects the identity of the games and the experience of the relationship.

The fair solution of taking turns leaves the identity of each game intact, providing an opportunity for each child to experience the other's imaginative world and regulating the exchange by the imposition of a rule based on a premise of equal respect. The inclusive solution, in contrast transforms both games through their combination: The neighbor game is changed by the presence of a pirate living next door; the pirate game is changed by bringing the pirate into a neighborhood. As each child thus enters the world of the other's imagination, that world is visibly transformed by their presence. The identity of each separate game yields to a new creation as the relationship between the children gives rise to a game that neither had separately imagined. While the fair solution protects identity and ensures equality within the context of a relationship, the inclusive solution transforms identity through the experience of relationship. The elaboration of these different views of self in relationship and the exploration of their significance for moral understanding and self-definition became the agenda for the research project in its second phase.

II. The Exploration of Divergent Data

"If we do not live just from moment to moment but try to be conscious of our existence, then our greatest need and most difficult achievement is to find meaning in life." Thus Bruno Bettelheim in defining the goal of development also states the problem faced by theorists of development, the imposition of meaning on change. That judgments of progress, stasis, and regression are made on the basis of value premises and from a perspective seems increasingly clear. But the extent to which a particular set of value premises and a particular perspective have governed not only the understanding of development but also the instruments for its measurement has not been equally apparent. The discordance heard between women's voices and theories of human development opened an avenue of exploration by revealing different conceptions of morality and self that were tied to different ways of perceiving relationships. The implications of these two perspectives for understanding both male and female development and for thinking about instruments of assessment pointed to the need for an enlarged developmental conception and new methods of analysis that could encompass and directly represent what previously appeared as anomalous data.

The systematic investigation of two moral orientations began with a study designed in conjunction with Michael Murphy to investigate the variables of gender, age, and type of dilemma that previously had been confounded in moral judgment research. The study hinged on the creation of reliable procedures for distinguishing different moral orientations and different forms of self-description in open-ended interview data. Nona Lyons in solving these problems demonstrated that it was possible reliably to distinguish considerations of justice and care in people's descriptions of "real-life" moral dilemmas, and Charlene Langdale demonstrated that Lyons's coding procedure could be used in analyzing responses to hypothetical moral dilemmas. In addition, Lyons constructed a manual for coding responses to an open-ended question about self-description by identifying a relational component that appeared in most people's self-descriptions and differentiating between two conceptions of self in relation to others: "separate/objective" and "connected."

The data used in these analyses were drawn from a sample of 144 males and females matched for high levels of intelligence, education, and occupation at nine ages ranging across the life cycle from six to sixty. Working with the data from an intensively interviewed subsample of 36 males and females (two males and two females at each of the nine ages), Lyons found that most people raised considerations of both justice and care in constructing and resolving moral problems and in evaluating the choices they made. However, one orientation generally was considered with greater frequency, reflected by the number of considerations presented within that mode. This difference observed in the frequency of considerations of justice and care led to the scoring of predominant moral orientation, and a parallel phenomenon of differential frequency was observed and used in scoring predominant mode of self-description.

The findings reported by Lyons revealed: (1) that considerations of justice and care could be distinguished in the ways people framed and resolved moral problems and in their evaluation of the choices they made; (2) that these two modes of moral reasoning were associated with different modes of describing the self in relation to others—with justice related to the depiction of self as separate in relation to others and care to the description of self as connected to others; (3) that major and minor modes of moral reasoning and self-description could be identified in most people's thinking; and finally, (4) that the use of these modes and their salience in people's thinking although not gender-specific were gender-related—while no individual was confined to any particular mode by virtue of gender and most people in fact used both modes, the women in this educationally advantaged North American sample tended to rely more on considerations of care and response in defining and resolving moral problems and to describe themselves in the connected mode, while the men, as a group, relied more on considerations of justice and rights and tended to define themselves as separate in relation to others.

The discovery that the voice that speaks of connection, not hurting, care, and response can reliably be differentiated from the voice that speaks of equality, reciprocity, justice, and rights and that these different modes of moral discourse appear in conjunction with different forms of self-description pointed to the common grounding of these distinctions in two perspectives toward relationships. These perspectives were clarified by the discovery that the two modes of moral discourse share a common moral vocabulary but that within each mode the meaning of individual words changes. This discovery then led to the recognition that these differences in meaning reflected a change in the perspective toward others and that these shifts in perspective denoted two ways of understanding relationships. Distinguishing the moralities of justice and care by delineating the different understanding of relationships embedded in each, Lyons defined the two perspectives toward others as the perspectives of *reciprocity* and *response*—one rooted in impartiality and the search for objectivity, the capacity to distance oneself and determine fair rules for mediating relationships, one grounded in the specific contexts of others, the capacity to perceive people in their own terms and to respond to their needs.

For centuries these two lines of morality have wandered through the Western tradition, appearing in the contrasts between reason and compassion, fairness and forgiveness, justice and mercy, and emerging repeatedly although by no means exclusively in contrasts between women and men. These distinctions imply an underlying division between thought and feeling, a separation between the process of judgment and the capacity for response. But the association with gender focuses the problem in this formulation since the implication that women are thoughtless and men without feeling clearly cannot be sustained. Instead there appear to be two modes of thinking that carry different implications of feeling and signify different ways of perceiving others and knowing oneself. Attention to women's thinking thus broadens the definition of self and the categories of moral thought, and this expanded conceptual framework provides a new way of listening to differences not only between but also within the thinking of women and men.

Such an extension in the conception of the moral domain has been advocated in philosophy by Lawrence Blum. He challenges the dominant Kantian position to argue that altruistic concerns and sympathetic emotions can be considered morally good. Similarly, in psychology Martin Hoffman, in turning to the study of empathy and altruism, points out that "Western psychology has evolved along lines seemingly antithetical to giving consideration for others a central place in the overall view of personality." Hoffman criticizes "the doctrinaire view . . . that altruistic behavior can always be explained in terms of instrumental, self-serving motives in the actor," the view, in short, that people are selfish and altruism always a guise. But the current inquiry, while sympathetic to these efforts and indebted to their clarification, begins with the awareness of two different perspectives toward relationships and asks whether the distinction between egoism and altruism, as well as the sharp division between rationality and emotion, both of which have informed the discussion not only of morality but also of love in the Western world, are not themselves embedded in a particular perspective toward relationships, one premised on a fundamental separation between other and self.

The existence of two moral perspectives and the way in which trying to see them as one blurs their representation were clarified by the work of Langdale. She analyzed the moral judgments made by the entire sample of 144 males and females of which the intensively interviewed group was a part. All participants in the study were asked to resolve two hypothetical dilemmas: (1) the Heinz dilemma constructed by Kohlberg as a dilemma of conflicting rights and (2) either the Kathy or the Sara dilemma, based on problems presented by women in the abortion decision study and constructed as dilemmas of conflicting responsibilities and relationships. The aim of the study was to investigate the interaction between the variables of age, gender, and type of dilemma and the presence and predominance of the two moral orientations. The "real-life" dilemmas that were generated by the members of the intensively interviewed subsample provided a measure of spontaneous moral orientation that made it possible to ascertain how the framing of standardized dilemmas affected the two moral orientations.

Using Lyons's coding procedures for distinguishing considerations of justice and care, Langdale found that in each dilemma (Heinz, Kathy, and Sara), both orientations appeared and could be reliably coded; that the use of these two orientations was significantly associated with gender across all the dilemmas, with care more predominant in the thinking of females and justice in the thinking of males; and that the two moral orientations appeared systematically across the life cycle with no significant differences in age. In addition to these overall findings of orientation distinction and gender difference, Langdale observed a variation in the frequency of the orientations across different dilemmas, with Kohlberg's Heinz dilemma eliciting the highest percentage of justice considerations in females and the self-generated "real-life" and the Sara dilemmas the highest percentage of considerations of care among males.

Since the representation of the two moral orientations in reasoning about the Heinz dilemma significantly differed in both sexes from their representation in the Real-Life dilemma, the Heinz dilemma, although the most frequently used dilemma in moral development research, did not appear to provide an accurate reflection of the way people thought about moral problems in their lives. For females, this disparity was far greater, given the predominance of care in their spontaneous moral orientation. But the pull toward justice reasoning which the Heinz dilemma displayed not only led to considerations of care being joined by or replaced with considerations of justice in the thinking of girls and women but also led to the almost complete disappearance of considerations of care from the reasoning of boys and men. Thus the responses of males to the Heinz dilemma would seem to confirm an equation of moral judgment with justice reasoning, while the responses of females would render that equation somewhat problematic, as demonstrated by the history of Kohlberg's research. However, the problem revealed by the women calls attention to a problem in Kohlberg's representation of men's moral reasoning: i.e., the presence of care considerations in men's thinking about real moral dilemmas.

The unexpected finding of a difference between the appearance of the two moral orientations in the two versions of the abortion dilemma further elucidates this problem by suggesting that the question posed by the investigator influences the judgments made. Although the issue of abortion remained constant in the dilemmas of Kathy and Sara, and although the story itself, although differently told, remained essentially the same, the question asked in each version differed. The open-ended question of the Sara dilemma ("What should Sara do?") elicited a representation of justice and care that did not significantly differ from the representation of these moral concerns in the real-life or actual moral dilemmas. In contrast, the Kathy dilemma posed a question that was analogous to that raised in the Heinz dilemma, in specifying a given resolution and inquiring about its justification ("Should Kathy have an abortion"?). Like the Heinz dilemma, although to a lesser extent, the responses to the Kathy dilemma, when compared with the measure of spontaneous moral orientation, showed an increase in justice considerations that were joined by women to considerations of care and associated in men's thinking with a decrease in care considerations. Thus the two moral orientations were sensitive to variations in the question, which affected the presence of care and justice reasoning for each sex in somewhat different ways. These effects, however, did not override the association of these orientations with gender.

The findings of gender difference in this sample were of particular interest since the sample had been selected to test Kohlberg's claim that gender differences found in moral reasoning could be attributed to differences in education and occupation. Yet in this sample where males and females were matched for high levels of intelligence, education, and professional status, gender differences in moral orientation remained. In interpreting these findings, it is essential to distinguish between Lyons's scoring of moral orientation and Kohlberg's scoring of moral stage. In support of Kohlberg's claim, there were no significant differences found in this sample between mean Kohlberg stage scores for males and females. There were, however, highly significant gender differences found in moral orientation, and these differences in moral orientation appeared on the Heinz as well as the other dilemmas.

The confusion between stage and orientation thus seemed to run deeper in Kohlberg's framework, complicating the discussion of gender differences but also revealing the problem in a unitary formulation of moral development. In untangling this confusion, Langdale found that individuals, primarily females (86 percent females, 14 percent males), with care represented in their predominant moral orientation have significantly lower Kohlberg stage scores than individuals, primarily males (69 percent males, 31 percent females) with care unrepresented in their predominant moral orientation (i.e., predominant care or split orientation vs. predominant justice orientation). The finding of significant gender differences in use of the two orientations together with the finding that the predominant representation of care is associated with significantly lower scores on Kohlberg's scale of moral development suggests that gender differences that have been reported on Kohlberg's measure derive not from the fact of gender *per se* but rather from the greater tendency of females to frame and resolve moral problems in the care orientation. The primary use of the care orientation thus creates a liability with Kohlberg's framework, lowering moral judgment scores by an average of 50 points and reflecting the fact that Kohlberg conceived moral development from a justice perspective.

The consequences of this conception for the assessment of moral development in both sexes is illustrated by the moral judgments at age fifteen of two children, Amy and Jake, whose judgments at eleven elucidated the divergence between the justice and care orientations. At eleven, when Amy was asked whether Heinz should steal the drug, she replied that he shouldn't steal but his wife shouldn't die either. Transforming the question from whether stealing could be justified to how Heinz could best care for his wife in this situation, she saw the moral problem arising not from a conflict of rights but from the druggist's failure of response. Her low score on Kohlberg's scale reflected this formulation since her shift in the focus of the dilemma from the relationship of law and life and to the relationships between the druggist, Heinz, and his wife turned her attention away from considerations of justice and rights. Considerations of care and response guided her strategy for resolving the problem.

At fifteen, Amy clearly understands the logic of both orientations and reflects their tension as she vacillates between them in judging Heinz's dilemma. Commenting that she "hated these dilemmas as much last time as I do now," she begins by questioning whether stealing was the best response in this situation. Thus when asked whether Heinz should steal the drug, she says, "I said the same thing [last time] if I remember what I said, which is that I really don't know." Yet then she switches direction, saying, "I mean, yes, I think he should steal the drug." Believing that another way beside stealing could be found for obtaining the drug or the money and yet noting the number of people in the world who are dying and starving, she finds no easy answer to the problem posed. The dilemma seems to her at once logically soluble and essentially implausible. Clearly life comes before profit in a hierarchy of values ("I think human life is a little more important than the man's profit"), but it remains unclear that stealing would solve either the more general problem of distribution or the particular problem of Heinz and his wife in this situation. Everything she knows about cancer suggests that it cannot be cured by a single treatment and that a drug for curing cancer would not be "sitting out on the shelf of the drugstore." If these events took place in a small town, as the narrative of the dilemma describes, then if the drug disappeared, Heinz would immediately be suspected. Imagining Heinz in jail after having saved his wife and deciding "it (was) worth it," she also imagines the wife alone, in need of money and additional treatment.

Returning to the question of stealing, she wonders about the druggist's perspective: "Maybe (his) property is important for some reason—there could be another side to the druggist's story." In the end, she concludes that it is not "as much a question of right and wrong as just what you feel, which is more important. It's a question of importance, not a truth." Her difficulty in seeing a unitary truth that would guide the resolution of this dilemma signifies the tension in her thinking between two ways of framing the question. Alternating between the question of whether life takes priority over profit, which admits a clear logical solution, and the question of how best to exercise care and avoid hurt, which requires moral imagination, she concludes that there is no single right answer: "I don't think you can say what's right and what's wrong in this situation."

Jake at eleven explained the logical priority of life over law and property by saying that property can be replaced and that the law can make mistakes. At fifteen, he begins by reiterating the value of life over money ("Money sort of comes and goes, and human life comes only once") but then imagines the complications that would arise if the druggist had children who were starving. No longer focusing simply on the inexorability of logic, he wonders not only about the druggist's situation but also what Heinz and the druggist are experiencing. Two perspectives are evident as he answers the question What if the druggist feels strongly about profit? by first saying simply that "he's got the wrong set of priorities" and then approaching the question from a different direction. Visualizing the situation and considering the feelings evoked by theft and by death, he responds to both feelings at the same time as he judges them to be incommensurate: "I just think what [the druggist] is going to experience is some sorrow and some anger over losing his money, and it's a shame that he's got to feel that, but at the same time that it's a lot, that is not as deplorable a thing as the idea of Heinz, his wife having to die and him having to deal with his wife's dying." Suddenly the problem in logic has been joined to a human story.

In terms of their Kohlberg scores at fifteen and eleven, Amy has gained significantly in moral development, while Jake appears not to have changed. The problems in this unitary representation are apparent when we consider how this judgment of development might affect the two children and their education. By focusing attention only on the adequacy of Amy's justice reasoning and ignoring her other considerations, one equates her development with her ability to accept a construction of reality that she finds problematic. In doing so, one may encourage her to rely on others' definitions and to put aside her own questions as naive or simply irrele- vant. For Jake, the focus on justice reasoning would serve to encourage in him the position that anyone who disagreed with his judgments had "the wrong set of priorities." His tempering of this view by imagining and responding to the druggist's experience would go unacknowledged—at worst it would seem to impede his development, at best to be of no moral consequence. The equation of moral development with progress in the justice orientation thus would render Amy more deeply uncertain and Jake more dogmatic. But it also would support the equation of moral education with education for justice, leaving considerations of care untutored. Set apart from the stream of development, these care considerations would come to sound increasingly naive and untested, especially as considera- tions of justice in contrast become increasingly practiced and more sophisti- cated.

To educate both moral voices and represent both orientations in the mapping of human growth means, however, to relinquish the comfort of a single right answer and the clarity of a single road in life. Yet if the opposite of the one is not the many but rather two lines that can be untangled, the prospect of chaos yields to a new way of envisioning development and a new set of questions. Among these questions are ones pertaining to the interplay of the lines and the dialogue of the voices—the circumstances in which this dialogue is heard and the conditions in which it is silenced. In exploring the various tensions created by two voices that speak differently about human relationships, we can see ways of speaking about differences without reducing them to the terms of invidious comparison. Then it becomes possible to ask about the origins of these voices in the experience of relationships and to explore the persisting puzzle of why they appear differentially in association with gender.

III. Remapping Development

In the opening pages of his book on *Attachment*, John Bowlby advises his reader that "the point of view from which this work starts is different. . . . The change in perspective is radical." The radical change in perspective is a change in the perspective toward relationships, a shift in the focus of attention from the inequality to the attachment of child and parent. Observing in children's responses to loss a capacity for love previously unimagined, Bowlby describes how the presence of this capacity in childhood transforms the account of human development. As he traces the formation of attachment to care-giving and responsiveness in relationships, he renders the process of connection visible as a process of mutual engagement. Proceeding from a different standpoint of observation and presupposing a different set of values, Bowlby aligns development with the strengthening of the capacity to love and measures growth in the ability to survive loss and separation without detachment. From this perspective, development hinges not on the achievement of separation but on the experience of attachment and the ability to sustain this experience through its symbolic representation.

It is notable that Bowlby's insights were gained by entering a world known mainly by women, the world of early childhood vulnerability to experiences of loss and separation. While the moral implications of this knowledge are in one sense apparent, these implications have not been integrated into our theories of human development. Instead the focus on the inequality of child and parent has been so insistent that the insights of attachment theory have been assimilated to its underlying premises. The values of autonomy, objectivity, fairness, and rights have become so deeply etched in the psychological imagination that development continues to be traced in the move from inequality to equality, dependence to autonomy, constraint to cooperation. As the radical implications of an alternative vision yield to this unifying perspective, the experience of love itself becomes cast in the language of object relations.

The present remapping of development begins by differentiating two dimensions of relationships which interweave and are often concurrent: the dimension of inequality/equality and the dimension of attachment/ detachment. Since both dimensions of relationship are inherent in the connection of parent and child, given the difference between them in size

and power and the shared vulnerability created by the attachment necessary for the child's survival, the experiences of inequality and attachment
are universal in human life. While the distinction between these dimensions of relationships appears in the ideals of justice and care to which they
give rise as well as in the different modes of self-definition which they
imply, their differences are most sharply focused by two opposites of the
word *dependence*.

Since dependence connotes the experience of connection, its axes extend
along the two coordinates of relationships—leading in one direction to
independence and in the other to isolation. These contrasting oppositions
of dependence—to independence and to isolation—illuminate different
ways of experiencing relationships—as impeding the development of autonomy and as protecting against isolation. Thus in contrast to the prevailing opposition between dependence and independence or autonomy in
theories of human development and in the instruments of psychological
assessment, the opposition of dependence to isolation informs an alternative vision, transforming the understanding of relationships not only in
childhood but also in adolescence.

The two opposites of the word "dependence" emerged in an ongoing
study of female adolescence conducted at a day and boarding school for
girls in upstate New York. The study was designed to map the terrain of
female experience that remains uncharted in the literature on adolescence.
In the context of a research interview that included questions about past
experience, self-description, moral conflicts, and future expectations, the
question "What does dependence mean to you?" appeared at the end of a
section about experiences of important relationships. The following answers illustrate the sharp contrast between the view of relationships conveyed by the opposition between dependence and independence and the
portrayal that emerges from the opposition of dependence and isolation
(both views were evident in the interview data):

> I think it is just when you can be dependent on or you can depend on
> someone, and if you depend on someone, you can depend on them to do
> certain things, like *to be there* when you need them, and you can depend on
> people *to understand* your problems, and on the other hand, people can
> depend on you to do the same thing.

> When you know that *someone is there* when you are upset, and if you need
> someone *to talk to*, they are there, and you can depend on them *to understand*.

> Well, sometimes it bothers me, the word, because it means that you are
> depending on somebody to make things happen. But also that you are
> depending on somebody else *to help you*, you know, either to make things
> happen for you that are good or just *to be there* when you need them *to talk to*
> and not feel that you are cutting into their time or that they don't want you
> there.

I wouldn't say total dependence but if we ever needed each other for anything, we could totally be dependent on the person and it would be no problem. For me, it means that if I have a problem, I can depend on her *to help me* or anything I need help with, she will *be there to help, whether she can help me or not, she will try,* and the same goes for me.

That I know if I go to her with a problem or something like that or not a problem but just to see her, even if she has changed and even if I have changed, that we will be able *to talk to* each other.

Dependence, well, in this case it would be just like I really depend on him *to listen* to me when I have something to say or when I have something I want to talk about, I really want him *to be there* and *to listen* to me.

In these responses dependence is assumed as part of the human condition, and the recurrent phrases, "to be there," "to help," "to talk to," "to listen," convey the perception that people rely on one another for understanding, comfort, and support. Focusing on their connections with others, not construed as a compromise of their integrity, these girls also describe the intention to be there for others and listen to them. The absence of opposition between dependence and independence is striking in the following response where the two words commingle, conveying a view of independence as enhancing and enhanced by relationships and defining a view of development as occurring through friendship, loyalty, love, and engagement:

I would say we depend on each other in a way that we are both independent, and I would say we are very independent but as far as our friendship goes, we are dependent on each other because we know that both of us realize that whenever we need something, the other person will always be there.

In contrast to the use of the word dependence to connote hanging from someone like a ball on a string—an object governed by the laws of physics, these examples convey a conviction of being able to count on someone, imagined as an active person, to respond. Being dependent then does not mean being helpless or powerless, inevitably fixed or without control, but rather signifies the knowledge or belief that one can trust someone, knowing that they are not fixed, to be there, to listen, and to try to help. Thus activities of care—being there, listening, showing a willingness to help and trying to understand—take on a moral dimension. As the knowledge that others will choose to care renders them lovable rather than merely reliable, so the willingness and the ability to care becomes a standard of self-evaluation.

This portrayal of care reveals its cognitive as well as its affective dimensions, its foundation in the ability to perceive people in their own terms and to respond to their needs. As this knowledge generates the power both to help and to hurt, the uses of this power become a standard of responsibility and care in relationships. In adolescence, when the advent of puberty and the growth of subjective and reflective thought change the experience of self and relationships, girls describe conflicts between responsibilities to themselves and to others. Seeking to perceive and respond to their own as well as to others' needs, they ask if they can be responsive to themselves without losing connection to others and whether they can respond to others without abandoning themselves. This search for an inclusive solution to these dilemmas of loyalty vies with the tendency toward exclusion expressed through the moral opposition between selfish and selfless choice—an opposition where selfishness connotes the exclusion of others and selflessness the exclusion of self. Thus the themes of inclusion and exclusion, salient in the childhood games girls play, extend to a reflective plane in adolescence, defining a line of identity and moral development that leads through changes in the experience and understanding of interdependence.

Within this framework of relationships, the central metaphor for identity formation becomes the metaphor of dialogue rather than that of mirroring. The emphasis on speaking and listening, on being heard and making oneself understood ties self-definition to an active engagement with others and turns attention to the process of communication. The themes of silence and voice that emerge so centrally in girls' descriptions convey the struggle to claim a voice and to find an opening that allows the subjectively known self to enter into relationships. But the imagery of silence and silencing also conveys the recognition of how readily this search can be foiled by a refusal to speak or to listen or by the cooptation of truth. While silence can be a way of maintaining integrity in the face of disconfirmation—a way of avoiding invalidation, the willingness to speak and risk disagreement is central to the process of adolescent engagement, making possible the reweaving of attachment and the transformation of relationships.

"I just wish to become better in my relationship with my mother, to be able more easily to disagree with her" . . . and this girl's wish to engage with others on her own terms rather than seeking connection by "making myself in their image" signifies both her temptation to yield to others' perceptions and her recognition that the exclusion of self like the exclusion of others renders relationships lifeless by dissolving the fabric of connection. Given the failure of interpretive schemes to reflect female experience and given the celebration of selflessness as *the* feminine virtue, development for girls in adolescence hinges on their willingness to challenge two equations: the equation of human with male and the equation of care with self-sacrifice. Together these equations have sustained not only a unitary conception of human development but also a problematic conception of human relationships.

By bringing a new imagery of relationships to the depiction of adolescent development, by tying identity formation to dialogue and morality to care and responsiveness in relationships, the study of girls and women enlarges existing theoretical conceptions, filling in a line that has been missing from the account of human development. Representing relationships along the two dimensions of inequality/equality and of attachment/detachment delineates two moral visions and informs two ways of describing the path of development: as a linear progression from inequality to equality, achieved by climbing a staircase of stages; and as an elaboration of human connection, achieved by enlarging and strengthening the web of attachments. As the concept of gender highlights two images of the human condition by standing both as a metaphor of difference and as a symbol of connection or interdependence, the asymmetry of gender in early family relationships suggests why these images of relationship may tend to have different meanings in male and female experience. At the same time the study of gender differences calls attention to the need to represent both images of relationships in describing human development.

Vygotsky, describing the process of internalization through which higher psychological functions develop, notes that these functions—voluntary attention, logical memory, and concept formation—originate as actual relations between human individuals. In the course of development, "an interpersonal process is transformed into an intrapersonal one." The remapping of development proposed here extends Vygotsky's description by delineating two dimensions of interpersonal connection that imply different concepts and different ways of thinking. This enlarged and more differentiated portrayal of human development changes the account of identity and moral development but also transforms the understanding of a series of relationships that previously have been imagined along a single dimension. By envisioning the relationships between parent and child, teacher and student, therapist and patient, researcher and subject not only in terms of their inequality but also in terms of their interdependence, it becomes possible to see how the parent is nurtured by the child, how the teacher learns from the student, how the therapist is healed by the patient, and how the researcher is informed by the subject. The moral implications of this transformation in the imagery of human connection suggests the power that lies in these divergent visions to generate a better mapping of human experience.

REFERENCES

Bettelheim, Bruno. "The Problem of Generations." In Erik Erikson (ed.), *The Challenge of Youth*. New York: Doubleday, 1965.

Blum, Lawrence. *Friendship, Altruism, and Morality.* Boston: Routledge & Kegan Paul, 1980.

Bowlby, John. *Attachment.* New York: Basic Books, Inc., 1969.

Gilligan, Carol. *In a Different Voice: Psychological Theory and Women's Development.* Cambridge: Harvard University Press, 1982.

Gilligan, C., S. Langdale, N. Lyons, and J. M. Murphy. "The Contribution of Women's Thought to Developmental Theory." Final Report to the National Institute of Education. Cambridge: Harvard University, 1982.

Hoffman, Martin. "Empathy, Role-Taking Guilt, and Development of Altruistic Motives." In T. Lickona (ed.), *Moral Development and Behavior.* New York: Holt, Rinehart & Winston, 1976.

Kohlberg, Lawrence. "Stage and Sequence: The Cognitive-Developmental Approach to Socialization." In D. A. Goslin (ed.), *Handbook of Socialization Theory and Research.* Chicago: Rand McNally, 1969.

————. *Essays on Moral Development. Volume One: The Philosophy of Moral Development.* San Francisco: Harper & Row, 1981.

———— and Anne Colby (eds.). *The Measurement of Moral Judgment: A Manual and Its Results.* New York: Cambridge University Press, 1985.

Langdale, Sharry. "Moral Orientations and Moral Development: The Analysis of Care and Justice Reasoning Across Different Dilemmas in Females and Males from Childhood to Adulthood." Ph.D. dissertation, Harvard University, 1983.

Lovejoy, Arthur O. *The Great Chain of Being.* Cambridge: Harvard University Press, 1936.

Lyons, Nona. *Seeing the Consequences.* Unpublished qualifying paper, Harvard University, 1980.

————. "Conceptions of Self and Morality and Modes of Moral Choice." Ph.D. dissertation, Harvard University, 1982.

————. "Two Perspectives: On Self, Relationships, and Morality." *Harvard Ed. Review,* Vol. 53, No. 2, May 1983.

Vygotsky, L. S. *Mind in Society.* M. Cole, V. John-Steiner, S. Scribner, and E. Souberman (eds.). Cambridge & London: Harvard University Press, 1978.

FEMINIST RESEARCH AND PSYCHOLOGY

Carol Nagy Jacklin

A conspicious characteristic of contemporary women's groups is a concern with process as well as product. Meetings, for example, are often evaluated as to goals achieved, efficiency, and feelings of the participants. A similar phenomenon seems to be occurring among women researchers. While there are many males making strides in the philosophy of science (e.g., Kuhn, 1962) and there are many excellent studies of the research process by male observers (e.g., in pscyhology, McGuire, 1973; Mahoney, 1975), it seems likely that were we to poll a random sample of female and/or feminist researchers we would find a larger number concerned with the process of research than we would find in a comparable random sample of male researchers.

In this paper I will look at some of the reasons feminist researchers have given for trying to understand the research process and some of the criticisms of that process. I will then talk about change in the research process as a function of feminist research. The substantive area I will examine is psychology but many of the changes I will describe are occurring in other disciplines as well. The changes are similar because the phenomena across disciplines is the same: Women are becoming the scholars, the researchers, the scientists on the one hand and the subject matter of scholarship, research, and science on the other. The paper therefore has three parts: 1. Understanding the research process, 2. Women as scientists and scholars, 3. Women (and girls) as subject matter of scholarship.

1. Understanding the research process

(1) Women may be trying to understand the research process because we have been excluded from that process. That is, we want to understand the process partly for political reasons, to help effect a change in the proportion of men and women in the disciplines. This political reason has

95

been called the "unfair employment practices" critique of science by Keller (1982), who sees it as simply allowing "equal opportunities" for men and women. One could imagine that achieving equal numbers of men and women doing science would not make much difference to science. However, a change in the proportion of men and women doing the scholarship of science might be revolutionary and improve and enrich the scholarly endeavor. I will return to this point below.

(2) Women researchers may be able to add to the understanding of the research process in a unique way. To paraphrase Margaret Mead: "Men will never understand themselves merely by looking at themselves within their own culture" (1978, 364). It may be that women can see the scientific enterprise more clearly than men because we have been left out of that enterprise for such a long time. A case in point is the psychology of women. Historically, myths have been perpetrated about women without the evidence and data psychology is generally bound by (Shields, 1975). In some *social* circumstances, myths are given the status of facts (see Weisstein, 1971, for a summary). Biology has also been the handmaiden to social values with regard to women and other minority groups (Sayers, 1982). But probably no discipline has been exempt. Mythology in the physical sciences may be as common, albeit on a different level (Keller, 1985), but that is beyond the scope of the present paper.

(3) A third concern with the research process is that women want to know what we are getting into. In *Three Guineas* (1938) Virginia Woolf struggles with this concern. She wants women to consciously decide whether and on what terms they will join the procession of educated men. "Above all," she asks, "where is it leading us, the process of educated men?" (62). There is a problem with Woolf's formulation of the issue. It contains a tacit assumption that if women join the procession of educated men already in progress, the procession will continue in the same direction. I disagree.

Let us for a heuristic moment imagine that every scientist in the procession was a woman, and that by an accident of history all these women were black. If through some revolution white males suddenly joined their ranks, it is easy to imagine that the enterprise would change. White males would bring to their work different perspectives, which would then translate to different questions and perhaps even different methods. Similarly, if women were represented in equal proportions in the research enterprise with men, the research enterprise would be different. It has often been demonstrated that a situation determines in part how people will act in that situation. However, significantly changing the kinds of participants in a given situation will also change how people act in that situation.

The way in which a science is governed by its participants is discussed in the next section. When the participants change, the process will change in two ways. One change will be a function of women being the scientists, the doers of research. And another change will be a function of women becoming the subject matter of the research. The changes that women make as scholars in psychology are analogous to changes women make as scholars in most disciplines. What happens when women (and girls) become subject matter may be partly idiosyncratic in each discipline. We will consider these two ways the participants govern the product in turn.

2. Women as scientists and scholars

What aspects of the research process are influenced by the participants of the process? Many, probably all, aspects are vulnerable to the interest, values, and biases of the researchers (Mahoney, 1976). We will consider some in more detail than others. Question-generation may be the most obvious and one of the most important areas where bias (interest, values) enter. Another important, but nonobvious, process is motivational. That is, how long do we continue with a problem, or issue? What is our threshold of convincibility? Both the question-generation and the motivational issue will be considered in some detail. Other research issues will be mentioned in passing with references for the interested reader.

Question generation is particularly vulnerable to bias in the research process. We study things we care about and that are relevant to our own lives.

"How do we choose the problem of interest? It is a rare one of us who starts with a broad literature review to find the most pressing new question to try to answer. While serendipity is highly operative, e.g., where were you trained? Who was your major professor? It is also the case that we tend to ask questions of interest to us that reflect areas important and/or problematic to us" (Wallson, 1981, 606).

Examples abound of sex bias in the particular questions asked of research (e.g., Keller, 1982). In fields dominated by male researchers and funded by male-dominated agencies, many times the research dollars are spent on male-related problems. One of the saddest examples is medical research. Breast cancer, the leading cause of death in women over 50, has only recently received research funds from federal funding agencies. Women's diseases are more likely to be studied by women, men's diseases by men (Kushner, 1975). In psychology, whole areas of research have grown with the advent of large numbers of women entering psychology. Research on sex differences and sex roles are two examples. In the fall of 1984 I sat in on my first meeting of the National Science Foundation (NSF) panel on Social and Developmental Psychology. This was the second time I had served on an NSF panel. The first time was in 1974 and it was a small grants panel. The small grants panel had no women members. Only two women applied for the grants and the topic addressed by one of the women applicants was considered a "women's issue." Neither application was funded. I am happy to report that women scientists have come a long way (if my NSF experience is not a biased sample, and I have no reason to believe that it is). The panel on which I now serve has six members and a chair. The chair is a woman, as are two of the other panel members. But more heartening to me are the proportion of applicants who are female. Although I did not count the numbers (and now wish I had), I would estimate that 30 percent of the applicants were female and perhaps the number of grant applications funded will be 30 percent to female investigators. Female applicants do ask different questions—they are more likely to ask questions and deal with problems that disproportionately affect girls and women. Another change is evident. Men as well as women are interested in understanding the social problems of women and girls. Women researchers have changed the questions being asked as legitimate research questions.

In addition to the general questions and issues one's research focuses upon, subtler forms of question-asking pepper the research process. Whether, for example, any study is analyzed for sex differences, no matter the field of study, is significantly related to the sex of the researcher (Harris, 1972). Not surprisingly, women researchers ask whether there are sex differences in psychology in studies as diverse as animal perception and human language. Male researchers are much less likely to do so.

Does the asking of different questions lead to a separate female-oriented psychology? It may, but it also leads to different conclusions about old psychological questions. Several traditional areas of psychology have been changed by the interest in sex differences. The study of motivation is one example. Although sex differences were reported in the 1930s, researchers stopped testing female subjects in response to finding sex differences. However, in the 1970s and 1980s new life has come into the study of achievement motivation as a function of trying to come to grips with the result of sex differences in that field of research (Maccoby & Jacklin, 1974). We will return to the example of the study of achievement motivation below.

In sum, one change in the research process as a function of women doing the research is that the questions addressed are different. Even the same topics of research may have small but important different questions asked about them. Sex bias in the research questions asked can be attributed in part to the sex bias in the proportion of male to female researchers in the field. Thus in question-generating we can expect to see a further change in the content of a discipline as women enter each field.

Many other steps in the research process have been criticized. How an area is conceptualized and operationalized can vary according to the views of the researcher (Parlee, 1975). What level and type of variable is used (Wallston, 1981), the interpretation of results (Parlee, 1975), subject selection and operationalization of variables (Grady, 1981) have all been shown to be possible sources of sex-bias. Pauline Bart (1971) has illustrated how response categories, can be sex-biased.

> The investigation by the pscyhoanalyst follows an interview schedule where the subject's role in intercourse could be classified as 'passive', 'responsive', 'resistant', aggressive', 'deviant', 'other', (Wenner et al., 1969). You can see that if a woman takes an active role in intercourse, she would have to be coded 'aggressive', 'deviant', or 'other'. It is when biases are built into the research itself that ideological underpinnings are clearest and the posture of being value-free is a patent absurdity. (740)

It is difficult to say which step in the research process is most open to bias, and the most likely candidate for showing the researcher's "ideological underpinnings." However, there is a subtle and pervasive vehicle of bias in research that is motivational and cuts across all these steps; I will call it persistence or "threshold-of-convincibility."[1] It may be the strongest vehicle for showing politics unconsciously in research.

While working on Maccoby and Jacklin (1974), I was chided by my co-author for not pursuing a secondary source quite as vigorously as I might have had I not agreed with the author's conclusion. She was right. I am more easily convinced of the truth of a conclusion if it agrees with my belief. My own threshold-of-convincibility moves with my prejudices or hunches. I was guilty of using my resources, in this case the library and my analytic skills, with different amounts of persistence, depending on my agreement with an author. Since that time, I have been continually struck by how scientists differ in our threshold-of-convincibility of all research. Similarly, our criticism of another's research and our persistence in following research leads depends on the conclusions of research.

The relationship between persistence of research effort and the conclusion of a study is not a simple one. Sometimes when scholars disagree with other research they ignore it. One striking example is research on female orgasm. As Bart (1971) and others have noted, Kinsey's work on female sexuality contained all the information necessary to counter Freud's position that there exist two types of female orgasm. Similarly, Masters and Johnson's work directly countered Freud's position. Both the Kinsey studies and the Masters and Johnson studies received very wide readership and critical acclaim. However, psychoanalytic writers have ignored these studies and continue to discuss two types of female orgasms (Lyndon, 1971).

Sometimes when researchers disagree with a conclusion, instead of ignoring a finding they are motivated to refute it. Parlee has been especially effective in refuting published sexist conclusions. In a review article about premenstrual syndrome, Parlee (1973) shows how myths build up without primary source data but later, with repetition, accrue the trappings of data support. In an excellent refutation of a widely cited article by Bronerman and his colleagues, Parlee (1972) painstakingly points out selective referencing and blatant errors. And in another excellent refutation Parlee (1975) gives instance after instance of incorrect use of secondary sources and bias in interpretation by Garai and Scheinfeld (1968). Parlee's threshold-of-convincibility was not met by these studies. Persistence was needed for these refutations and Parlee effectively used it. Ignoring conclusions one disagrees with or working hard to refute them are two very different activities. I don't know what criteria researchers apply in deciding whether to ignore or refute findings they disagree with.

Threshold-of-convincibility and persistence may be even more important in one's own work. How long we stay with a topic, how hard we work to try to understand an area of research, and how quickly we feel we have solved a problem or understood it are extremely subjective decisions, decisions that are certainly affected by one's baises or politics.

A case in point can be seen in education-related research. Are nursery school and elementary school classrooms feminine and therefore unfair to boys? On the basis of one study, in which classroom objects (such as blackboard, page of arithmetic; school desk, book,) were labeled as masculine or feminine by second and third graders, Kagan (1964, 1051) concluded, "In sum, more young girls than boys viewed school activities as congruent with their sex role, and consequently, they should be more highly motivated to master academic tasks." In a popularization of this work, Kagan (1969, 41) states, "The ratio of boys to girls with reading problems ranges as high as six to one. One reason for this difference is that the average American six-or seven-year-old boy sees school as a feminine place. On entering school he meets female teachers who monitor painting, coloring and singing, and put a premium on obedience and suppression of aggression and restlessness. These values are clearly more appropriate for girls than for boys—boys naturally resist the complete submission it [school] demands."

There is a sharp contrast between Kagan on the one hand and others working in this area in the persistence with which they have pursued their work. Serbin and Connor and their colleagues have done study after study analyzing the nursery school setting and the effects that teachers' behaviors and classroom equipment have on the cognitive abilities and social behaviors of boys and girls (e.g., Serbin et al., 1973; Conner & Serbin, 1978, Serbin et al., 1982). Similarly Dweck and her colleagues (Dweck et al., 1978) have studied the contingent responding of teachers to girls' and boys' academic and nonacademic behavior in the classroom. Parsons and her colleagues (Parsons et al., 1982) have studied classroom behavior of the teachers, school-related expectations, and behavior of the parents and their effects on boys and girls.

It is true that Kagan is male and all the other researchers cited are female. But the sex of experimenter does not tell the whole story. The Kagan work is much older than the work by Serbin, Connor, Dweck, or Parsons. Still, asking the same research question, these psychologists have attacked the problems with different amounts of persistence. When one is willing to say the issues are settled is partly a function of one's prior beliefs.

Alternative research strategies have also been suggested by feminist critics as something new that women can add to the male research enterprise. Although different formulations have been given of these alternative strategies, they fall into roughly two categories: (1) arguments for research methods that bring the scientist closer to the subject matter; (2) arguments for the importance of doing value-laden vs. value-free research which includes taking the responsibility for the social effects of one's research. We will consider these in turn. One spokeswoman for bringing the scientist and subject closer together is Rae Carlson (1972). She has suggested that the general research strategy in psychology and the social sciences was "agentic" and that feminists (and women in general) could add a "communal" dimension to social science. In using the distinction of Baken (1966) to describe methodology, Carlson argues that the agentic male features are "separating, ordering, quantifying, manipulating, controlling" while the communal female features "involve naturalistic observation, sensitivity to intrinsic and qualitative patterning of phenomena studies, and greater personal participation of the investigator" (20). Other labels for this same distinction have been "wet" vs. "dry." The "wet" approach is seen as feminist and again as being more involved in the subject matter. The wet approach is richer in that it does not impose simplified unnatural order, but seeks to understand the complex natural order of things as they are (Bart, reported in Wallston, 1981).

The question of whether an artificial order is being put on the raw data is a recurring theme. Keller's (1982, 1985) criticism of hierarchical theory building in science explicitly argues that hierarchical thinking itself is a masculinist fallacy. She argues that the scientific enterprise has been distorted to see hierarchy where none exists. She contrasts Francis Bacon's view of science, i.e., binding nature to our service, with a contemporary feminist perspective of "letting the material speak to you," "getting a feeling for the organism" (McClintock, quoted in Keller, 1982, 599). Objectively, hierarchy may exist or it may not. Keller argues that masculinist scientists have tended to impose hierarchy in social and physical science to the detriment of their own scientific contributions.

How can we evaluate these alternative research strategies? Is it better to "get close to the data" or keep an objective distance? Surely the answer depends upon the research question being asked. If the question is description of a process or description of an organism, then clearly the closer one can get to the process or the organism the better. Anthropologists have "communal" methods, as Carlson (1972) has pointed out. They are trying to describe different cultures. In biology, ethologists use communal methods, and in psychology many developmentalists use communal methods. Is the "wetter" communal method the better method? Again it depends upon the question being asked. Do feminists ask different questions? Often they do. But many males are asking questions that would be better answered with "wetter" methods (Keller, 1985). We have become myopic with regard to our methods as we have with our equipment. Methods and equipment have often dictated our questions and surely that is a mistake. "The narrowness of our methods may also shape the way we ask questions and that is where the broadening of acceptable methodologies becomes quite important" (Wallston, 1981, 602). The methodology chosen should be the best possible for answering the particular question chosen.

We will now consider arguments for the importance of doing value-laden vs. value-free research. The general position of scientists is often that their job is to discover and the politician's job is to decide how these discoveries are to be used. In an eloquent book, aptly titled *Disturbing the Universe*, Dyson (1979) describes the joys and sorrow of working on nuclear energy, defense, and bomb building. Even given the complex ethical issues, he concludes that scientific work is somehow independent of the human costs. Feminists generally disagree. "I would argue that we need to consider the possible outcomes of our work at the onset. If I ask this question, how might the possible answers be used? I believe we have that responsibility as scientists, although it is not always an easy one. . . . it is difficult, if not impossible, to separate scientific and political concerns" (Wallston, 1981, 609). The same message is given in feminist literature. "Your scientists were so . . . childish. Carefully brought up through a course of study entered on early never to ask consequences, never to consider a broad range of effects, never to ask on whose behalf" (Piercy, 1976, 196).

Science does have political consequences. To pretend otherwise is absurd. The decision becomes whether to steer clear of issues that are politically important or try to grapple with the politically important problems and their possible conclusions. Many feminist scientists opt for the latter.

3. Women and girls as subject matter

In order to see how girls and women as subjects are changing psychology, I need to give a very brief description of the intellectual origins of psychology. Psychology has three intellectual origins. Each has a different model or view of the scientific enterprise and therefore a different model of the intellectual goal of psychology. These models are (1) Physiological/ philosophical individual model, (2) Medical, normal/abnormal model, (3) Educational testing of individual differences model. We will consider these in turn.

(1) Individual model

Physiology and philosophy together in the person of Wilhelm Wundt founded the first laboratory of psychology about one hundred years ago. From Wundt's laboratory through the classic schools of psychology and learning theories (most notably behaviorism) to cognitive psychology today, we have one intellectual model. That underlying model is that the goal of psychology is understanding a representative single individual's mind or a representative single individual's behavior. The variations between real live humans or the variability of the same human on different days is believed to be "noise" or random error. The "mind" and the laws of behavior are seen as universal (Keller, 1937). (Not surprisingly, given the researchers involved, the universal mind to be understood was always housed in a white male body.)

(2) Normal/abnormal model

The second intellectual origin of psychology is the medical study of psychiatric disorders. Freud was not the first in this line, but is the most famous early name. What medical research and clinical psychological research had then and now is the underlying model of two kinds of individuals: normal ones and abnormal ones. Variation between normal individuals is not something interesting to this underlying model. Variations between abnormal individuals are only noteworthy if they present a new abnormal pattern to be labeled.

(3) Individual differences model

The third intellectual origin of psychology is the educational-testing movement. This began with the commissioning of Alfred Binet to develop the first intelligence tests in France. Binet was asked to devise a way to distinguish between individuals who were bright and lazy and those who were not bright. The testing movement grew rapidly in the United States under Lewis Terman and the development of his Stanford-Binet tests. In the earliest days and in what has been described as "differential psychology" of the 1920s and 1930s the point of testing was to measure the variability of individuals. In educational testing, the differences between individuals are not error, but the point of testing. This is the only area of psychology that has included females as subjects from the beginnings of the research. In fact, in the early work by Binet and Terman it was found that girls scored higher than boys. The early testers were not only cognizant of sex differences, they tried to eliminate them by eliminating questions on which girls as a group scored higher than boys as a group. (One can't help but wonder what would have happened if the sex differences had been reversed).

The original three intellectual models of psychology have not had equal influence on contemporary psychology. By far the most influential model has been that of physiology/philosophy, the individual model. Understanding an "ideal" individual mind is still the underlying aim of most research psychologists. This is true even though clinical psychologists hold most of the Ph.D. degrees in psychology. Most of the work coming from educational testing is performed in schools of education and not in departments of psychology in America.

What then is the contribution of including girls and women as the subject matter of psychology? The existence (even occasionally) of sex differences makes the whole enterprise more complicated. It makes the underlying world view of a simple ideal individual too simple. Complication is inherent in human behavior. However, the complication of sex differences points out a flaw in the model of believing that one individual can (even ideally) stand for all individuals. It moves the study of individual differences out of the educational testing ghetto and into mainstream psychology. The discovery of sex differences by researchers studying motivation, memory, and perception makes it much more difficult to ignore the variation among normal individuals.

Conclusion

I have reviewed reasons feminist scholars give for trying to understand the research effort. These reasons include (1) the political goal of trying to change the proportion of men and women engaged in research; (2) the goal of understanding the research process in order to evaluate whether we want to join the research enterprise; and (3) the goal of adding a new dimension to science since women have been excluded from it as scholars and subject matter.

I have argued that women change the research process and thus their disciplines as a function of being the doers of the research and as a function of being the subject matter of the research. One important way in which women make a difference as scholars and scientists is generating different kinds of questions for research. Other specific sources of bias reviewed include conceptualization of problems, operationalization of measures, the nature of the control groups chosen, and sampling. I have suggested that the most ubiquitious sources of bias are question-generation and a motivational issue. The motivational bias that enters into all stages in the research process is the threshold-of-convincibility of the scientist or scholar. One's threshold-of-convincibility leads to persistence of the vigor of pursuit in one's own research and the criticism of others' research.

The alternative research strategies suggested by some feminist researchers are better ways to study some research questions but not others. For example, deciding to do fieldwork or laboratory work seems not a feminist/masculinist issue but a decision to be made depending on the research question asked by the investigator. I urge with Grady (1981) that "many issues of sex bias can be addressed by making research in psychology more scientific. To the extent that the ideal of objectivity is realized, research tends to be "sex fair" in many fundamental ways, as the early feminists hoped" (634). In sum, at the very least women and feminist scholars have made a difference to psychology and other disciplines in changing the questions raised and in having a somewhat different threshold-of-convincibility for many research issues. Included now as legitimate areas of study are issues that would not have seemed legitimate science a decade or two ago. Violence in the family, rape, female sexuality, math anxiety are only a few topics that have been common research issues because of women and feminist scholars. Whether particular methods are feminist or make a different contribution to science is thus far not clear.

The ways in which psychology is changed by including females as well as male subjects is somewhat more complex and idiosyncratic to the discipline. When sex difference (or any group difference) appears a different model may be necessary than the prevailing "idealized individual" model of much of psychology.

Feminists' concern with the research process, whatever the reasons, will help to change the process itself. We are changing the questions and increasing the variability of research methods used. I believe generating different questions and areas and having a different threshold-of-convincibility in traditional areas will be revolutionary. Women are moving into new disciplines in unprecedented numbers. When I was an undergraduate and graduate student in psychology, I had no women teachers. That would be a very unusual situation for a student of psychology today. We are becoming researchers and scholars in more than token numbers. Much more needs to be done, but even the begininings of this revolution of women has changed psychology forever.

NOTES

1. I wish to thank Carolyn Kaufman for suggesting this phrase.

REFERENCES

Bakan, D. 1966. *The duality of human existence: an essay on psychology and religion.* Chicago: Rand McNally.

Bart, P. B. 1971. Sexism and social science: from the gilded cage to the iron cage, or, perils of Pauline. *Journal of Marriage and the Family*, 734–45.

Carlson, R. 1972. *Understanding women: implications for personality theory and research. Journal of Social Issues* 28, 17–32.

Connor, J. M., & Serbin, L. A. 1978. Behaviorially-based masculine and feminine activity preference scales for preschoolers: correlates with other classroom behaviors and cognitive tests. *Child Development* 48, 1411–16.

Dweck, C. S., Davidson, E., Nelson, S., and Enna, B. 1978. I Sex differences in learned helplessness. II The contingencies of evaluative feedback in the classroom. III An experimental analysis. *Developmental Psychology* 14, 268–76.

Dyson, F. 1979. *Disturbing the universe.* New York: Harper & Row.

Garai, J. E. and Scheinfeld, A. 1968. Sex differences in mental and behavioral traits, *Genetic Psychology Monographs* 77, 169–299.

Grady, K. E. 1981. Sex bias in research design. *Psychology of Women Quarterly* 5, 628–36.

Harris, S. L. 1972. Who studies sex differences? *American Psychologist* 27, 1077–78.

Kagan, J. 1964. The child's sex role classification of school objects. *Child Development* 35, 1051–56.

———. 1969. Check one: male, female. *Psychology Today* 3, 39–41.

Keller, E. F. 1982. Feminism and Science. *Signs* 7, 589–602.

———. 1985. *Reflections on gender and science.* New Haven: Yale University Press.

———. 1937. *The definition of psychology.* New York: Appleton-Century-Crofts, Inc.

Kuhn, T. S. 1962. *The structure of scientific revolutions.* Chicago: University of Chicago Press.

Kushner, R. 1975. *Breast cancer.* New York: Harcourt Brace Jovanovich.

Lydon, S. 1971. The politics of orgasm. In M. H. Garskof (ed.), *Roles women play: readings towards women's liberation.* Belmont, CA: Brooks/Cole Publishing Co.

Maccoby, E. E., & Jacklin, C. N. 1974. *The psychology of sex differences.* Stanford: Stanford University Press.

Mahoney, M. J. 1976. *Scientist as subject: the psychological imperative.* Cambridge, Mass.: Ballinger Publishing Co.

McGuire, W. J. 1973. The yin and yang of progress in social psychology: seven koan. *Journal of Personality and Social Psychology* 26, 446–56.

Mead, M. 1978. The relationship between research by women and women's experimental roles. *Psychology of Women Quarterly* 2, 363–65.

Mednick, M. T. S. & Weissman, H. S. 1975. The psychology of women-selected topics. *Annual Review of Psychology* 26, 1–18.

Parlee, M. B. 1981. Appropriate control groups in feminist research. *Psychology of Women Quarterly* 5, 637–44.

———. 1972. Comments on "roles of activation and inhibition in sex differences in cognitive abilities" by B. M. Broverman, E. L. Klaiber, Y. Kobayashi and W. Vogel. *Psychological Review.*

―――. 1975. Psychology. *Signs* 1, 119–38.

―――. 1973. The premenstrual syndrome. *Psychological Bulletin* 80, 454–65.

Parsons, J. E., Kaczala, C. M. & Meece, J. L. 1982. Socialization of achievement attitudes and beliefs: classroom influences. *Child Development* 53, 322–39.

Piercy, M. 1976. *Woman on the edge of time*. New York: Fawcett Crest.

Serbin, L. A., O'Leary, K. D., Kent, R. N. & Tonick, I. J. 1973. A comparison of teacher response to the preacademic and problem behavior of boys and girls. *Child Development* 44, 796–804.

Serbin, L. A., Sprafkin, C., Elman, & Doyle, A. 1982. The early development of sex-differentiated pattern of social influence. *Canadian Journal of Behavioral Science* 14, 350–63.

Shields, S. A. 1975. Functionalism, Darwinism, and the psychology of women: a study of social myth. *American Psychologist* 739–54.

Wallston, B. S. 1981. What are the questions in the psychology of women? A feminist approach to research. *Psychology of Women Quarterly* 5, 597–617.

Weisstein, N. 1971. Psychology constructs the female, or the fantasy life of the male psychologist. In M. H. Garskof (ed.), *Roles women play: readings toward women's liberation*. Belmont, CA: Brooks/Cole Publishing Co.

Wenner, N. K., Cohen, M. B., Weigert, E. V., Kvarnes, R. C., Chaneson, E. M. & Fearing, J. M. 1969. Emotional problems in pregnancy. *Psychiatry* 32, 389–410.

Woolf, V. 1938. *Three guineas*. New York: Harcourt, Brace & World, Inc.

The Sticking Power of Stereotypes

SCIENCE AND BELIEF

A POLEMIC ON SEX DIFFERENCES RESEARCH

Ruth Bleier

The natural sciences may well be the last of the research disciplines to feel the impact of critical feminist scholarship. Compared to most of the social sciences and the humanities over the past decade, relatively few women's studies scholars and scholarly works have appeared in the natural sciences. Biological scientists have, however, not been so reticent in their investigations and the presentation of theories that have great relevance for dominant cultural representations of women as biologically flawed for the skills our society values. The central question in this area of research has been that of sex differences in behaviors and characteristics and the presumed biological bases for those differences. The scope of the literature on sex differences is enormous, and the critical literature on sex differences research is growing. In this space I can only touch upon a few of the more well known or recently publicized and influential studies. (For a more detailed examination of many of the issues in sex differences research, see Bleier, 1984; Kimball, 1981; Lloyd and Archer, 1976; Maccoby and Jacklin, 1974; Wittig and Petersen, 1979.)

Research on sex differences in human behaviors and cognitive functioning has become prominent over the past decade in a number of fields—psychology, sociology, political science, primatology, neuroendocrinology, and reproductive physiology. Sex differences research is doubtless based upon the ordinary experience and observation of obvious asymmetries in roles and socially recognized achievements between women and men,

Some material in this chapter has appeared in R. Bleier (ed.), *Feminist Approaches to Science,* New York: Pergamon, 1986.

I usually use the term *sex differences* because that is the name given to this flourishing field of research. Under discussion, however, are *gender differences,* the sets of attributes socially and culturally constructed on the basis of the birth assignment as female or male.

generally speaking, in our culture. Attention in the social and biological sciences has focused on presumed sex differences in mathematical and visuospatial skills and in aggressivity as explanatory factors for perceived differences in social achievements.

Biologists have attempted to specify the biological origins of such presumed sex differences in cognition and motivation. Sociobiologists of the E. O. Wilson school locate the differences in genetic-evolutionary adaptive mechanisms; neuroscientists, in brain hemispheric asymmetries and prenatal hormonal effects on the developing brain.

Common to all such efforts are certain assumptions: that there are absolute measurable, consistent sex differences in achievement, behaviors, and cognitive abilities in this country (where most studies I shall cite have been done), that such differences are consistent across cultures, and that such differences—because they are universal—must have a biological basis. The evidence that is available does not support any of these assumptions.

It is important to recognize that the existence of biologically based sex differences in cognitive functioning and achievement is a viewpoint, a stance, not demonstrated fact. It constitutes an unquestioned assumption for studies rather than a hypothesis to be tested and challenged. As such, like any other assumptions concerning human behaviors and characteristics, it reflects and embodies individual and social values.

Scientists (like everyone else) are frequently unable to see the contradictions and inconsistencies in the frameworks they themselves have constructed. We live in a culture built on a particular set of gender assumptions and structured to amplify if not produce gender asymmetries and inequalities, and we come to view these differences as part of the natural world. We tend to ignore the fact that other cultures have different sets of gender asymmetries, that they place different values and significances upon those differences, and that *their* world, obviously, appears as "natural" to them as ours does to us. If women (or blacks or Native Americans) are denied equal educational, training, and job opportunities, and at the same time are exposed to a cultural ideology and consistent, ubiquitous cultural representations of their inferiority, their achievements (as recognized and measured by the dominant group that sets the standards) will indeed turn out to be unequal, "different," and inferior.

An enormous literature is devoted to the measurement of gender differences in cognitive functioning. The studies produce inconsistent and contradictory results since different tests are used and since test results vary according to which particular subject populations are chosen, suggesting the importance of a large number of variables that are not taken into account by those looking for "innate," biological explanations. Nonetheless these measures also produce results suggesting that the differences between boys and girls or men and women, if real, are also trivial. The important questions to answer are: Why then is so much attention paid to the measurement and explanation of differences *between* the sexes that are trivial and easily explainable on the basis of the extraordinarily wide gap in the socialization, education, and training processes of girls and boys? Why is so little attention paid to the very real and enormous differences that exist *among* girls, *among* boys, *among* people in general in educational and general life achievement, development, and satisfaction—a problem clearly accessible, to a large degree, through changes in social policies and priorities.

Otherwise meticulous scientists who have made important and fundamental contributions to their fields have shown serious suspensions of critical judgment in interpretations of their own and others' data to make them fit what has become a ruling paradigm of the 1970s and 1980s. That paradigm is that significant cognitive sex differences exist and that these differences may be attributed to biological sex differences in the development, structure, and functioning of the brain. Support of the paradigm involves the process of ignoring the obvious and the known (the complexity of human development and experience) in favor of a constructed reality (of biologically based gender differences), legitimized by an elaborate network of interdependent hypotheses, as I shall demonstrate. Few of the hypotheses and assumptions have any independent scientific support but together, supported by each other, they create the illusion of a structure with weight, consistency, conviction, and reason.

The illusory structure is the scientific case for the biological basis for gender differences in cognitive functioning and other socially valued human characteristics. In support of this paradigm, scientists have been making increasing numbers of unsubstantiated conjectures that are then taken up by other scientists as confirming evidence for their own conjectures, a process that repeats itself like the infinite series of images produced by two facing mirrors.

The profound and troublesome truth is that no single part of the paradigm is known to be descriptive of reality nor are the assumptions on which the entire paradigm is based. It is the task of this paper to show how this is so, by analyzing some research in three areas prominently featured in the sex differences literature: aggressivity, brain asymmetries, and mathematical/visuospatial ability.

Historical Context

The women's movement since the late 1960s and early 1970s has forced into public scrutiny and public policy questions of gender inequalities in employment, educational, and sports opportunities and in legal and social status. I believe that the heightened interest in biological sex differences as either explanation for or justification of the myriad forms of gender asymmetries is not unrelated to the social-political context of the 1970s and 1980s. I do not claim, however, that this is a new form of sensitivity of science to social events and values. History shows otherwise, and the brain has frequently been the site of battle in controversies over sex or race differences.

That social values and beliefs affect the work of scientists is hardly surprising. It would in fact be naive to believe that scientists, unlike other human beings, are unaffected in their thinking by their life histories and by the values and realities of our culture. This is a subject that has been explored extensively by philosophers and historians of science and sociologists of knowledge (Mendelsohn et al., 1977; Osler, 1980; Provine, 1973). It is not difficult today to see clearly the biases of the most reputable brain scientists in the middle and late nineteenth century, a period of antislavery and women's rights turmoil, in their finding female and "Negro" brains to be inferior and underdeveloped. James Hunt, president of the London Anthropological Society, wrote in 1863 that "there is no doubt that the Negro's brain bears a great resemblance to a European female or child's brain and thus approaches the ape far more than the European, while the Negress approaches the ape still nearer" (Fee, 1979, 421). Stephen Jay Gould has shown how the most prominent brain scientists of the period, obsessed with numbers as indicators of scientifc rigor, used craniometry to "confirm all the common prejudices of comfortable white males—that blacks, women, and poor people occupy their subordinate roles by the harsh dictates of nature." They used numbers "not to generate new theories but to illustrate a priori conclusions" (1981, 74). The esteemed Carl Vogt wrote in 1864:

> By its rounded apex and less developed posterior lobe the Negro brain resembles that of our children, and by the protuberance of the parietal lobe, that of our females. . . . The grown-up Negro partakes, as regards his intellectual faculties, of the nature of the child, the female, and the senile white. (Gould, 1981, 103)

In 1861 Paul Broca wrote:

> We might ask if the small size of the female brain depends exclusively upon the small size of her body. Tiedemann has proposed this explanation. But we must not forget that women are, on the average, a little less intelligent than men, a difference which we should not exaggerate but which is, nonetheless, real. (Gould, 1981, 104)

G. Le Bon, whom Gould calls the chief misogynist of Broca's school, wrote in 1879:

> In the most intelligent races, as among the Parisians, there are a large number of women whose brains are closer in size to those of gorillas than to the most developed male brains. This inferiority is so obvious that no one can contest it for a moment; only its degree is worth discussion. (Gould, 1981, 104–5)

It is, however, difficult to see clearly something that is happening in science *today* and to believe that *today* social values, resistance to current dramatic changes in traditional gender roles, can affect the questions that scientists find interesting to ask, the methods they use, the interpretations they make of their data, and the alternative interpretations they do not consider. Another problem is that we tend to see the scientific truths of today as the final valid truths, the culmination of the previous centuries' unavoidable and primitive follies and approximations. Yet today's truths, today's science, are as relative, as changing, as incomplete, as certain to be superseded in coming decades as they ever were. Our understanding of biological facts and concepts based on that understanding have always changed over time and there is every reason to believe that they will continue to do so.

An example from primatology may be instructive in showing how speculation becomes established as a paradigm that is not demonstrated or challenged but accepted as self-evident. On the subject of the relationship between competition and reproductive success, Darwin had suggested that male dominance and intermale competition or female choice may be critical factors in sexual selection. But Huxley was convinced that intermale competition and not female choice was significant in sexual selection and that there was a relationship between male dominance rank and reproductive success (Fedigan, 1983). This speculation was accepted as theory without testing and has prevailed as the priority-of-access-to-estrous-female model of reproductive success. It is a theory that has been, in fact, very difficult to substantiate since dominance has been a murky, ill-defined concept and since reproductive success in males can only be *inferred* from observed mating behavior. Commitment to this unsupported theory required an inability to see that in troops and species with dominance hierarchies, the females also have dominance hierarchies, that females select their mating partners and often do not select dominant males, and that measuring reproductive success in females requires neither mystery nor inference. One can count their offspring from the time of birth through the suckling and often the postsuckling period. Actual observations of social relationships within troops could have produced rich and testable hypotheses about possible connections between dominance and reproductive success.

For my purposes here it is irrelevant whether or not there is such a correlation. It is significant, however, that recent studies testing the hypothesis have produced contradictory results, with some finding correlations and some not (Fedigan, 1983).

Aggressivity

Following experimental work in rodents demonstrating a relationship between pre- and peri-natal hormonal levels and the incidence of fighting behaviors in the adult (Conner and Levine, 169; Edwards, 1969), there has been interest in the possible relationship between androgen levels and "aggressivity" in humans. The first problem in this area of research is semantic, beginning with the literature on rodents and ending with that on humans. In rodents what is measured are the fighting behaviors of animals, but what is discussed and interpreted is "aggressivity," an undefined characteristic that has a range of subjective meanings for investigators and readers alike. It is a term, however, that invites extrapolation to human behaviors. Then, different human studies use different (and arbitrary) measures of aggressivity, which range from the general phenomenon of fighting in wars to criminal activity to playground characteristics of children. In research on sex differences in aggressivity, however, the underlying issue being addressed is the difference in achievement in publicly visible or leadership positions in business, politics, the arts, academia, etc.

Possibly the most widely cited studies in the literature on sex differences in aggressivity in humans are those of Anke Ehrhardt and John Money on "tomboyism" in girls exposed as fetuses to high levels of androgens (Ehrhardt and Money, 1967; Ehrhardt et al., 1968). The 25 fetally androgenized teenagers that constituted the subject population for Ehrhardt's and Money's two studies were born with masculinized genitalia, usually resembling a penis and scrotum closely enough that the children were considered to be boys for a while—all but one case required clitoridectomy and reconstruction of the labia and vagina. The authors found a higher level of "tomboyism" in the subjects than in controls. By tomboyism the authors meant a preference for outdoor play and athletics, for boys as playmates, and for boys' toys; little interest in dolls or in infant care; preference for functional clothes (pants rather than dresses); an interest in career equal to or greater than that in marriage. The tomboyism reported in these studies has been widely and uncritically interpreted as reflecting "masculinization" of the developing brain and as being a measure of aggressivity, induced by androgens.

It is a measure of the degree to which "membership in a culture blinds us to the constructed nature of that culture's reality" (Kessler and McKenna, 1978) that Ehrhardt and Money and subsequent scientists accept at face value the idea of "tomboyism" as an index of a characteristic called "masculinity," presumed to be as objective and innate a human feature as height and eye color. Yet the attribution of masculinity or maleness to physical activity, athleticism, and freedom of body movement is an anachronistic nineteenth-century, white EuroAmerican value judgment, not a scientific truth. Its necessary complement is the nineteenth-century prescription of a presumably innate characteristic called femininity: physical restraint, restriction of body movements, physical and athletic incompetence, passivity, "niceness," and preoccupation with maternalism and nurturant activities. This is but another example of psychology's turning "the nineteenth-century nurturing imperative into a twentieth-century factual, female attribute" (Westkott, 1984).

This concept of tomboyism further implies that if little girls do not conform to the cultural stereotype, there must be something wrong with them: disordered hormones or chromosomes or gender identity. Such value judgments form the unexpressed assumptions for the research and they affect what data are collected and how and what interpretations are made of the data. The finished work then provides a body of "knowledge" that places the stamp of *science* on a set of unexamined social values and judgments concerning gender. Science and culture together structure gender and gender characteristics in and by the very process of their explorations of presumed biological origins of gender differences.

Furthermore, the social science and biological literature on sex differences in aggressivity has uncritically supported the belief that Ehrhardt and Money demonstrated a cause and effect relationship between *in utero* effects of androgens on the brain and subsequent behaviors. One need only read the original reports to see that the authors did not demonstrate an effect of androgens on the developing brain in the production of "tomboyism," that the authors themselves concluded in their initial reports of their studies that this was only one of several possible interpretations of their findings, and that the subsequent rapid incorporation of this tentative hypothesis into the literature as a demonstrated fact had more to do with the social and political climate of the 1970s and 1980s than with rigorous scientific inquiry.

The first study of Ehrhardt and Money (1967) was of ten girls with progestin-induced fetal androgenization and the second (Ehrhardt et al., 1968) was of fifteen girls with the adrenogenital syndrome (AGS). In their first paper, Ehrhardt and Money raised the "question of whether tomboyishness may not be a frequent characteristic in the development of middle-class suburban and rural girls who have both the space and tradition of the outdoor life" (96). They concluded, "It will require more than ten cases and better control of at least the socioeconomic variable before one can answer with confidence the question of the extent to which prenatal hormones can affect subsequent behavior" (98). In their second paper, they wrote:

> It is not possible to estimate on the basis of present data, whether individual differences in degrees of tomboyism may have reflected differences in parental attitude. Each parent knew of the child's genital masculinization at birth. This knowledge may have insidiously influenced their expectancies and reactions regarding the child's behavioral development and interests. . . (166)

Yet, on the basis of the same data on the same 25 patients, Ehrhardt and Money wrote a number of subsequent articles and a book that ignored their cautious qualifications at the time of original publication of the data and became ever more assertive that the results demonstrated the behavioral effects of androgenization of the fetal female brain. In their book, written four years later in 1972, they wrote, "The most likely hypothesis to explain the various features of tomboyism in fetally masculinized genetic females is that their tomboyism is a sequel to a masculinizing effect on the fetal brain" (Money and Ehrhardt).

Following a subsequent similar study of 17 female AGS patients in 1974, Ehrhardt and another colleague concluded that their findings "suggest strongly that it is the fetal exposure to androgens that contribute to the typical profile of behavior exhibited by AGS females" (Ehrhardt and Baker, 1974). Five years later, still on the basis of the same work, Ehrhardt and another colleague concluded that, more than "suggesting strongly," the studies demonstrate that the "effects of prenatal androgens *have been established* [emphasis added] for the sex-dimorphic behaviour clusters" (Ehrhardt and Meyer-Bahlburg, 1979).

Aside from the reservations originally expressed by the authors themselves, there are a number of other reasons for questioning any claim that tomboy behaviors (i.e., aggressivity) were demonstrated to be a product of androgen effects on the fetal brain. I shall mention only a few here. The first is that the authors did not consider the effects on a child's choices and identifications of knowing that she has or had a penis and scrotum, the one sure sign of being a boy. The first plastic surgery was not done in some cases until 3 and 1/2 or even 7 and 1/2 years of age, and usually further vaginal surgery was necessary at the time of adolescence. For both themselves and their parents, surely the ambiguity of their situation in this extremely gender-polarized society would have some effect on their preferences and choices in play, playmates, clothes, and attitudes toward motherhood and career. When gender becomes so fragile and arbitrary a concept that it depends on plastic surgery, perhaps parents and children alike recognize the wisdom of taking all options toward full human development. That is, it would seem arbitrary indeed, under the circumstances, not to sanction or encourage boy-type activities in a child born with a boy's genitalia, the one absolute indicator on the basis of which gender is assigned at birth. It also seems relevant that, in the first study of 10 girls, the only girl who preferred dolls, showed no preference for outdoor play or boys' toys or clothes, and did not consider herself a tomboy was the only one without masculinized genitalia. The authors also did not appear to consider that the intense medical and psychological scrutiny and interventions that the patients had undergone since birth, all centered on their genitalia, could have affected their behaviors and attitudes.

While Ehrhardt and Money noted the possible importance of parental attitudes and family traditions, they did not formally explore the attitudes or study the siblings of the patients. Yet their anecdotal comments are revealing. They recorded, in their first study of 10 patients, that one mother considered herself a tomboy as a child and reported that *both* her daughters, the patient and her unaffected sister, were tomboys. They added that it "was anecdotally evident . . . that some of the sisters of index cases were tomboyish. . ." (97). Since some (number unspecified) of the 10 patients had *no* sisters, and we know that some (number unspecified) of the patients (only nine of whom were tomboys) had sisters who were tomboys, it seems rather clear that tomboyish behaviors may have been characteristic rather than exceptional in this small sample of families. The data as they are reported or implied do not easily invite the elaborate, and scientifically dubious, explanation of an androgen effect on the developing fetal brain.

Brain Asymmetries and Cognitive Functioning

Recent years have seen a heightened interest in finding sex differences in brain structure and function to explain presumed sex differences in cognitive functioning. The focus has been mainly on the question of hemispheric lateralization in cognitive processing. The predominant theory is that women are more lateralized than men to the left hemisphere in verbal processing and that men are more lateralized than women to the right hemisphere in visuospatial (and, therefore, presumably, mathematical) processing. Women are considered to use both hemispheres more than men do in processing visuospatial information.

It is, first of all, noteworthy that the majority of studies in this area are flawed for one reason or another and that there is no agreement among them on the question of sex differences in lateralization of cognitive processing, as two exhaustive reviews of the literature have documented

(Kimball, 1981; McGlone, 1980). It is also not clear that tests for lateralization measure lateralization of cognitive processing rather than hemispheric differences in attentional or memory storage mechanisms (Hardyck et al., 1978).

But the most serious interpretive problem is that, even if sex differences in functional lateralization *were* demonstrated, there is no evidence that there is any relationship between hemispheric lateralization (or hemispheric bilateral symmetry) of functioning and performance. There are studies that find sex differences in lateralization but no sex differences in performance, studies that find a sex difference in performance but no sex difference in lateralization, and studies that find no sex differences in either lateralization or performance (Kimball, 1981). The assumption is that the (questionable) demonstration of right hemispheric lateralization of visuospatial processing in males accounts for their presumed superiority in visuospatial skills. But no independent evidence supports this assumption. It is instead a product of circular reasoning: men are superior in visuospatial skills because their right hemispheres are specialized for visuospatial cognitive processing; we know that right hemispheric specialization provides superior visuospatial skills because men are better at visuospatial skills than women, who use both hemispheres for visuospatial processing. To put this another way, if it is true that women use the left as well as the right hemisphere for processing visuospatial information, there is no intrinsic reason to believe that that situation makes for inferior processing. If the hemispheres have some degree of lateralization of processing information and if the left is indeed specialized for analytical processes, as the dominant theory maintains, there is no reason to believe that left hemispheric analytical processing is a disadvantageous complement to right hemispheric visuospatial processing. The only reason for believing this is that, presumably, men do not do it and women do.

Some recent studies purport to add evidence for this dominant belief in sex differences in lateralization and cognitive processing.

De Lacoste-Utamsing and Holloway (1982) reported that the splenium, the caudal part of the corpus callosum, which carries nerve fibers connecting the two hemispheres, was larger in five female brains obtained at autopsy than in nine male brains. No mention is made of the ages or circumstances of death in these subjects, factors of possible relevance to the measurements. While the authors state that a larger sample size and information on the numbers and types of axons in the splenium are needed before further interpretation of these results can be made, they do offer their interpretation of the significance of their findings. Since there is some evidence that the splenium is the site of the interhemispheric transfer of visual information, the authors write:

If we are to believe that a larger splenium implies a larger number of fibers interconnecting cortical areas and that the number of interhemispheric fibers correlates inversely with lateralization of function, then our results are congruent with a recent neuropsychological hypothesis that the female brain is less well lateralized—that is, manifests less hemispheric specialization—than the male brain for visuospatial functions (1432).

But there is no evidence that the number of fibers connecting the two sides is in any way related to degree of symmetry or asymmetry between the two sides. The larger number of fibers tells us nothing on that issue but does suggest that there is an increased amount of transfer of information between the two hemispheres. This appears to be an intuitive assumption on the part of the authors that is likely to be wrong or irrelevant. But even if there *were* a known relationship between number of fibers and symmetry, there is still no evidence whatsoever that links the degree of symmetry or asymmetry with visuospatial ability. But the wording (quoted above) implies a link between symmetry and superior function by the use of the terms "less well lateralized" and "less hemispheric specialization." If one were to rely on a different set of intuitive judgments in the interpretation of these findings, one could just as easily suggest that because their splenium is larger than men's, suggesting richer interhemispheric interchange of information and, therefore, more bilateral representation of visuospatial perception, women would be superior to men in visuospatial skills if they received the same training and experience (in three-dimensional perceptual/motor skills) during childhood as the majority of boys and men do. In short, it is equally possible that bilateral representation improves visuospatial perception. *No one knows.*

Finally, it should be noted that even the experimental "findings" themselves of the de Lacoste-Utamsing and Holloway study are questionable. Using magnetic resonance images of the brain (similar in appearance to x-rays) from 37 subjects, we have repeated the measurements of the corpus callosum made in the original study. We found no sex differences in the size or shape of the splenium of the corpus callosum (Bleier, Houston, and Byne, 1986). Rather, we found an enormous range of variability in the size and shape of the callosum regardless of gender or age. The biological and experiential forces shaping the corpus callosum during fetal and postnatal growth and development are unknown as is the functional significance of the shape or size of any portion of the callosum.

Left-handedness, Testosterone, and Mathematical Ability

Another study (Geschwind and Behan, 1982) reported an association between left-handedness, certain disorders of the immune system, and developmental learning disabilities such as autism, dyslexia, or stuttering, which are more common in boys. On the basis of their own findings and those of Chi et al. (1977), in their studies of human fetal brains, that several convolutions of the right hemisphere develop one to two weeks earlier during gestation than those on the left, Geschwind and Behan proposed that testosterone has the effect *in utero* of slowing the development of the left hemisphere. Aside from the fact that there is no evidence for such a proposal, it is important to note that Chi et al., in the study quoted by Geschwind and Behan, examined and did measurements on photographs of 507 brains and on serial sections of 207 brains from infants of 10-44 weeks' gestational age and found *no significant sex differences* in any of their measurements. If there were such an effect of testosterone on the developing brain, there would be detectable sex differences in the rate of growth or development of the left hemisphere. Geschwind and Behan further state, "Delayed growth in the left hemisphere as a result of testosterone would account for the greater frequency of left-handedness in males." (5099) But one is then led to wonder why are not *all* boys left-handed, since ordinarily they are all exposed to testosterone from their own testes and adrenals during development, and what is to account for the fact that the overwhelming majority of boys are right-handed?

Ignoring the obviously contradictory findings by Chi et al. on *human* brains, Geschwind and Behan offer as supporting evidence for their hypothesis the work of Diamond et al. (1981) that the right posterior cortex (the layers of nerve cells on the surface of the hemispheres) is thicker in male *rats'* brains than in females'. It is interesting to examine this study since it fits into the paradigm pattern that is the subject of this paper. The study found a 3% difference between the two sides (with the right cortex thicker than the left) in areas 17, 18a, and 39. In female rats they found the right cortex to be thinner than the left in these areas, but the differences were statistically insignificant. Diamond et al. noted that other studies have shown that areas 17 and 18a process visual information, and they suggested that ". . . in the male rat it is necessary to have greater spatial orientation to interact with a female rat during estrus and to integrate that input into a meaningful output." We see in this interpretation an unsupported conceptual leap from the finding of a thicker right cortex in the male (in three areas) to the assumption of "greater spatial orientation" in male rats. Yet there is no evidence that female rats have a "lesser" or somehow deficient spatial orientation or that "spatial orientation" is related to any asymmetry of the cortex. I am not aware of studies showing that female rats get lost or fall off cliffs.

One suspects that beliefs in men's superior visuospatial abilities, in their reported functional lateralization to the right hemisphere, and in the inferiority of women's visuospatial skills and their *lack* of right hemispheric lateralization became hidden premises for the interpretation of the findings in this study on rats. The results of the study are then used by others as evidence for their own otherwise unsupported conjectures that testosterone enhances right hemispheric development and, therefore, superior mathematical ability in boys and men.

Whatever the significance of a thicker right cortex may be for the rat's behaviors (a significance that is presently unknown), it surely is even more obscure what significance the rat's thicker right cortex has for *human* brains or behaviors. It is extraordinarily simplistic even to suggest such an extrapolation from the rat to the human cortex or behaviors in view of the enormous qualitative and quantitative leaps that the human brain and behavior have undergone in evolutionary development.

Though Geschwind and Behan did not study (or report) the incidence of giftedness in their population, in two news reports of their work in *Science* (Marx, 1982; Kolata, 1983), Geschwind suggested that testosterone effects on the fetal brain can produce "superior right hemisphere talents, such as artistic, musical, or mathematical talent" (1983, 1312). This proposal was greeted with enthusiasm by two investigators who had earlier reported a larger number of male seventh-graders (260) scoring above 700 on the mathematics section of the Scholastic Aptitude Test (SAT) than female seventh graders (20), and had suggested an "endogenous" (i.e., innate) superior mathematical ability in boys (Benbow and Stanley, 1980, 1983). Criticisms of this work have been numerous (Chipman, 1981; Beckwith and Woodruff, 1984; Fox, 1984; Schafer and Gray, 1981), and I shall not repeat them here, but it is important to acknowledge that there is no known measure, including the SAT, of "innate" intelligence or mathematical ability, nor is it clear how innate intelligence or mathematical ability *could* be measured or could even exist apart from learning and experience.

Nonetheless, following Geschwind and Behan's findings and speculations, Benbow and Stanley returned to their sample of students scoring over 700 and were "delighted" (Kolata, 1983) to find that 20 percent of the subjects are left-handed (twice the usual incidence), a figure they evidently find more significant than that 80 percent of them are *not*.

The body of work I have summarized has significance far beyond an ordinary controversy among academics. A combination of valid and irrelevant findings, flimsy evidence, and unsupported conjectures (strengthened by the omission of contradictory evidence) are assembled by the researchers themselves and taken up by the national news services and major news media as demonstrating that male mathematical superiority may be from "math genes" and "in-womb hormones" (*Newsweek* and *Capitol Times*). The news item in *Science* on Geschwind's findings and subsequent speculations carried a prominent bold headline, "Math Genius May Have Hormonal Basis" (Kolata, 1983). Except for the rare and irrepressible talents, the effects of such "scientific" declarations of innate intellectual limitations of being female can be only devastating.

Other Conceptual Problems

I should like to make it clear, first, that I do not wish to deny the possibility of biologically based structural or functional differences in the brain between women and men. My point is that, to date, no sex differences in cognitive function have been shown to be independent of learning and experience, and the very few sex differences in brain structure reported in the literature have no known relationship to cognitive functioning. Furthermore, even were structural or functional differences to be demonstrated, it would still have to be shown that these have any explanatory relevance for the vast differences between the sexes in social position and recognized achievements in our culture. Interpretations that claim otherwise go beyond the available evidence and have achieved acceptance only because they fit smoothly into a currently dominant paradigm of the biological basis of cognitive sex differences. They make it possible for millions of people to suspect "that their social prejudices are scientific facts after all" (Gould, 1981, 28).

My objections to this body of research are, however, even more fundamental since I question the concept itself of sex differences in cognitive functioning as well as the validity of the accepted concept of gender. We tend to forget that gender is an attribute that is assigned at the moment of birth primarily on the basis of the presence or absence of a penis. The rest of the trappings of gender categories are "social accomplishments" (Kessler and McKenna, 1977), a set of attributions culturally prescribed on the basis of the original birth assignment, and these include gait, gestures, facial expression, interests, appearance, clothes, behaviors, expectations, and potential roles and tasks. These have nothing to do with biological capacities and they are different for different cultures. Yet we—and science—come to view the socially accomplished attributes as *natural*, for which biological explanations are appropriate. Having arbitrarily assigned a different set of gender characteristics and behaviors to women and to men in our culture from the time of birth, we then assiduously investigate whether gender differences exist, measure the differences we find, and then look for their origins in biology.

But the next problem is that, even in the face of the vast differences in education, training, and experience between girls and boys, women and men (differences that are finally diminishing), the measured cognitive differences are surprisingly small and cannot be considered to be sex or gender differences. Many studies find *no* differences, since the experiences and culture of the tested populations influence the test results (among Alaskans, for example, no sex differences are found in visuospatial abilities). When sex differences are found, they are "typically on the order of one-quarter of a standard deviation" (Springer and Deutsch, 1981, 129). This means that, on the average of studies, 50 percent of the men score below 40 percent of the women. It means that women and men, boys and girls have the same overlapping range of scores, and there may be a small difference in the *means* between the two populations. It means that a few girls or women score better than all but a few boys or men, and vice versa. This does not fit a reasonable definition of a *gender* difference. No score predicts the gender of the subject; knowledge of a subject's gender does not predict her/his score—not even the range of possible scores, which would be *identical* for both genders. "To emphasize these differences is, therefore, a particular selective viewpoint . . .", says the psychologist John Archer (1976, 254). And one wonders why such extraordinary attention is focused on mean sex differences that are irregularly found and trivial in comparison with the enormous differences that are found *within* each group, within any population that is measured. Part of the reason is, as the anthropologist Marilyn Strathern says, that gender is not just an endproduct of biological and social forces; we put gender to work: "It frequently carries a heavy symbolic load, relevant for how men and women regard one another, but also to how society regards itself." (1976, 68). Gender attributes reflect basic structural divisions in our social, political, and economic worlds. Now, at a time when the borders between these divisions are under assault, one way to protect them is by finding that the divisions, like the attributes, are rooted in nature, in biology.

It does not seem a worthy project for science to continue measuring trivial sex differences in mean scores on cognitive tests and then to attempt to justify these, along with differences in social achievement, as biological. If we are trying to understand social issues, like differences in achievement, we could ask, "Why is it that the difference in the participation rates of women and men in scientific fields is so large when sex differences in intellectual abilities are so small?" (Kimball, 1981, 333). Or, if we are really interested in variations in cognitive functioning and achievement, then we might ask, Why within any population, as defined by age or class or race or sex, do we find such an enormous range of cognitive style and ability? Since there are boys *and* girls at the highest end of the range of scores for reading and mathematics ability, and girls *and* boys at the lowest end, do these dramatic differences not hold greater promise for yielding suggestive hypotheses concerning cognitive functioning (if that is indeed the question of interest) than the elusive and small differences between some populations of girls and boys?

Since we are unable to explain cognitive functioning, intelligence, mind, or consciousness in terms of brain structures or functions (i.e., we do not know how or what brain activity gives rise to cognitive functioning or consciousness), why do we assume we can explain presumed *sex differences* (or race or class differences) in cognitive functioning in terms of brain structures and functions? If we have no information that relates verbal or visuospatial abilities to either symmetry or asymmetry in brain structures and functioning, why do we assume we can relate presumed *sex differences* in verbal or visuospatial abilities to presumed sex differences in symmetry or asymmetry of brain structures and functioning? If we are unable to even begin to explain the enormous range of differences in verbal or visuospatial or mathematical abilities *within* any given population of people, within any group of girls or women and within any group of boys or men on the basis of brain structure or function, why do we think it is possible to explain the small "sex differences" that have been reported in some (but by no means all) studies of boys and girls or men and women on the basis of brain structure or function? Since we have not even begun to understand the degree to which biological factors interact with environmental factors— e.g., how the structure (and subsequent functioning) of developing neurons interacts with sensory input and learning from before birth and through adult life—in cognitive and behavioral processes, how can we claim that hormones in a particular dose at a particular time of fetal life induces mathematical superiority?

The amount we do not know about the ontogenetic development of human behaviors, skills, and characteristics in general is enormous. As much as we do know and are learning about neuronal processing of information and the organization of sensory systems in processing sensory input, we still do not know much about the ontogeny of hemispheric functional lateralization, mind, consciousness, or learning, and the relationship of these to either neuronal structure and function or to environmental input. In the face of this basic ignorance, it is premature, illogical, and presumptuous to believe we can now explain presumed *sex differences* in the development of such processes.

Alternative Hypotheses

The evidence that we have permits one important conceptualization of the development of cognition and behavior: biological and environmental factors are inextricable, and in ways that make meaningless and futile any efforts to separate out and measure how much of human behaviors can be attributed to biology—genes or hormones—and how much to environment and learning. Reductionist and linear approaches—attempting to find single and final ultimate causes and explanations for human behaviors and characteristics—deny the extraordinary complexity of the intricate web of processes that define what is uniquely human: our mind, its creativity, and its nearly limitless capacity to learn.

From the earliest stages of development, the fetus represents not simply an unfolding of genetic expression but a continuing changing process of interaction between biological and environmental elements that are themselves changed in the process. Genes and other biological elements (cells, tissues, hormones) are in continuous interaction with each other and with the developing fetus as a whole, are affected by their particular position within the fetus, and are, in the process of interaction, themselves transformed from one moment to the next to new states of being. The fetus, in continuing and changing interaction with myriad elements in its maternal environment (which, in turn, is in continuing and changing interaction with its external environment), exerts effects on the development, functioning, and expression of the unique collection of individual units of which it is composed—limbs, organs, tissues, cells, proteins, and genes: a true hermeneutic circle, no part of which can be fully understood in isolation from the rest. An understanding or awareness of the context is necessary to understand and interpret the functioning of the parts; the parts provide a material base for understanding the functioning of the whole fetus within its environment.

Such processes of interaction and transformation are no less true for the brain, the organ of mind and behavior. We know that neuronal migration, positioning, survival, growth, and synaptic functioning are not "simply" programmed genetically since these basic patterns can be disrupted by deviations from the normal range of fetal environmental influences, as they may be caused by viruses, drugs, or metabolic abnormalities. Furthermore we know, from experimental work with animals and studies of the human brain, that the brain and its neurons *require* sensory input for normal structural and functional development to occur. Without input of light and visual stimuli to one or both eyes of cats and monkeys, neurons processing visual information fail to develop normal dendrites and normal connections (Wiesel and Hubel, 1963a, 1963b, and 1974). Similarly, the auditory system depends upon environmental stimulation for normal development. Auditory neurons remain structurally and functionally immature in mice reared with partial or complete sound deprivation, and profound structural changes in auditory neurons were found in a child born with sensorineural deafness (Trune, 1982; Webster and Webster, 1977, 1979).

The human brain is born relatively more immature than that of any other primate or other mammal. It doubles in size by the end of the first year of life and quadruples by the end of the fourth year. That means that the major growth of the human brain occurs precisely during that period of development that it is exposed to a massive new input of sensory information from the external world. The major increase occurs in the size and complexity of the neurons and their dendritic and axonal ramifications and, therefore, in the extent and complexity of synaptic connections among neurons. For example, in the cortex of rodents and cats, there is a tenfold or greater increase in neuronal connections in the month following birth (Jacobson, 1978). In humans, the major expansion in the synaptic network takes place in the first two years of life, though growth continues to adulthood (Schadé and van Groeningen, 1961). Then, mind itself, as an emergent property of the brain (Sperry, 1980), acts as another force influencing neuronal and brain functioning.

It is because learning and environment are inextricable from the structure itself of neurons and because we have a mind, each the unique product of our unique and complex histories of development and experience, that I claim the futility and meaninglessness of efforts to reduce human behaviors to biological parameters. Our biology does not significantly constrain our potentialities. Rather it is the cultures that our brains have created that most severely limit our visions and the possibilities for the fullest possible development of each individual.

REFERENCES

Archer, J. 1976. Biological explanations of psychological sex differences. In B. Lloyd and J. Archer (eds.), *Exploring Sex Differences.* New York: Academic Press.

Beckwith, J. and Woodruff, M. 1984. Letter to the Editor. *Science 223:* 1247–48.

Benbow, C. and Stanley, J. 1980. Sex differences in mathematical ability: fact or artifact? *Science 210:* 1262–64.

Benbow, C. and Stanley, J. 1983. Sex differences in mathematical reasoning ability: more facts. *Science 222:* 1029–31.

Bleier, R. 1984. *Science and Gender: A Critique of Biology and Its Theories on Women.* New York: Pergamon.

Bleier, R., Houston, L., and Byne, W. 1986. Can the corpus callosum predict gender, age, handedness, or cognitive differences? *Trends in NeuroSciences 9:* 391–94.

Chi, J., Dooling, E., and Gilles, F. 1977. Gyral development of the human brain. *Ann. Neurol. 1:86–93.*

Chipman, S. 1981. Letter to the editor. *Science 212:114–16.*

Conner, R. and Levine, S. 1969. Hormonal influences on aggressive behavior. In S. Garattini and E. Sigg (eds.), *Aggressive Behavior.* Amsterdam: Excerpta Medica.

De Lacoste-Utamsing, C. and Holloway, R. L. 1982. Sexual dimorphism in the human corpus callosum. *Science 216:1431–32.*

Diamond, M., Dowling, G., and Johnson, R. 1981. Morphological cerebral cortical asymmetry in male and female rats. *Exp. Neurol.* 71:261–68.

Edwards, D. 1969. Early androgen stimulation and aggressive behavior in male and female mice. *Physiology and Behavior* 4:333–38.

Ehrhardt, A. and Baker, S. 1974. Fetal androgens, human central nervous system differentiation, and behavior sex differences. In R. Friedman, R. Richart, and R. Vande Wiele (eds.), *Sex Differences in Behavior.* New York: Wiley & Sons.

Ehrhardt, A. and Meyer-Bahlburg, H. 1979. Psychosexual development: an examination of the role of prenatal hormones. *Sex, Hormones and Behavior* 62:41–57.

Ehrhardt, A. and Money, J. 1967. Progestin-induced hermaphroditism: IQ and psychosexual identity in a study of ten girls. *Journal of Sex Research* 3:83–100.

Ehrhardt, A., Epstein, R., and Money, J. 1968. Fetal androgens and female gender identity in the early-treated adrenogenital syndrome. *Johns Hopkins Medical Journal* 111:160–67.

Fedigan, L. 1983. Dominance and reproductive success in primates. *Yearbook of Physical Anthropology* 26:91–129.

Fee, E. 1979. Nineteenth century craniology: the study of the female skull. *Bulletin of the History of Medicine* 53:415–33.

Fox, L. 1984. Letter to the Editor. *Science* 224:1292–94.

Geschwind, N. and Behan, P. 1982. Left-handedness: association with immune disease, migraine, and developmental learning disorder. *Proc. Natl. Acad. Sci.* 79:5097–100.

Gould, S. 1981. *The Mismeasure of Man.* New York: Norton.

Hardyck, C., Tzeng, O., and Wang, W. 1978. Cerebral lateralization of function and bilingual decision processes: is thinking lateralized? *Brain and Language* 5:56–71.

Jacobson, M. 1978. *Developmental Neurobiology.* New York: Plenum.

Kessler, S. and McKenna, W. 1978. *Gender. An Ethnomethodological Approach.* New York: Wiley.

Kimball, M. 1981. Women and science: a critique of biological theories. *International J. Women's Studies* 4:318–38.

Kolata, G. 1983. Math genius may have hormonal basis. *Science* 222:1312.

Lloyd, B. and Archer, J. (eds.). 1976. *Exploring Sex Differences.* New York: Academic Press.

Maccoby, E. and Jacklin, C. 1974. *The Psychology of Sex Differences.* San Francisco: Stanford University Press.

Marx, J. 1982. Autoimmunity in left-handers. *Science* 217:141–44.

McGlone, J. 1980. Sex differences in human brain asymmetry: a critical survey. *The Behavioral and Brain Sciences* 3:215–63.

Mendelsohn, E., Weingart, P., Whitley, R. 1977. *The Social Production of Scientific Knowledge.* Boston: Reidel.

Money, J. and Ehrhardt, A. 1972. *Man and Woman, Boy and Girl.* Baltimore: The Johns Hopkins University Press.

Osler, M. 1980. Apocryphal knowledge: the misuse of science. In M. Hanen, M. Osler, and R. Weyant (eds.), *Science, Pseudoscience and Society.* Waterloo, Canada: Wilfrid Laurier University Press.

Provine, W. 1973. Geneticists and the biology of race crossing. *Science* 182:790–96.

Schadé, J. and Groeningen, W. van. 1961. Structural organization of the cerebral cortex. *Acta Anatomica* 47:74–111.

Schafer, A. and Gray, M. 1981. Sex and mathematics. *Science* 211:229.

Sperry, R. 1980. Mind-brain interaction: mentalism, yes; dualism, no. *Neuroscience* 5:195–206.

Springer, S. and Deutsch, G. 1981. *Left Brain, Right Brain.* San Francisco: W. H. Freeman.

Strathern, M. 1976. An anthropological perspective. In B. Lloyd and J. Archer (eds.), *Exploring Sex Differences.* New York: Academic Press.

Trune, D. 1982. Influence of neonatal cochlear removal on the development of mouse cochlear nucleus. I. Number, size and density of its neurons. *Journal of Comparative Neurology 209*:409–24.

Webster, D. and Webster, M. 1977. Neonatal sound deprivation affects brain stem auditory nuclei. *Archives of Otolaryngology 103*:392–96.

Webster, D. and Webster, M. 1979. Effects of neonatal conductive hearing loss on brain stem auditory nuclei. *Annals of Otolaryngology 88*:684–88.

Weisel, T. and Hubel, D. 1963. Effects of visual deprivation on morphology and physiology of cells in the cat's lateral geniculate body. *Journal of Neurophysiology 26*:978–93.

Weisel, T. and Hubel, D. 1963. Single-cell responses in striate cortex of kittens deprived of vision in one eye. *Journal of Neurophysiology 26*:1003–17.

Weisel, T. and Hubel, D. 1974. Ordered arrangement of orientation columns in monkeys lacking visual experience. *Journal of Comparative Neurology 158*:307–18.

Westkott, M. 1984. Out of the shadows. *Women's Review of Books 1*:7–8.

Wittig, M. and Petersen, A. 1979. *Sex Related Differences in Cognitive Functioning.* New York: Academic Press.

THE TASK OF A FEMINIST ECONOMICS

A MORE EQUITABLE FUTURE

Barbara R. Bergmann

Men and women have typically played very different roles in the economy. This difference in economic roles has made an enormous difference in their lives—in how much power and prestige they can achieve, in the possibilities of developing and expressing any talents they possess, in whom they spend their time with, in their chances of having interesting and creative work, in the likelihood that they will suffer deprivation in the course of their lifetimes.

In the past, most economists, although obviously aware of such glaring differences, have not viewed them as matters of professional interest, much less as matters of any grave professional concern. We are now emerging from this period of almost complete indifference because of three interrelated developments. The first is the accelerating increase in women's participation in paid work. The second is the increase in the numbers of women raising children alone. The third is the revival of the ideology of feminism, which has created a demand for changes in public policy.

As might have been expected, those economists who have taken an interest in the economic implications of sex roles have formed themselves into two opposing factions. Feminist economists (of both sexes) have documented the severity of the problems women face in economic life, are attempting to develop the outlines of what they claim will be a more equitable future, and are trying to formulate policy proposals that might bring us closer to a workable yet equitable system. On the other hand, nonfeminist economists (of both sexes) have busied themselves in defend-

Portions of this chapter derive from articles by the author appearing in *Academe* and the *Journal of Economic Education*.

ing and justifying the old regime, in shouting "vive la difference," and in declaring the feminists' proposals for the amelioration of women's condition to be devoid of economic sense.

Two books by economists have recently been published that review at length the major economic issues involving women from a feminist viewpoint. One is my own book, *The Economic Emergence of Women* (1986). The other is *The Economics of Women, Men, and Work* by Francine Blau and Marianne Ferber (1986). The major statement from the nonfeminist camp is Gary Becker's *A Treatise on the Family* (1981). Becker explains, justifies, and even glorifies role differentiation by sex.

Currently, most economists are probably in the nonfeminist camp, which continues hostile to any suggestion that the economic position of women needs improvement. The profession continues to be overwhelmingly male. Women economists are still under pressure to conform to traditional male attitudes. Moreover, most economists have an ideological commitment to the free enterprise system and spend their professional lives trying to disprove assertions that it does not function well. These economists are predisposed to give short shrift to women's complaints that the market system treats them unfairly, and to oppose women's demands that the government should interfere in the marketplace on women's behalf. Marxist economists, on the other hand, are committed to advancing the revolution against capitalism, an event they project will do away with all inequities all at once. Having this splendid goal in mind, most Marxists have shown little interest in spending energy fighting inequities that women suffer in the here and now.

Economists' resistance to feminists' claims of unfairness also owes something to the assumptions economists have traditionally made about the nature of economic life. Mainline economists conduct their analyses under the assumption that economic activity is the free interaction of rational beings, whose only concern in buying and selling goods, services, and labor is to advance their material advantage. Economists make a professional practice of ignoring the fact that people, even those with above-average rational abilities, may have stereotyped attitudes about women, may have false beliefs about women's abilities, may be influenced by tradition or religion, or may be proud of having been born with the superior status of a male, a status they may desire to protect.

The rational beings posited by economic theorists are burdened by none of this sexist baggage, and are assumed not to undergo the cost and bother of paying attention to irrelevant considerations in deciding whom to hire or buy from or sell to or lend to. If such beings notice the sex of the persons with whom they are carrying on transactions and allow sex to influence their behavior, then mainline economists feel forced to conclude that paying attention to sex yields a material advantage and is therefore legitimate behavior. Feminists consider such assumptions ludicrously unrealistic.

The New Home Economics

Ironically, the first economists in recent times to take an interest in sex roles in economics was a group that was conservative and largely male. In the 1960s economists centered in the University of Chicago, who sardonically called their work "the new home economics," broke with the tradition of ignoring women's economic activities and started to take an interest in the unpaid production of services for the family by family members. Their analyses have dealt with the determinants of who marries whom, of the division of labor within families, of fertility, and of divorce.

To say that the "new home economists" are not feminist in their orientation would be as much of an understatement as to say that Bengal tigers are not vegetarians. In their discussions of sex roles, members of the school are fond of invoking the theory of "comparative advantage," developed originally to explain the import and export of commodities and the specialization of countries in certain lines of economic production to the exclusion of others. They apply this theory to the division of labor between the sexes to explain why women specialize in housework—and presumably will do so until the end of time.

Feminists have strongly criticized this application of the theory of comparative advantage on the grounds that the alleged advantage of men in market work is derived from discrimination against women in the market and traditional male refusal to take on a fair share of unpaid domestic work when the wife takes a job.

The "new home economics" (NHE) has somewhat retarded the development of feminist economics by seeming to preempt large areas of relevant subject matter and attacking the issues with what looked to be a sophisticated methodology. Some women economists, seeing that matters of concern to them as women were being addressed by the NHE group, have been drawn in to adopt the NHE assumptions and points of view. Feminist thinking about the family involves a refusal to accept some of the key assumptions of the NHE group. For example, feminists refuse to assume as the NHE group explicitly does, the unfailing benevolence of the "head of household" (a term feminist economists and other social scientists fought successfully to ban from the U.S. Census and may someday succeed in ousting from social science literature). Nor are feminists willing to concede that biological motherhood necessarily entails more responsibility for child rearing than does fatherhood.

Why Are Economic Sex Roles Changing?

There is considerable agreement that the major economic factor leading so many women to abandon the role of housewife and take paid jobs is the long-term upward trend in productivity. This has raised the demand for labor, and hence the real wages available to women. The parallel growth in men's wages should work in the opposite direction, but the rise in women's wages appears to have dominated. June O'Neill's review (1981) of cross-section and time-series estimates of the effects of wage changes on labor-force participation shows that wage changes explain much of the increase in women's participation rates over time, although not all.

The improvement in household equipment has made housework easier, reducing the value of women's time at home (see Margolis, 1984). Some writers, notably sociologist Valerie Oppenheimer (1979), stress the growth in the number of jobs considered to be suitable for women. Clair Brown (1982) has emphasized the importance of the desire to consume newly available products.

All of these factors stem from technological change. It is these advances that have progressively raised the productivity of labor, and so the real wage of women. They have given birth to the new products that reduced the strain of housekeeping. The lure of these new products has kept the marginal utility of money high, even as income rose. Thus the economic forces unleashed by the industrial revolution are of prime importance in motivating the changes in sex roles. Other explanations—higher divorce rates, improvements in women's education, changes in attitudes—are probably of secondary importance, or are effects as much as causes.

Many popular accounts of the rise in women's labor-force participation cite families' "need" for more income. This explanation seems inconsistent with the long-term rise in husbands' real incomes, which have raised the standard of living of one-earner families. One reason for the popularity of the "needs" explanation is the fall in real wages of the last decade. Another is the deprivation felt by one-earner families when they compare their standard of living to that enjoyed by two-earner families in the same social group. Finally, the "needs" explanation may express the desire of women who take jobs to cite family benefits rather than their own ambitions or desires.

The economic forces promoting women's emergence into the money economy appear at this juncture to be irreversible. It certainly appears unlikely that the old-fashioned family structure, with women playing the part of lifelong housewives, can be revived as the dominant form.

Economic Causes and Consequences of the Decrease in Birth Rates

The fourfold fall in the birthrate since the beginning of the nineteenth century is clearly implicated in the transformation of women's economic role. However, disentangling cause and effect is not easy.

The advances in contraceptive technology and the wide availability of relatively pain-free and legal abortion with low medical risk are recent phenomena and cannot explain a trend that has lasted two hundred years or more. Economic explanations are more plausible. Folbre (1983) is one of those who argue that the reduction in the proportion of the population in agriculture, and the changeover from small family businesses to large capitalist enterprises has reduced the economic benefit of having children. The institution of government-run social security systems have also reduced the need for people to depend on their children to support them in old age. Recent increases in the proportion of young people going to college have increased the financial costs of having children.

Women in the labor force want fewer children than women at home, because the economic opportunity cost of another child in terms of lost wages and opportunities is more obvious. Conversely, the fewer children a woman has, the more likely she is to be at a job. However, this latter effect is not large. Bureau of Labor Statistics data for 1984 show that 71 percent of married women with one child were in the labor force. This percentage drops only to 65 if she has two, and to 59 percent if she has three. Women's labor force participation rates are still increasing, and most of the increase comes from the entry to the job market of women with young children.

Controversies about the Labor Market

The economic activity which is most crucial to a person's place in life in the modern world is the selling of that person's labor. That women are less successful in the labor market than are men is something agreed to by economists of all factions. After all, women in the United States who are college graduates average the same pay at a full-time job as men who dropped out before completing high school. What the economists do not agree on, however, is the interpretation of these facts.

Traditional economists are skeptical of women's complaints of employment discrimination. After all, the "economic man" who is an employer is assumed to want to maximize his profits. If there are any female workers who are as productive as male workers in a certain occupation, and if, as is the case, the employer can get women cheaper than men, then there must be some employers who will hire them for that occupation. So if we see any occupation from which women are absent, a mainline economist tends to assume that either women themselves have shunned the occupation as not compatible with "their" home responsibilities, or that employers have shunned women workers because of evidence of women's low productivity in that occupation.

Those mainline economists who do concede that discrimination might possibly exist in the economy tend to describe it as a personal "taste" of the employer and rush to deduce from allegedly universal principles that it can be no more than a temporary aberration.

Feminist economists, on the other hand, see employment discrimination not as a personal foible of the individuals who make hiring decisions, but as deriving from a system of social organization in which woman's role is as a servant of men. The existence of this tradition influences the behavior of individuals, men and women, even as they carry on their economic business. Although the traditional social system which underlies employment discrimination is both ancient in origin and geographically universal, feminist economists believe that a world without it is both feasible and desirable.

Feminist economists, many of whom see sex discrimination in employment as the most important item in the catalog of women's oppression, have worked to demonstrate the forms sex discrimination takes, to measure its effects on men and women, to pinpoint the practices in which it is embodied. Many such investigations have indeed shown systematic differences in the way employers treat male and female employees, after differences in education and experience are accounted for. Feminist economists (again, it must be emphasized, of both sexes) differ from their nonfeminist and antifeminist colleagues in their unwillingness to explain away such systematic differences as simply evidence of the women employees' inferiority on one count or another.

What Causes Occupational Segregation by Sex?

In all societies, women have been assigned primary or exclusive responsibility for child care and housework, and this has changed little in recent years. The traditional view is that occupational segregation in paid work derives from women's gladly accepted assignment to primary responsibility for housework and child care. Some would argue that different economic assignments for men and women, both at home and in paid work, are dictated in biology, and that women's comparative advantage in home tasks is a matter of natural differences between the sexes in talent, aptitude, and tastes. (Tiger and Shepher [1975] argue, for example, that attempts to reduce economic specialization by sex are for this reason doomed to failure.) Others, such as the sociologist Talcott Parsons (1970), have argued that setting up economic assignments according to sex is simply an efficient way to structure a society and an economy. It is sometimes claimed that both sexes stand to gain from sex-linked economic assignments.

Traditional economists have argued that women have made a rational choice to take less education and training—"accumulate less human capital"—than men and have kept away from occupations that have intensive human-capital requirements. Women have also been motivated to choose occupations in which exit and subsequent reentry are relatively easy and in which overtime, travel, locational transfer, and demanding duties are not required (see Mincer and Polachek, 1974 and Polachek, 1981).

Feminists argue that much if not all of the occupational segregation in paid work results from continuing and current discrimination on the demand side of the labor market. Although many women tamely subside into the occupations traditionally marked out for them, a substantial number are available for any jobs in male-dominated fields that open up to them. But many jobs and promotions remain off limits to women. The research into staffing patterns in individual workplaces of Bielby and Barron (1984) suggest that segregation by sex on the job is so extreme that it could not be accounted for solely by women's volition. Some women who do get nontraditional jobs are harassed sexually and in other ways by men who are unwilling to see women invade the job territory they claim as exclusively men's (see MacKinnon, 1979). The result is that women's labor market success is compromised, in terms of position, status, and wage.

Some economists have argued that employers increase their profits when they segregate workers by race and sex. Gordon, Edwards, and Reich (1982) see discrimination as one of the strategies capitalists use to keep the working class divided. Phelps (1972) suggests that excluding individuals because people of their race or sex have lower ability on average—so-called "statistical discrimination"—may in some circumstances improve the quality of workers an employer hires. Bergmann and Darrity (1980) cite employers' efforts to avoid having women or blacks in positions where they act as the superiors or even the equals of white men. Such interactions contravene societal notions of who is superior and who inferior and may result in productivity-lowering conflicts in the workplace.

Why Are Women's Wages So Low?

Becker (1957) was one of the first to speculate about how discrimination lowers the wages of a group. He conjectured that employers who had a "taste" for shunning members of the group would extract a bribe from them, in the form of low wages, before consenting to associate with them as their employer. Whether or not Becker's bribe idea is a good explanation of blacks' lower wages, it plainly lacks plausibility when applied to women.

I have presented an alternative explanation of how discrimination lowers wages: Occupational segregation—the exclusion of women from certain sets of jobs—affects supply and demand. Discrimination, in the form of limitations put on the jobs women are allowed to compete for, maintains women and men in separate labor market segments. In each segment supply and demand set wages. The women's segments are relatively more crowded because of the power of men to keep the best and most extensive part of the labor market turf free of female competition (See Bergmann, 1974 and 1986.)

Some economic theorists reject outright the idea that women's low wage levels result from discriminiation. They cite Becker's (1957) suggestion that firms that discriminated and excluded the relatively cheap labor of women and blacks would put themselves at a fatal competitive disadvantage. Since such discriminating firms would tend to fail and thus to disappear, the occupational segregation and low wages we observe for women must have other explanations. This theory, although widely accepted by economists (see Madden's summary, 1985) is contradicted by the fact that many successful firms have been convicted of long-standing discrimination in the courts (see Bergmann, 1986 for details). Perhaps the secret of discriminators' continuing success is that their rivals discriminate too. Or, as suggested above, discrimination may increase profits.

Those economists, notably Mincer and Polochek (1974), who have rejected discrimination as a cause of women's lower wages, have rested their case in the past on differences between the sexes in human capital and in motivation. However, in empirical studies, including those of Mincer and Polochek, differences between the sexes in schooling, training, experience, absenteeism, breaks in career, attitudes, and other variables explain only a part of the sex gap in wages. A review of these empirical studies, as provided in Treiman and Hartmann's *Women, Work, and Wages* (1981), shows that most studies fail to demonstrate that even half of the gap can be attributed to nondiscriminatory causes.

Empirical studies of discrimination using regression methods on variable sets that contain no direct measures of discrimination are never conclusive. It is always possible to speculate that certain variables—which would properly measure women's allegedly lower productivity and less vigorous pursuit of success—are missing or improperly measured in any particular study, but would explain the sex differences in wages if they were there. (For example, see Fleisher and Kneiser, 1985.) On the other hand, variables that would measure men's inferiority to women in certain respects (such as men's greater propensity to alcoholism, criminality, and driving accidents, all of which tend to lower success in the labor market) are typically not included either.

Another explanation offered for women's low wages is Polochek's conjecture (1981) that women gain an economic advantage by voluntarily choosing certain occupations in which intermittent labor-force participation inflicts relatively little loss in pay. However, England's work (1982) suggests that the conjectured advantage is nonexistent, because the wages in the occupations in question are so low.

Gary Becker (1985) appears to have abandoned the human capital explanation of the sex-gap in wages, remarking that the increase in women's human capital over the last few decades has closed the gap considerably less than might have been expected. He speculates instead (without empirical support) that women earn less because they are tired from housework, while men come to their jobs refreshed from their time off the job. He does not specify whether he means that women seek less demanding jobs, or are less productive in the jobs they hold than are men. Nor does he take account of male activities that bring men to the job in less than top-notch condition. Nor does he remark on ethical problems inherent in these customs.

The Controversy about Pay Equity Wage Adjustments

The suggestion, originating with feminist lawyers and trade unionists, that pay in the traditional women's occupations should be raised (by collective bargaining, court order, or legislative fiat) has posed a difficult issue for feminist economists. These suggestions for "pay equity" or "comparable worth" come from those impatient at the slow progress in gaining for women wages which are comparable with those of men of similar educational attainments.

Economists have been trained to believe that the "worth" of a worker is measured in the marketplace by that worker's actual wage, and they distrust appeals to any other standard. Even many feminist economists tend to shy away from advocating the administered reform of wages. They are inclined rather to attack the wage gap between men and women by working more vigorously and more effectively toward the elimination of occupational segregation by sex.

Those in favor of pay equity argue that the verdict of the market has been distorted by employer discrimination and that the pay scales that a discriminatory market dictates are by no means optimal. The job evaluation procedures used in deciding pay equity adjustments amount to evaluations of the human capital required in each job. Revamping wage rate patterns so that jobs requiring equal endowments of human capital are paid equally improves the wage structure rather than degrades it (see Bergmann, 1986, Chapter 8). Pay equity may get us closer to the wage structure we would have if there were no discrimination against women, claim its proponents.

The major line of argument against pay equity is economists' traditional warning against interfering in the free market. Wages fixed by other than market forces are "arbitrary." Bad effects forecast by the foes of pay equity include labor surpluses in the female occupations, greater unemployment for women, and inefficiencies in the use of labor (see O'Neill, 1984, and Gold, 1983). Unemployment among women might well increase in the longer run if pay equity realignments were widely implemented. However, Australia's massive pay realignment, reviewed in Gregory and Duncan (1981), resulted in little or no displacement.

Housewives' Place in the Economy

The occupation of housewife is still the largest single way of making a living, despite its continual decline in relative importance over the last century. The housewife occupation has of all occupations the greatest economic and physical risks associated with it. Some of the most frequently mentioned issues concerning housewives—including housewives in the GNP or paying them a cash wage—are probably of the least practical importance.

There is, of course, no reason why housewives could not be included in the GNP. Other productive activities which are carried on without money payment, such as the producing of food eaten on farms, are included. The most sensible way of valuing housewives' services would probably be to attribute to them the wages of household servants. However, this would be politically embarassing, especially since the whole point of the enterprise would be to lend dignity to the housewives' work efforts.

The pay-for-housewives idea takes a number of forms. The pay might come from husbands, either directly or through taxes or employer deductions on a husband's pay rebated to the wife. The major effect would be psychological, possibly giving at least some housewives greater dignity and perhaps a greater say in the family budgeting process.

Alternatively, the pay of the housewife might come out of general tax revenues, possibly in the form of paying for child care in the home. This would cause a redistribution away from single people and two-earner couples toward families maintaining housewives. Presumably, such payments would encourage women to be housewives, something it is difficult to understand feminists advocating.

More serious issues concerning the housewife relate to the violence that "workers" on this "job" not infrequently encounter from their husbands, the alimony and child support that would do justice to long-term housewives whose marriage breaks up (dealt with in the next sections), and the treatment of housewives by the social security system.

The U.S. system for public old-age pensions was designed in an era in which most families had a husband at work and a wife at home. Women were expected to be supported in old age through the benefits earned by their husbands. The increasing prevalence of divorce made that system of old-age support for women increasingly problematic. While the treatment of divorced wives by the social security system has been liberalized, there has arisen a demand that housewives should be enabled to accumulate credits toward a pension in their own account in their own name.

Economic Issues in Divorce

Through the first half of this century, few mature women took paid jobs, and it was thought demeaning for a married woman to have to do so. When a man married, he assumed an obligation of lifelong support to his bride. Divorce was granted only when one of the parties was proven to have committed some fault, such as desertion or infidelity. Where the husband wished a divorce, and where the wife was innocent of any fault, he had to persuade the wife to sue him. To get her to do this, he might offer to enter into an obligation to pay her either alimony or a lump sum. If she agreed, some real or concocted fault attributed to him would be presented as the grounds for the divorce. The legal theory of alimony was that, even though the marriage had dissolved, the husband owed a continuation of support over the innocent wife's lifetime.

Two things have changed: the grounds for divorce, and the movement of married women to paid work. Most states have adopted divorce laws that do not require a showing of fault. A divorce is granted (perhaps with some modest lapse of time) if there is merely a declaration by one of the parties of unwillingness to continue in the marriage. This has done away with any need on the part of the husband to buy his way out of a marriage with an alimony agreement (see Weitzmann, 1985). Moreover, now that a majority of prime-age married women are in the labor force, fewer people believe that the divorced husband has an obligation to make substantial contributions over a long period of time to the ex-wife's living expenses.

There are, however, justifications for alimony under current conditions.

During the marriage, the wife may have sacrificed, perhaps irreversibly, her pursuit of labor market success to give the husband full support in developing his own career. She may have supported the family during the husband's schooling. If they have had any children, she has most likely taken most of the burden in caring for them. Her willingness to play such a role was promoted by what she thought was a promise of lifetime support. Where the wife has played such a role, Sawhill (1985) argues, there is a rationale for the award of substantial post-divorce alimony payments from the husband to the wife, essentially reimbursing her for the loss of earning potential that resulted from her marital activities.

The Support of Single Mothers and Their Children

Because of divorce, separation, and out-of-wedlock births, millions of women with children live without the economic support of a man. While some of these women have managed to latch on to a job that pays enough to support themselves and their children above the poverty line, almost half of all single mothers, including some working mothers, are poor. This may be true because of race or sex discrimination in the labor market, because they lack anyone to care for their children while they work, or because of lack of experience, education, confidence, or energy. Some single mothers may feel that they ought to stay home with their children.

Since the 1930s welfare grants have been available to support single women and their children. The welfare system has been criticized as providing benefits so low that they keep single mothers and their children in poverty, as encouraging out-of-wedlock births, and as discouraging work effort. However, efforts to reform it that have been going on since the 1960s have not produced a satisfactory system, for reasons reviewed by Aaron (1973).

Besides wages and welfare, financial support for single parents can come from child support payments from the absent parents. As of 1983, only 45 percent of mothers living with children whose father was absent from the home had a court-ordered award of child support. Of those with awards, only about half received all the payments to which the award entitled them. Many awards were for very small amounts; they averaged $1,800 per year.

In recent years, there has been increased emphasis by public authorities on the collection of child support. There is increased vigor in pursuing for child support payments men who have fathered children out of wedlock. Technological advances in the biological sciences have made the process of deciding parenthood claims far surer. There is a greater willingness to use computerized records to track the locations of absent fathers, whether divorced or not, and to use court-enforced payroll deductions to extract child support payments from them.

A well-ordered system of securing child support payments from absent biological parents in amounts that would defray an appreciable share of the cost of bringing up a child hold considerable promise of reducing poverty among single mothers. Child support awards are not lost when the mother takes a job, the way welfare grants are. So the work-inhibiting aspect of welfare would be avoided if child support could take the place of welfare. When the mother works, a child support award added onto her wage might put most single mothers above the poverty line. Garfinckel and McLanahan (1987) discuss these newer ideas on how to support single mothers and their children.

Who Will Do the Housework?

Family well-being depends on the performance of the chores that create a safe, healthy, and comfortable life—putting meals on the table, caring for the children, keeping clothing and living quarters clean. The organization of family care services is undergoing considerable change, as the number of housewives dwindles. When the wife takes a paid job, the family has the problem of what to do about the services that the housewife has been providing. The wife may simply continue to do them, pretty much as before. Or the husband may increase the share of the housework he does. The couple can reduce the amount they have to do themselves by lowering their standard of housekeeping, or by purchasing a larger proportion of the family care services they use.

Husbands are in a good material position to resist employed wives' demands for a more equal division of hours of housework because of the difference in their salaries. It is a rare wife who makes enough at a job to support herself and her children in any degree of comfort. If she carries the fights about housework too far, and the couple separates or divorces, her standard of living is going to be severely cut. Her social status will also be reduced without a husband. By contrast, the income the husband has to devote to himself will increase, and the demographics are such that he will have little trouble finding a new wife.

On the choices that the family makes in reorganizing family care a great deal will depend. If the wife continues to do the same chores as before, plus her paid work, the overload may sour life for her and the whole family. Resort to the purchase of services on a large scale may change the whole tenor of family life.

Families are wrestling with these decisions as they try to find the life style suitable to their taste and situation. As they do, they are forced to confront and reconcile the sometimes conflicting interests of husband and wife. While Becker (1981) sidesteps these conflicts by postulating an altruistic head of household who makes all decisions in everyone's best interest, Hartmann (1981) and Folbre (1984) have addressed the causes and nature of these conflicts directly. How these problems are dealt with will establish the degree of fairness between the spouses, whether wives can live as full and free a life as husbands, the daily lives of children, the amount of friction between spouses, the prevalence of divorce. Even the shape of the economy will be affected. If most family-produced services are replaced by purchased services, a large number of service jobs will be created, many of them in small enterprises.

Juster (1985) presents the latest results of surveys on the time that husbands and wives devote to paid work and household work. The evidence suggests that as wives have increased their participation in paid employment they have reduced the time they spend in housework. Yet there seems to have been little increase in the contribution of services by husbands. To take up part of the slack, many families have increased their purchase of services. They are buying child care, and they now eat less home-cooked food.

In the United States and the capitalist West, a free competitive economy makes possible the movement of resources into producing housework substitutes in step with families' increasing willingness to buy housework substitutes. It is possible that much of the housework problem will dissolve by a process of "industrialization."

Should the Government Provide or Subsidize Child Care?

A considerable majority of families with mothers employed full time now purchase child care, although some manage to avoid this by utilizing care given by the husband, grandmother or other relative, or by leaving the children by themselves.

In Europe, as Kammerman and Kahn's review (1981) shows, government provision of free or subsidized child care is common. In the United States, governmental programs supporting pre-school child care are highly controversial. In the past, there has been considerable agitation for a more active governmental role in providing or subsidizing pre-school child care, and it may well revive once the current wave of conservatism passes (see Hewlett, 1986).

In the United States, the demand for government-run and government paid-for child care runs up against two sources of opposition. One obvious source is the people who are devoted to the perpetuation of the system of sex roles that devotes women to homemaking, a system which accords the husband primacy in the family on the basis of his role as sole earner. The second source of opposition in the United States is from those who think that as a rule it is best if people buy what they need or want from profit-making private enterprises out of their own incomes.

The provision of child care centers on a free or subsidized basis to all families would help both mothers and children. The children would be saved from the inadequate care to which some of them are consigned in the absence of government aid. Government-sponsored child care centers would help mothers by redressing the traditional difference between the sexes in child care responsibilities.

The Task of a Feminist Economics

The task that feminist economists have set for themselves is to produce the design for a more equitable future. What really distinguishes feminist economists is their view that the present assignment to economic duties based on sex is unfair and should be eliminated. They tend to believe that such a system of assignments can be eliminated with little or no loss in economic efficiency or quality of life, and possibly some considerable gain. However, even if it were to be found that some temporary or permanent loss in total output were to be suffered as a result of the disappearance of sex roles, feminist economists would advocate absorbing that loss in the name of equity.

I remember a discussion on women's place in the economy which occurred during a conference on equity a number of years ago at the Institute for Advanced Study at Princeton. Sex role issues are very infrequently broached on such occasions; such discussions usually center on studies from which data on females have been excluded. However, on this occasion, the talk happened to turn to the place of women in the Russian economy. The elderly male expert on the Soviet economy who was present explained rather plaintively that the penetration of women into the ranks of the professions and the skilled crafts had occurred in Russia only because of the wholesale slaughter of the male population—in the Revolution, in two world wars, and in the Stalinist purges. In short, he characterized female progress in Russia as the dismal and undesired side effect of a series of historic atrocities. I was unable on that occasion to resist remarking that I hoped it would not require such an extreme sequence of events to bring about sex equality in America. I continue to hope so.

In fact, the major preoccupation of feminist economists is precisely to try to sketch visions of a system of work and family relations which will be fair to men, women, and children, and to try to devise methods, short of mayhem, to get us from here to there.

REFERENCES

Aaron, Henry. 1973. *Why is welfare so hard to reform?* Washington, D.C.: The Brookings Institution.

Becker, Gary S. 1957. *The economics of discrimination.* Chicago, Illinois: University of Chicago Press.

———. 1981. *A treatise on the family.* Cambridge, Massachusetts: Harvard University Press.

———. 1985. Human capital, effort, and the sexual division of labor. *Journal of Labor Economics,* vol. 3, no. 1, part 2 (January): S33-S58.

Bergmann, Barbara R. 1974. Occupational segregation, wages, and profits when employers discriminate by race or sex. *Eastern Economic Journal,* vol. 1 (April/July): 561-73.

———. 1986. *The economic emergence of women.* New York: Basic Books.

Bergmann, Barbara R., and William Darity, Jr. 1980. Social relations in the workplace and employer discrimination. *IRRA 33rd Annual Proceedings.*

Bielby, William T., and James N. Barron. 1984. A woman's place is with other women: segregation within organizations. In Barbara F. Reskin, ed., *Sex segregation in the workplace.* Washington, D.C.: National Academy Press.

Blau, Francine, and Marianne Ferber. 1986. *The economics of women, men, and work.* Englewood Cliffs: Prentice-Hall.

Brown, Clair (Vickery). 1982. Home production for use in a market economy. In Barrie Thorne and Marilyn Yalom, eds., *Rethinking the family: some feminist questions,* 151-67. New York: Longman.

England, Paula. 1982. The failure of human capital theory to explain occupational sex segregation. *Journal of Human Resources,* vol. 17 (Spring): 357-70.

Fleischer, Belton M., and Thomas J. Kneiser. 1985. *Labor economics: theory, evidence, and policy.* 3d ed. Englewood Cliffs, New Jersey: Prentice-Hall, Inc.

Folbre, Nancy. 1983. Of patriarchy born: the political economy of fertility decisions. *Feminist Studies,* vol. 9, no. 2 (Summer): 261-80.

———. 1984. The pauperization of motherhood: patriarchy and public policy in the United States. *Review of Radical Political Economy,* vol. 16 (winter): 72-88.

Garfinkel, Irwin and Sara McLanahan. 1987. *A new American dilemma: the plight of single mothers and their children.* Washington, D.C.: Urban Institute.

Gold, Michael Evans. 1983. *A debate on comparable worth.* Ithaca, NY: Industrial and Labor Relations Press.

Gordon, David M., Richard Edwards, and Michael Reich. 1982. *Segmented work, divided workers: the historical transformation of labor in the United States.* Cambridge: Cambridge University Press.

Gregory, Robert G., and Ronald C. Duncan. 1981. The relevance of segmented labor market theories: the Australian experience of the achievement of equal pay for women," *Journal of Post Keynesian Economics,* vol. 3 (spring): 404-28.

Hartmann, Heidi I. 1981. The family as the locus of gender, class and political struggle: the example of housework. *Signs: Journal of women in culture and society,* vol. 6, no. 3 (spring): 366-94.

Hewlett, Sylvia Ann. 1986. *A lesser life: the myth of women's liberation in America*. New York: William Morrow and Company, Inc.

Juster, F. Thomas. 1985. A note on recent changes in time use. In F. Juster and Frank P. Stafford, eds., *Time, goods, and well-being*, 313–22. Ann Arbor, Michigan: Institute for Social Research, University of Michigan.

Kamerman, Sheila B. and Alfred J. Kahn, eds. 1981. *Child care, family benefits and working parents: a study in comparative policy*. New York: Columbia University Press.

MacKinnon, Catherine. 1979. *Sexual harassment of working women: a case of sex discrimination*. New Haven, Connecticut: Yale University Press.

Madden, Janice Fanning. 1985. The persistence of pay differentials: the economics of sex discrimination. In Laurie Larwood, Ann H. Stromberg, and Barbara A. Gutek, eds., *Women and Work: An Annual Review, Volume I*, 6–114. Beverly Hills: Sage Publications, Inc.

Margolis, Maxine L. 1984. *Mothers and such: views of American women and why they changed*. Berkeley, California: University of California Press.

Mincer, Jacob and Solomon W. Polachek. 1974. Family investments in human capital: earnings of women. *Journal of Political Economy*, vol. 82, no. 2(March/April):S79–S108.

O'Neill, June. 1981. A time-series analysis of women's labor force participation. *American Economic Review*, vol. 71, no. 2 (May):76–80.

———. 1984. The comparable worth trap. *Wall Street Journal*, 20 January, p. 28.

Oppenheimer, Valerie K. 1979. *The female labor force in the United States: demographic and economic factors governing its growth and changing composition*. Westport, Connecticut: Greenwood Press.

Parsons, Talcott. 1970. *Social structure and personality*. New York: Free Press.

Phelps, Edmund S. 1972. The statistical theory of racism and sexism. *American Economic Review*, vol. 62 (September):659–61.

Polachek, Solomon W. 1981. Occupational self-selection: a human capital approach to sex differences in occupational structure," *Review of Economics and Statistics*, vol. 58, no. 1 (February):60–69.

Sawhill, Isabel V. 1983. Developing normative standards for child-support payments. In Judith Cassetty, ed., *The parental child support obligation*, 79–114. Lexington, Massachusetts: Lexington Books.

Tiger, Lionel and Joseph Shepher. 1975. *Women in the kibbutz*. New York: Harcourt, Brace, Jovanovich.

Treiman, Donald J., and Heidi I. Hartmann, eds. 1981. *Women, work, and wages: equal pay for jobs of equal value*. Washington, D.C.: National Academy Press.

Weitzman, Lenore J. 1985. *The divorce revolution*. New York: The Free Press.

WHAT RESEARCH ON THE POLITICAL SOCIALIZATION OF WOMEN CAN TELL US ABOUT THE POLITICAL SOCIALIZATION OF PEOPLE

Virginia Sapiro

In her discussion of feminist social science Margrit Eichler writes: "At its best, feminist writing fulfills three functions: it is critical of existent social structures and ways to perceive them, it serves as a corrective mechanism by providing an alternative viewpoint and data to substantiate it, and it starts to lay the groundwork for a transformation of social science and society." Although she correctly argues that, strictly speaking, these three "processes of criticism, correction and transformation form a logical sequence but not a chronological one" (Eichler, 1980, 9), the history of feminist writing in most social science fields and, probably, the history (biography) of many individual feminist social scientists, is marked by a progression of emphasis from criticism to correction and finally, at its best, to transformation. This progression only makes sense; in most cases one must notice errors before setting out to correct them and, ultimately, to transform the field.

Feminist work on political socialization has followed precisely this path, although within the field of political science the process of transformation remains relatively underdeveloped, especially in comparison with research fostered in related disciplines such as psychology and anthropology.[1] It is particularly important to understand the growth and impact of feminist research on political socialization because its focus and concerns should logically fall so close to the core of both women's studies and the study of political socialization. Women's studies and feminist research revolve around such specifically political concepts as power and authority, autonomy, liberty, and equality. It emphasizes socialization as the explanation for how individuals come to fit or not to fit—into specific sex-gender systems.[2]

As for the field of political socialization, the questions posed by the continued stratification and segregation of females and males would seem to be crucial to those who focus on the learning of political values, attitudes, roles, and behavior.

This paper explores the development and impact of feminist research on political socialization, focusing almost exlusively on the development of political orientations and behavior at the mass level. It begins with a look at the feminist criticism, correction, and transformation during the last decade and more of feminist political science. It then turns to the question of future transformations by identifying some themes and approaches in feminist social research that might help advance not just the study of women's political socialization, but political socialization more generally. One of the points I wish to stress is that as the field of feminist studies has developed, it has become clear that it can not only transform our understanding of women or gender; it can also transform the way questions are asked and answered more generally in our home disciplines.

Criticism and Correction

Feminist critics of the first generation of influential political socialization literature cannot say that questions of gender and, particularly, the political development of women were ignored, although precious little research effort was devoted to this area. This literature can be—and has been—justly criticized for numerous inadequacies stemming from sexism in its specific form of androcentrism. By the early 1970s feminists in political science joined the efforts of those across the social sciences and published critical reviews of the extant literature (Bourke and Grossholtz, 1974; Goot and Reid, 1975; Jacquette, 1974; Morgan, 1974). Because the field of political socialization was, at the time, quite young and relatively small and because the number of research reports that mentioned questions of gender was even smaller, these critiques tended to focus on a very few central works, but works that nevertheless continue to be part of the field's "required reading."[3]

The complaints of the critics may have sounded severe to those outside the community of feminist scholarship and fresh and revealing to those inside at the time they were issued, but with the hindsight of another decade's worth of women's studies research they now appear fairly limited: They constituted calls for relatively small-scale but crucial correctives to the field's approach to women. These early criticisms revolved around three related points. First, there was not enough research on the political socialization of females.[4] Second, what writing there was was often male-biased or, as more critics would say today, androcentric. Some of this bias is best illustrated by the third emphasis of the criticisms: methodological problems in research and interpretation.

Some of the most influential reports of "sex differences"—the primary mode of gender research—offer very shaky evidence to arrive at conclusions that reflect and reinforce conventional wisdom on male and female roles and behavior. Without replowing the length of old furrows, two examples offer particularly good illustrations. Robert Lane's book *Political Life* (1959) has become infamous for speculating about the nature of the female political personality in the absence of any discernible evidence; when he did do empirical work on the development and structure of political thought he used a male-only sample (Lane, 1962). Second, differences between males and females were often exaggerated in a number of ways. Where gender differences were observed in political activities or interests, those of females were sometimes depoliticized by labeling them or attributing them to social or personal concerns rather than political ones (e.g., Lane, 1959; Greenstein, 1961). Especially in the absence of testing for statistical significance, very small and sometimes inconsistent gender differences were sometimes interpreted as offering clear evidence supportive of conventional wisdom (e.g., Easton and Dennis, 1969, and, for a much later example, Stevens, 1982). Despite the warnings of feminist critics, these sometimes dubious conclusions remain alive and well in the footnotes of later writing.

Most of the research on gender questions in political socialization falls into one of two categories: the identification and explanation of gender differences in political attitudes and behavior, and the effects of gender related variation in family structure and relationships on political socialization. A brief discussion of both themes follows. One point that will be stressed is that although much of the literature suffers from androcentrism, some of the early works raised some questions and pointers that were never followed up adequately from within the mainstream of the field but, rather, have been pursued fruitfully by women's studies scholars in other fields. Had more students of political socialization understood women and therefore the politics of gender and sex-gender systems as central to the political world, they might have been led earlier to this rich and growing literature. As I shall argue later, this lack has left its mark not just on understanding of the political socialization of women, but on the field as a whole.

Early Socialization Research: Gender Differences

Gender differences research made its first appearance in writing on political socialization in the book that is generally identified as the first in the field: Herbert Hyman's *Political Socialization* (1959). Hyman begins his work by pointing to the importance of "regularities in the political behavior of adult individuals and stable *differences between groups of adults* (Hyman, 1959, 17)."[5] Rather than taking these patterns and especially, group differences as a result of "transient stimulation in [the adult's] contemporary environment," Hyman turns to childhood and writes that "one is naturally directed to the area of learning; more specifically to the socialization of the individual, his learning of *social patterns corresponding to his societal positions* as mediated through various agencies of society (Hyman, 1959, 18).[6] He therefore suggests that an important strategy for the study of political socialization is investigation of the development of social group differences including, for example, race, class—and sex. Hyman therefore begins his inventory of empirical research with an exploration of "subgroup" differentiation, focusing first on gender differences.

Although empirical research on political socialization continued to note "subgroup" variations, especially differentiation by race and class, but also by gender, the full theoretical and sociopolitical import of analyzing individual development into group patterns often appears vague or lost in discussion of the research, and especially in the case of gender analysis. A comparison of racial versus gender analysis illustrates the point. The field of political socialization developed during the era of the black civil rights movement, the passage and implementation of the Voting Rights Act, black militancy, race riots, and clear political symptoms of alienation and frustration among blacks. The analysis of race was not generally very theoretically sophisticated in terms of understanding the specificity and conditions of racial oppression, dominance, and inequality, but the historical context did impress itself upon researchers enough so that these concepts informed the scholarly analysis at least to some degree.

Analysis of gender roles and differentiation in political socialization rarely showed even this degree of understanding of the socioeconomic condition of women or of the reality of contemporary sex-gender systems. Whereas researchers might display some understanding of racial oppression and inequality, of the effects of dependence, systematic subordination, and discrimination, at least for black males, the same was not true for analysis of women.[7] It is common in mainstream political science writing to begin discussion of women by noting how long it is since women gained "full rights as citizens," referring to the Nineteenth Amendment to the Constitution, and then to appear to take the notion of "full citizen" at its word. Other than feminists, few if any political scientists showed awareness of systematic discrimination and dependence, the relative poverty of women compared with men, their comparatively high dependence upon the public sector for support, or any of the other facts of unequal life that are central to the basic framework employed by feminist scholars. By and large, researchers in the field seemed to accept the view that is dominant in the society around them: Women are relatively underdeveloped as political animals, but this is not indicative of any important structural problem in society or in the political system.

The lack of attention to the realities of the social structure sometimes manifested itself in curious ways. For one example, one common and often reported finding was that girls were less likely than boys to identify public or political figures as an ego-ideal, and more likely to pick people in their immediate environment (Hyman, 1959; Greenstein, 1965). None of these reports noted that other than Eleanor Roosevelt, there were precious few female figures that would have been presented to girls as realistic ego ideals with the force that boys are offered hosts of presidents, generals, or Founding Fathers. Log cabin myths aside, the dictum that "any little boy can grow up to become president" might raise some skepticism in the minds of little boys; the best girls could do was hope to marry one.

The scant attention to the kinds of questions that are of special interest to students of women's studies is, as argued above, in large part due to sexism, including a devaluation of women as citizens who should be a part of the principles of rights and self-governance in a democratic society. It is equally important to note that the types of questions feminists are primarily interested in are off the track of primary emphasis of political socialization research for other reasons as well. Perhaps most important is the theoretical framework that guided much of the field, especially the portion of it that seemed to stir the most interest among early students of political socialization: Eastonian systems analysis and questions of system support.

One of the most important goals of political socialization research was to understand how citizens came to be a part, and indeed the basis, of a stable political system, and especially a stable democratic system. Research therefore emphasized how individuals become assimilated into the dominant political culture and its institutions and how they become functioning and supportive members of political society. Although great emphasis has been placed on participatory values, including not just the propensity to take part in elections and certain other forms of political behavior, but also the acquisition of a sense of political efficacy, partisanship, and other cognitive and affective underpinnings of behavior, these values were regarded as important primarily for their role in determining the stability of the system and citizen-government relations. Thus a lack of participation caused concern primarily, although by no means exclusively, insofar as it might indicate a degree of alienation that might be threatening to the political system.

Within this framework the typical findings that females showed less propensity to participate in politics, to understand or show interest in government, or to have a sense of political efficacy than males did not appear indicative of a serious problem, especially because females tended to show relatively high levels of trust in and acceptance of political authority, and because psychological research tends to report women as being less aggressive than men, which many political scientists accept as an explanation for lower levels of politicization among women than men.[8] The fact that this combination might suggest more of a "subject" than "citizen" mentality (Sapiro, 1983) does not imply any obvious threat to the political system.

The significance of this framework for understanding political socialization, especially of females, finds its most explicit expression in David Easton and Jack Dennis's *Children in the Political System* (1969). Their research was oriented more clearly than most toward understanding system support and persistence. They pointed out that for purposes of their work they were not interested in sex differences in order to understand "the continuity of the wider cultural sex typing of political role behavior," "their explanatory power about possible leadership and policy," or on the "effects upon the individual and . . . his [sic] relationship to others that are the result of the political manifestations of his sex roles," although they recognized that these are important questions. "Our main effort is directed toward understanding what possible consequences sex differences might have, not for allocative politics but for system politics . . ." (Easton and Dennis, 1969, 336). They found that sex differences were small, that females seemed less developed as citizens, and that this difference posed no threat to the political system as it existed. From the point of view of systems persistence one might argue (although Easton and Dennis did not) that these findings are indications of "successful socialization"; in a political and social system based on gender inequality and subordination of women, females appeared as supportive of political authority as males but less likely to be oriented toward assuming an active attitude toward this authority than males.

I do not mean to suggest that an emphasis on system support and maintenance is inappropriate as a topic of inquiry for political scientists, even feminist political scientists. It is, however, a very limited view of the importance of politics and political socialization, and ill-conceived insofar as it is the primary interest not just of some scholars in the field but of a very large portion of it. Mere system persistence is a strange object to pose as a primary goal of political socialization, particularly in a political culture that otherwise values such objects as representation, responsiveness, and other democratic values.

System persistence and maintenance, in fact, are important themes in feminist social science, including that which focuses specifically on socialization. Feminist research, after all, asks how systems that are structured around inequality, especially in power and authority patterns (including autonomy and self-determination) persist and how they can be changed. It inquires about how people—in this case women—can come to accept a sex-gender system that grants them subordinate and limited status and even to participate in the persistence of this system. The difference is that women's studies researchers take allocative politics and the welfare of individuals and groups as their central concern, and they understand sex-gender systems as essentially political systems and not as something essentially distinct, existing in a remote, although related private domain.

The problem with the dominant framework used in the field of political socialization is that many of the questions which are most crucial for understanding women and politics cannot be asked or must be seriously underplayed. Moreover, and just as important for seeing the relationship between feminist research and the traditional disciplines, these questions, which hit at the heart of the relevance of politics to people, remain relatively untouched with regard to anyone. As M. Kent Jennings and Richard G. Niemi write, whether one uses a framework that is concerned primarily with how political socialization satisfied "the requirements of political structures" or, alternatively, "the requirements of individuals" makes a substantial difference in the kinds of questions we ask and the kinds of conclusions we can draw (Jennings and Niemi, 1974, 13).

To summarize, early work on gender differences in political socialization tended to suffer from two problems: androcentrism and the predominant type of systems analysis used by the field as a whole. The former led to problems noted throughout the social sciences by feminist critics. Females tended to be compared with a male norm and defined in terms of family roles and relationships and traditional views of femininity. The socialization of political gender roles and values was neither regarded as especially important to understand in and of itself nor as a type of "case study" of socialization or the socialization process that could have wider implications for understanding political socialization. The latter reinforced these tendencies by defining the prevailing political system and structures rather than the political, social, and personal needs of people and the possibility of change as the objects of interest. There were certainly exceptions in the earlier years of political socialization research (e.g., Heiskanen, 1971; Orum, Cohen, Grasmuck, and Orum, 1974; Jennings and Niemi, 1974). One of the more interesting developments in the area came as some political scientists began to focus on the relationship of gender and what are generally defined as "gender roles" to political learning over the life cycle as well as the impact of gender ideology on political learning (e.g., Jennings, 1979; Fulenwider, 1980; Jennings and Niemi, 1981; McGlen, 1980; Sapiro, 1983).[9]

This type of research has value not just for the advances they bring to our understanding of the political relevance of gender, but also for the added sophistication they bring to understanding the links between everyday social and economic life and politics. Unfortunately, little of this has yet had a significant impact on the dominant framework of political socialization research, at least as far as we might judge from textbook treatments of the field.

Family Structure, Divisions of Labor, and Political Socialization

Gender divisions of labor are central interests of women's studies. They have also played a significant role in political socialization research, generally through one of two foci: the impact of gender divisions of labor in the family on the political socialization of children, and the relationship of individuals' roles in gender divisions of social and economic labor to their own political values and behavior. I will discuss each successively.

From the early days of the study of political socialization the impact of family structure and some underlying family values played important roles in research, although psychological and psychoanalytic concepts often had the relatively vague "hand me down" look they often do when concepts filter from one discipline to another. Studies speculated about the relative effects of "authoritarian" versus "democratic" families on the political development of the young. It was generally accepted that contemporary (1950s–1960s) American families were democratic, although the list of indicators of family power structure, particularly with regard to gender relations, was very limited and certainly not sensitive to the types of power and authority questions feminist research on the family raises.

Fred I. Greenstein was influential in posing the argument that children first draw their image of and reaction to political authority from their views of their own fathers. Later research debated the point, but it seemed obvious to most observers that if such transference plays a role, in normal circumstances the male parent and not the female parent serves as the basis for children's views of authority. There was no speculation as to whether the father image might be less important if governmental authority itself had a less partriarchal visage; that is, if political figures were not so over-whemingly male (Greenstein, 1961, 1975; Jaros, Hirsch, and Fleron, 1968). Sex-gender systems receive little explicit treatment in these works; one must read between the lines to find that the normal family is what might be called a "democratic patriarchy"—no apparent contradiction in terms as far as most of the writings are concerned—and that this is the type of family structure that best serves the purpose of developing democratic citizens.

The point is reinforced in some studies that look explicitly at questions of mothers and fathers as authority figures in the family. The most revealing in this regard is Kenneth P. Langton's (1969) study of political socialization among Jamaicans and Americans. His work, which begins with a comparison of the effects of single-parent maternal vs. dual parent ("nuclear") families is grounded in traditional psychological views of the role of the father in child development (by which is generally meant male development) and the role of "appropriate" versus "cross-sex" identification and imitation. Langton cites the stream of literature suggesting that living in mother-only families harms sons in that it leads to "debilitating conflicts over their cross-sex identification," and makes them insecure over being the "sole male provider" (Langton, 1969, 32). These male "providers" were high school students. Such males are less achievement-oriented and display "decidedly effeminate behavioral patterns," are more infantile, dependent, and submissive (Langton, 1969, 31). In other words, these males conform to the traditional picture of the normal, healthy female. He also draws on prior research on the two-parent but "wife-dominant" home in the United States (in at least one case, based on the child's report of who is boss in the family) and concludes that these too are debilitating, at least for males. His discussion does not recognize questions of gender ideology or societal expectations and treatment of one-parent versus two-parent families but, rather, emphasizes apparently more "natural" and psychoanalytic explanations of cross-sex identification and the overprotectiveness of mothers unmediated by a father.

Langton's conclusions based on both the Jamaican data on single- versus two-parent families and American data on husband versus wife dominance finds that "mother-dominated families" and those in which children perceive the mothers as dominant are associated with relatively low levels of political efficacy, interest, and participation among males but primarily in families of lower social status.[10] Langton's conclusion was, "In short, boys appear to thrive politically in a patriarchal environment—at least in the lower classes—while there is little evidence that the conjugal power structure has a politically relevant impact upon female offspring" (Langton, 1969, 49).

Both this conclusion and the elaboration on it show how much research on political socialization can miss in the absence of the type of analysis emphasized in feminist research. There is no question of whether boys thrive, at least in the terms used here, in a patriarchal environment because of some essential psychological characteristics of human relationships—a conclusion toward which the book seems to lean—or because this family structure is consistent with the more general social structure and value system. The effects of the relative structure of familial and other institutional gender structures is a centerpiece of feminist research, which not only would not ignore such questions, but also is aware of ways in which patriarchal socialization creates important kinds of dependencies and weaknesses in males themselves (e.g., Chodorow, 1978).

The type of framework Langton uses leads him to exaggerate the "debilitating" effects of alternatives to patriarchal families; although he notes that the relationship is weakened and even reversed within the subsamples of higher social status, this point is underplayed and certainly unexplained. Finally, of signal importance to feminist research, this type of research framework and analysis claims to look at political development of the young, but in fact is neither sensitive to nor can comprehend the political development of young females. If it only helps to account for variation within one gender group, the theory and explanation must be more rigorous in its attention to gender-specific social phenomena or it is not helpful. All we learn in this particular treatment is that if living in non-patriarchal families is debilitating for boys because of the pressure of "cross-sex" identification for them to become "feminized," and conjugal power is politically irrelevant to girls, who will become (debilitatingly?) feminized anyway, it is probably best for families to be patriarchal. It is important to note that feminist critics of the mainstream of developmental psychology's treatment of gender point out that the most widely accepted theories in that field have offered explanations for why males would come to identify with males, but they cannot account for female identification with females (Rohrbaugh, 1980). If supposedly general theories fail in such a substantial way, there is little reason to trust their truth for either sex.

Another body of political socialization literature looks at a different question in the relative roles of mothers and fathers in the socialization of children. This looks at the "division of political labor" in transferring political values to the young; in other words, if parents differ in their political values or identities, whose influence on children will be stronger? (Langton and Jennings, 1969; Jennings and Niemi, 1974; Beck and Jennings, 1975). These studies show more awareness of the possible links between historical development of societal gender roles and values and the impact of the family on children. They also find that mothers exert at least as strong an effect on their children's political development as fathers do.

As students of political socialization have been increasingly interested in political learning throughout the life cycle, some have focused on the effects of assumption and enactment of gender-related roles in the family and economy on the development of political values and behavior. One of the few early studies to investigate the process and timing of gender-related political learning concluded that we cannot account for gender differences in political learning from the evidence of childhood and speculated that part of the explanation might rest with the effects of adult "situations" (Orum, Cohen, Grasmuck, and Orum, 1974). Research employing over time analysis of the same individuals, indeed, shows that some political gender differences actually *increase* following adolescence (Jennings and Niemi, 1981). Although a fair amount of research has investigated the relationships of roles such as motherhood or homemaking to political values and behavior (e.g., Andersen, 1975; Welch, 1977; McGlen, 1980), some have looked at these relationships much more explicitly in terms of political learning rather than as what might be regarded more as immediate constraints on the individual, although they are undoubtedly that too (Jennings, 1979; Jennings, and Niemi, 1981; Sapiro, 1983; Andersen and Cook, 1985; Sapiro, 1986).

These studies set the stage for important advances both for the specific question of gender differences in political learning and for the field as a whole. They move political science research on learning away from simple "sex differences" research; as I have argued elsewhere, use of the dichotomous gender variable in empirical political research is laden with traps for the unwary (Sapiro, 1983). Political scientists have certainly been slower than, for example, their colleagues in psychology and social psychology in this respect, although beside the role analysis discussed above some have also looked at the effects of variation in gender ideology (Fulenwider, 1980; Sapiro, 1983) or the sets of personal characteristics often combined to indicate "masculinity," "femininity," and androgyny (Hershey, 1977; Hershey and Sullivan, 1974).

These studies also bring into focus questions and problems that need to be investigated more seriously for political learning per se. The impact of family dynamics and structures on individuals—female and male—and the surrounding society cannot be understood without careful attention to sex-gender systems either for women or men. Women's studies has turned assumptions about the relationships between "private" and "public" life into research questions, thereby providing a new opportunity for the study of political learning to rise above a conventional wisdom that has often been defined through gender stereotypes. Further, they tend to be less isolated from the contributions of colleagues in other disciplines, a problem that afflicts scholars throughout the generally segregated world of scholarship. In order to look at these different kinds of questions, women's studies scholars are also transforming our understanding of political learning and how it works. In order to illustrate this point in more detail, it is necessary to look at some of the current questions and theories raised within women's studies to see how they might enter into and transform the field of political socialization.

Transformations

Gender in the Scheme of Things

Political scientists have restricted their work largely to traditional "sex differences" investigations, comparing the behavior and values of males and females, sometimes in general and sometimes within the broad categories of education, employment, or family role classifications. Gender itself tends to be treated in a relatively simple atheoretical manner, without much attention to its meaning or components. It is difficult to imagine that many interesting hypotheses can be generated about the relationship of political learning to gender if the nature of gender itself is not carefully investigated.

A considerable amount of work on the meaning and structure of gender has been developed outside of political science which may be very useful in the study of political learning. One of the most interesting concepts used recently is that of gender schemas, or the structure of interconnection among different ideas about perceptions of gender (Bem, 1983; Deaux and Lewis, 1984). Deaux and Lewis (1984) argue that gender stereotypes, which are applied to self or others, are composed of interrelated beliefs about traits, role behavior, occupations, and physical appearance. Cues about gender or a component of a gender schema will trigger cues about other components. Bem describes a schema as a "cognitive structure, a network of associations that organizes and guides an individual's perceptions. A schema functions as an anticipatory structure, a readiness to search for and to assimilate incoming information in schema-relevant terms." A gender schema, according to Bem, includes not just content-specific information about definitions and expectations about male and female, but also a heterogeneous network of ideas that are "more remotely or metaphorically related to sex, such as the angularity or roundedness of an abstract shape and the periodicity of the moon" (Bem, 1983, p.604). Even these metaphorical or abstract ideas are important elements of political thinking, as Jean Laponce demonstrates in his analysis of the meanings (including gender-related meanings) of left and right (Laponce, 1970).

The utility of the concept of gender schemas is that it does not start out with any notion of an inherent meaning of gender, but rather easily allows understanding it as a web of ideas that depends on cultural contact, individual experiences and situations, and expectations about the future. In terms of political learning and socialization, it emphasizes the ways in which particular political ideas and actions may be conceptually associated with gender and what the significance of these associations might be. Further, as Bem points out, analyzing the development of schemas is amenable to combining the theoretical approaches of both social learning and cognitive development, particularly important in political science, which has tended to make very little use of developmental frameworks. The drawbacks of ignoring developmental frameworks are particularly apparent in the study of gender in light of some of the exciting and controversial work done in other fields (e.g., Gilligan, 1982).

This emphasis on the learning and significance of associations of ideas or webs of significance linking politics and gender (Sapiro, 1983) opens the way to go beyond the narrow constraints of sex differences research, which asks only whether males and females do the same things or think the same thoughts, to an understanding of the historically flexible and context-specific meanings of both politics and gender. Julie Matthaei's (1982) economic history of women offers a good example relating to women's labor when she shows how, in the late nineteenth and early twentieth centuries women could engage in what might superficially appear to be radical departures from traditional gender roles in work but which, instead, were interpreted as extensions of women's domestic and "feminine" roles and therefore posed little threat to the prevailing ideology of gender and labor. (For a more current example, see Feree, 1979). It is possible to see politics in the same way. Women may well engage in many of the same activities as men, but these may be regarded as non-political extensions of women's roles (à la Lane) when they are done by women. Women may therefore enter new roles without offering a real challenge to gender ideology. Likewise, the massive expansion of the state in this century into "nurturance" functions such as social welfare services has led to an increased involvement of men in these areas of life (primarily through political and management functions) without significantly altering conceptions of masculinity, although it is true that, for example, in the Cabinet the offices associated with these functions are generally regarded as "softer" areas, a word with feminine significance in cultural terms. These offices, not surprisingly, hold lower status than the "harder" (more "masculine") offices associated with defense and the treasury.

The relevance of gender to politics does not simply lie, for example, in whether the proportion of women and men who vote in presidential elections, hold certain attitudes toward the president or presidency, or even run for the office of president is the same. Experimental research continues to show that women and men can engage in the same activities or display the same characteristics but still be perceived differently, depending on the circumstances (Brown and Geis, 1984; for an explicitly political example: Sapiro, 1981-82). People have gender but so, linguistically and conceptually, do activities, ideas, and institutions. Gender continues to connote status, both of people and of these other aspects of life. A transformed and sophisticated understanding of gender can help us understand how gender fits into the scheme of things political, and how the contours of political life rest in part on the significance of gender.

The question of association of ideas within schemas is directly relevant to the large body of research within political science on belief systems, another variant of the problem of interrelationships of ideas. Within political science, analysis of belief systems usually takes one of two forms, both of which rely on survey research. The first, using open-ended questions, investigates the conceptual framework people use to understand political parties and "left" and "right." The second, using techniques based on intercorrelation of responses to closed-ended questions, looks at the degree to which people within a particular sample display connection between one attitude or belief and others.[11] Unfortunately this type of research has not generally explored explicitly the process of political learning or socialization. Past empirical work has found women's political belief systems to be less sophisticated than men's in many countries (e.g., Jennings and Farah, 1980). Sapiro (1983) found that women's conceptual frameworks for politics, thus measured, depend in part on their gender roles and gender ideology.

Some research in women's studies on the association of ideas suggests both some important gender-related questions political scientists have ignored as well as others with implications extending well beyond the study of gender. First, gender and sexual ideology are related to other political beliefs and attitudes (Burt, 1980; Granberg and Granberg, 1981; Sapiro, 1983). Because the foundations of sexual and gender ideology are established very young and because these are so central in personal identity, it would seem that investigating the connections between these and other political beliefs, attitudes, perceptions would teach a considerable amount about the development of both gender and political schemas.

Women's studies research also points out limitations in political science research on gender differences in belief systems or schemas. More specifically, those studies which conclude that women display less sophistication or interconnection in their patterns of ideas focus on very limited ranges of ideas. Claire Fulenwider (1980), for example, finds more constraint among certain elements of a gender ideology and personal identity among women than men, although a number of studies suggest that men are more rigid in their application of traditional gender ideologies than women are. Barbara Finlay's (1981) analysis of abortion attitudes found a sample of college women's and men's attitudes toward abortion choice to be similar, but the structure of attitudes was different. The framework men used was more simple and related to their degree of conventionality in sexual and social matters, while women's were also tied to questions of the value of children in their own life plans and to their views of life and the right to life. Conventional observers might argue this indicates women's "personalism" as compared with men's more "sophisticated" and "political" abstract conceptual thought. We might suggest in contrast that the structure of women's ideas, at least in these examples, is more sophisticated and politically and personally useful in that they show evidence of women's tendency to be able to integrate "private" and "public" questions. The lesson for other studies would be to investigate more rigorously the connections between "abstract" ideas and the choices individuals make in their personal and political life.[12]

Finally, empirical research on the nature of prejudice and stereotype outstrips much political science research on political thinking in investigating the development, use, and change of schematic frameworks or ideology and belief systems. Some good examples are offered by studies that show the relationship between stereotype and reality in the distribution of social roles, as well as the circumstances under which certain cues call up stereotypic responses and those under which individuals can break through their present schemas (e.g., Locksley, Borgida, Brekke, and Hepburn, 1980; Beattie and Diehl, 1979; Locksley, Hepburn, and Ortiz, 1982; Deaux and Lewis, 1984; Eagly and Steffen, 1984). The special appeal of this research is that it suggests strategies for looking not just at the dynamics of individuals' cognitive frameworks, but those which are derived from the cultural myths on which people are raised in any given historical epoch. As such they point to one of the "holy grails" of social science: a means of combining, in empirical research, a concern for both individual and more social or cultural level analysis.

Politics in the Scheme of Things

One of the battles waged by feminists, including scholars, is over the question of what constitutes politics and the political. Just as a massive amount of the labor women perform is often not considered "work" because it either does not take place under the institutional conditions men associate with work, because it does not receive direct financial reward, or—perhaps most important—because it is seen as voluntary service to loved ones, so much of what might be regarded as women's political work is regarded as social or personal because it does not take place under the institutional conditions men associate with politics, because it does not receive the obvious political reward of power, or because it is seen as stemming from the "nonpolitical" value of nurturance or social commitment. Further, as numerous observers have pointed out, we have come to make relatively clear distinctions between institutions, interactions, values, and events that are considered political and those that are not. Within the study of government even finer distinctions are made: Some questions are "political" while others are "judicial" or "administrative."

Feminist scholars cannot help being aware that the definition of the political is an essential problem to investigate, not just as it is done in the usual cursory way in introduction to political science classes, but as a key element in political thinking and action. The distinctions between public and private, political and nonpolitical or, at a higher level, between political, judicial, and administrative are important because they help to define particular problems and also who should be concerned with them and what means may be used to solve them. These distinctions and how they are developed in the minds of individuals are important both for understanding political thinking in general and, more specifically, political thinking with direct relevance to gender questions. I have already suggested that women have long been able to become active in politics without necessarily challenging the "maleness" of politics by understanding and shaping their political activity as an extension of their "appropriate" domestic concerns. Indeed, research shows that under certain circumstances motherhood draws women into political concern and activities (Sapiro, 1983; Jennings, 1979), just as in the late nineteenth century the "professionalization" of homemaking led many women to expand their concerns from domestic to "social" housekeeping (Matthaei, 1982). More often than not, however, definitions of the political have been used against women by defining certain activities or institutions as out of bounds for them, by depoliticizing (conceptually, at least) women's concerns and activities, or by defining women's problems as private and individual and therefore, out of bounds for state attempts at amelioration.

This last point has taken on special practical significance in the last decade during the debates between left and right over women's rights, the welfare state, relations between family and state, and reproductive and sexual policies. Feminists have certainly been aware that whether people understand their problems as personal and individual ("I do not have enough education"; "I am not capable of having an impact") or social and political ("There is systematic discrimination against people like me"; "People like me have been taught to avoid competence") makes considerable difference for whether a group's condition will be improved. Feminist scholars have been particularly keenly aware of how supposedly "private" institutions such as the family or "private" social interactions must be subjected to political analysis. These "private" institutions shape and are shaped by the larger political system, they reflect and help maintain or change the distribution and application of political values.

Equally important, many of the most crucial policy issues of politics, and certainly those with the most direct gender relevance, turn on how people define the domain of politics and political activity. Students of political socialization and learning have spent far too little time finding out how people develop their frameworks for understanding the domain and functions of politics and government and what the significance of these different frameworks is. Instead, it has often seemed as though the researcher "knows" what politics is, and then checks to see whether respondents are right or wrong.

One of the most interesting developments in research on the political framing of gender is the recent emphasis on group identity and consciousness (Miller, Gurin, Gurin, and Malanchuck, 1981; Gurin, 1985; Klein, 1985; Gurin and Townsend, 1986; Conover, 1986; Sigel and Welchel, 1986). These studies are part of a larger trend toward investigating social groups, their status relationships, and interaction as frameworks for individuals' political thinking. Scholars concentrating on gender and politics have been among the leaders of this move in political science. Although this approach has not yet been taken up to any great extent by students of socialization, we should expect much more work in this area soon.

Conclusion: Learning in the Field

Item: Throughout the 1970s research on women and politics noted that as women's education came to match that of men and as women entered paid employment in increasing numbers, especially in jobs previously reserved for men, women's and men's political behavior and attitudes would look more and more alike, presumably because women would begin to "look more like" men. Beginning with the 1980 presidential election, we entered an era in the United States in which women's and men's political attitudes became more differentiated than they had appeared to be since poll taking began. This phenomenon was known as the gender gap. Both major parties responded in 1984, the Democrats by nominating a woman to be Vice President, and the Republicans by engaging as convention speakers as many women as they could.

Item: In 1984 Geraldine Ferraro became the first woman nominated by a major party to run for Vice President. The first major issue of the campaign, and one which emerged before the acceptance speeches had been made, was how the nominees should pose themselves when they appeared together. The first major decision was that they would not engage in the timeworn tradition of clasping hands together over their heads to show their mutual solidarity and determination. Instead, they looked nervous and awkward.

These two stories of politics in the 1980s point out some of the important weaknesses in the study of political learning as it has been done in political science, but they also suggest some contributions a transformed field can make in the future.

The phenomenon of the gender gap created great confusion among most political analysts. Conventional wisdom states that women are either by nature or by training inclined to be more pacifistic and social welfare-oriented, less violence-prone, more conservative and more idealistic (as compared with "realistic") than men in their approach to politics. On the other hand, differences between male and female attitudes had never had such clear, persistent, and practical significance for American politics as they have had since 1980. At the same time, despite the universality of this conventional wisdom at least in Western political cultures, similar gender gaps have not been apparent in other nations. Further, changes in the status and roles of women in the last two decades led most people to speculate that as women's education and participation in the labor force came to resemble men's, and as feminist ideology had greater impact on American life, political gender differences would fade even more.

The study of political learning should be able to help account for such phenomena as the gender gap. There have been too many pieces of the puzzle missing. Students of political socialization have tended to slight investigation of the development and application of the conceptual frameworks people use to understand the substance of politics. They have particularly ignored the context-specificity of the use of conceptual frameworks, thus making analysts incapable of knowing whether people have changed, the situation has changed, or both. Even judging the context of people's political responses is difficult; policy researchers considering gender, for example, have become increasingly aware that apparently neutral public policies can affect women and men very differently.

Political science moved ahead when its practitioners began to understand that day-to-day life roles and activities such as work, marriage, and parenthood have an impact on the way people approach politics and government, but because political science focuses so thoroughly on the second part of the equation and because the impact of women's studies has been rather less than that in some related social sciences, the treatment of the "independent variables" tends to be crude and unsatisfactory. At the most basic level, for example, the increasing labor market figures for women do not, in and of themselves, offer much reason to hypothesize that women and men are converging in their private roles and experiences and therefore, that these should be offering the basis for similar political outlooks or activity. Both domestic and paid labor remain highly gender-segregated, which means that both domestic and more public economic and social roles should continue to provide a different training ground and different sets of constraints on women and men as they approach politics. Indeed, because of this segregation one might speculate that as women gain some amount of independence through their paid labor, they should be freer to diverge from men in their awareness and expression of their own interests.

The contours and meanings of day-to-day experiences and commitments need to be treated as thoughtfully and rigorously by political scientists interested in learning as they are in women's studies, not just in order to understand women's lives but men's lives as well. This need is underscored by the increasing emphasis on learning throughout the life course, which focuses attention on critical life events such as entering employment, marriage, or parenthood, retirement, or widowhood. Such analysis is becoming—must become—more complicated than it has been in the past for a number of reasons.

It was once assumed that there was a fairly standard "life cycle" of events individuals experienced, running from the end of education to the beginning of employment and marriage to retirement and old age. The first serious realization that this cycle is only one of many which are "normal" was made by women's studies scholars. Until recently, paid employment, especially full-time employment, was a feature of a minority of adult women's lives, and many women began their careers at a later time than men do. This timing was generally called a "delay" on women's part because the male pattern was considered the norm from which women deviated. Reliance on the male model of life stages also meant that critical events that are particularly common and important in vast numbers of women's lives but not men's were often ignored; the two most important of these are the time when children leave home, which alters women's responsibilities and routines more substantially than men's, and widowhood, which affects far more women than men. These obvious differences must not obscure the fact that even when women and men apparently experience the same life events, as when they are married, become parents, employees, or retire, their actual roles and experiences are very different.

Life course patterns and timing have changed throughout history, and numerous changes have been apparent in recent years. The rise in education levels, divorce, and remarriage have affected both women and men. Increasing numbers of women are having children without first marrying. It is becoming more common for men to change careers, more common for women to establish careers, and the age of retirement is shifting. By the early 1980s half of all mothers of two-year-olds were in the work force. Institutions of higher learning are reporting that the average age of students, and especially female students, is rising as alternatives to completing one's education in consecutive years are becoming more widespread and acceptable. Public policy has even begun to reflect the increasing acceptance of life course flexibility with antidiscrimination policies based on age and changes in retirement and pension policies.

Above all, if research on political learning is to comprehend the connections between day-to-day and political life, researchers must be aware that not only are critical personal experiences usually defined as "roles" more complex and flexible than they are usually treated, they are also meaningful in large part through subjective aspects. People differ not only across the sexes but within each sex with respect to how salient and central the various personal and economic roles are to their senses of identity (Mackie, 1983). The impact of women's private roles on their approaches to politics depends not just on what roles they hold, but how they interpret these roles (Sapiro, 1983; Feree, 1980). It is likely that the same is true of men.

Current work on the subjective and ideological nature of social roles and their timing offers some intriguing suggestions for the study of political learning through adulthood. Recent emphasis on the timing of women's critical life events and their comparison with male standards has led some investigators to turn from discussion of "life cycles" and other similar phases to "social clocks." Helson, Mitchell, and Moane (1984), for example, point out what any woman (or man?) who has deviated from the standard course of life-event timing—what they call "normative schedules"—probably knows. There is a social and cultural definition not just of what roles adults are supposed to assume and how they are supposed to be enacted, but of when these roles should be assumed and when they should be developed in specific ways. Individuals know when they are "on time" and "off time" according to the normative schedule that applies to their sex and class. The social clock, therefore, provides a means of comparison between self and other or self and expectations which, as they say, serves to integrate personal and social processes through time.

Feminists have become well aware of the importance of the social clock for women's political situation. Societal expectations for careers and political activism are that these work according to a stereotypic masculine clock; because women's young adult time is supposed to be dominated by domestic activities (thus freeing young men to follow their appropriate schedules), their own expectations for activism and success are diminished. As mentioned above, women's economic and employment careers are generally discussed in terms of "delays" and other indications of deviation from the male norms. This is one reason why as important as policies designed to combat sex discrimination are for women, policies aimed at age discrimination may be even more important, at least for current generations of women.

The idea of the social clock can make an important contribution to understanding political learning among both sexes. For a brief example, it is likely that the economic difficulties and high interest rates of the late 1970s and 1980s denied to individuals in some classes the ability to purchase a first home at the age they might have expected given the normative schedule that had developed for people of their class in recent decades. What impact might this have on individuals' orientation toward themselves, society, and politics? The answer depends on how they answer the key question Helson, Mitchell, and Moane claim is the trigger for the import of social clocks: How am I doing for my age? If the answer is "Not well," another question follows: Why not and what can be done about it? One of the appealing aspects of the social clock for theories of learning is that it offers a means of applying cognitive developmental frameworks of learning to adult life through the explicit role of identity and social comparison. This view suggests that normative social values may be impressed on individuals as social learning theories would argue, but also that individuals play an active role in accepting, rejecting, and applying these values, as developmental models argue.

The Geraldine Ferraro story suggests some other aspects of political learning that need more investigation by political scientists. Women's studies scholars, and especially those in social psychology, have long emphasized the politics of verbal and nonverbal language and social interaction. They have argued that many of the important practical principles of power and politics are learned and applied at a very young age in the fairly automatic and non-conscious application of day-to-day social interaction. The ways people speak, act, and interact reflect and help to maintain systems of power, deference, status, and function within society at the most basic levels. The clearest indication of political equality and the integration of women into political life as the equals of men is not, feminists argue, when people answer survey questions to indicate that they believe in equality or in women's participation in high power positions, but rather, when their automatic interactions indicate the fracturing of the old structures of systematic deference and dominance and when interaction of male and female colleagues in settings such as politics and the workplace do not become confused with the interaction of male and female intimates in more private settings.

That the Democratic nominees for President and Vice President in 1984 could not engage in a traditional political ritual (the victory clasp) because, by social norms, it would be interpreted as a variant of a traditional courtship ritual (holding hands) shows how important these forms of interaction and the norms on which they are based can be for politics. Likewise, there was some initial confusion over whether the nominees should follow the nearly universal political ritual of having the (potential) head of state walk ahead of all subordinates, or whether they should follow the chivalrous principle of ladies first. Many newspapers reported that at least in their early days, the two people nominated to work in one of the most powerful and responsible offices in the world were reduced to looking like an awkward couple on their first high school date. If any event should illustrate the power of gender socialization, its impact on politics, and the importance of social interaction in political learning, this must. Unfortunately most political scientists interested in political socialization have ignored language and social interaction in part because it appears to them "social" rather than "political" and in part, one suspects, because it cannot be studied adequately through the predominant research method used by the field, survey research.

Conclusion

Throughout this paper I have suggested ways in which the field of political socialization has failed not only to study the political learning of women adequately, but also has failed to take advantage of some of the contributions made by women's studies that could increase knowledge of political learning more generally.

It is curious that the study of *gender* and politics has generally been regarded as the study of *women* in society, even when it is performed through analysis of sex differences, or comparisons of women and men. People could, of course, read these studies just as easily with an eye toward finding out how men approach politics as to find out how women do. (In the process, this would lay to rest the old canard, "If there is 'women's studies,' why is there not 'men's studies'?") The problem is that because men are considered the norm in politics, most people understand the relevance of gender as a question of how much women do or do not diverge from the male standard. It is no wonder that most analysts of the "gender gap" focused on women as the explanation for change and difference rather than looking at both sides of the equation.[13] The point is that gender is an important part of *people's* identity and day-to-day lives, and we would do well to understand how gender influences *people's* approaches to politics.

The potential contribution of women's studies, however, goes beyond questions of either women or gender. The nature of the substance that women's studies investigates and the institutional development of women's studies as an interdisciplinary field (crucial for those of us in particularly male-dominated disciplines such as political science) focuses attention on some problems and issues of personal and political life and learning that have been ignored by others, it takes a different perspective, and it has given rise to concentration on different kinds of research methods. Women's studies has now been developing both within traditional disciplines and in its own space for at least fifteen years. The mainstream of the traditional disciplines suffer from not taking advantage of our experience and expertise.

NOTES

1. In political science, unlike psychology, "socialization" does not necessarily imply a particular model of learning or development.
2. For the first discussion of the meaning of "sex-gender systems," see Rubin, 1974.
3. Notable among these are Lane, 1959; Greenstein, 1961, 1965; Easton and Dennis, 1969; and Hess and Torney, 1967.
4. By the publication date of these early critiques there had been very few articles or books devoted specifically to research on gender and political socializa-

tion, and many of those were published too late for the critics to be aware of them. Other than those cited above, the bulk of the literature at the time was composed of Dowse and Hughes, 1971; Heiskanen, 1971; Hyman, 1959; Iglitzin, 1974; Jennings and Niemi, 1974; Langton, 1969; MacLeod and Silverman, 1973; and Orum, et al., 1974.

5. Hyman placed textual emphasis on the word "adult"; I have deleted that and for our purposes, substituted emphasis on group differences.

6. Again, emphasis has been changed.

7. I say black *males* because, as is often noted, when people have discussed the problems of blacks, for example with regard to employment and their rights, they are generally focusing on black *males*, whereas when people discuss the problems of women, they are often talking primarily of *white* women. For further discussion, see Hooks, 1981.

8. This is indicative of another difference between feminist students of politics and others. Feminist political scientists tend to reject the notion that aggression is necessarily a basis for politicization, and specifically political action and values that are of benefit to the political community.

9. Some of these are discussed more completely in the next section.

10. It is important to note that the indicator of class or status is education. Although research often finds more traditional gender and sexual ideology among lower- than higher-class people, Anne Locksley has concluded that the key explanatory factor is education and not class. See Locksley, 1982. Other research suggests that the correlation between class and sexual and gender roles and ideology may have decreased over time, at least in the United States. See Caplow and Chadwick, 1979; Weinberg and Williams, 1980.

11. The former can be used to analyze individuals while the latter cannot.

12. At least one study, however, suggests that women's attitudes are more related to a general ideology or set of principles while men's are more related to their personal economic interests. See Stout-Wiegand and Trent, 1983.

13. The question most people asked was why women became so disproportionately unfavorable toward the Reagan administration rather than why men became so disproportionately favorable.

REFERENCES

Andersen, Kristi (1975). "Working Women and Political Participation, 1952–1972." *American Journal of Political Science* 19 (August), 439–53.

―――― and Elizabeth A. Cook (1985). "Women, Work, and Political Attitudes." *American Journal of Political Science* 29 (August), 606–25.

Beattie, Muriel Yoshida and Leslie Diehl (1979). "Effects of Social Conditions on the Expression of Sex-Role Stereotypes." *Psychology of Women Quarterly* 4 (Winter), 241–55.

Beck, Paul Allen and M. Kent Jennings (1975). "Parents as 'Middlepersons' in Political Socialization." *Journal of Politics* 37 (February), 81–107.

Bem, Sandra Lipsitz (1983). "Gender Schema Theory and Its Implications for Child Development: Raising Gender-Aschematic Children in a Gender-Schematic Society." *Signs* 8 (Summer), 598–616.

Bourke, Susan C. Jean Grossholtz (1974). "Politics as an Unnatural Practice: Political Science Looks at Female Participation." *Politics and Society* 4 (Winter), 255–66.

Brown, Virginia and Florence L. Geis (1984). "Turning Lead Into Gold: Evaluations of Men and Women Leaders and the Alchemy of Social Consensus." *Journal of Personality and Social Psychology* 46 (April), 811–24.

Burt, Barbara R. (1980). "Cultural Myths and Supports for Rape." *Journal of Personality and Social Psychology* 38 (February), 217–30.

Caplow, Theodore and Bruce Chadwick (1979). "Inequality and Life-Styles in Middletown, 1920–1978." *Social Science Quarterly* 60 (December), 367–86.

Chodorow, Nancy (1978). *The Reproduction of Mothering.* Berkeley: University of California Press.

Conover, Pamela Johnston (1986). "Group Identification and Group Sympathy: Their Political Implications." Paper prepared for delivery at the Annual Meeting of the Midwest Political Science Association, Chicago.

Deaux, Kay and Laurie L. Lewis (1984). "Structure of Gender Stereotypes: Interrelationships among Components and Gender Label." *Journal of Personality and Social Psychology* 46 (May), 991–1004.

Dowse, Robert and John Hughes (1971). "Girls, Boys, and Politics." *British Journal of Sociology* 22 (March), 53–67.

Eagly, Alice H. and Valerie J. Steffen (1984). "Gender Stereotypes Stem from the Distribution of Women and Men Into Social Roles." *Journal of Personality and Social Psychology* 46 (April), 735–54.

Easton, David and Jack Dennis (1969). *Children in the Political System: Origins of Political Legitimacy.* New York: McGraw-Hill.

Eichler, Magrit (1980). *The Double Standard: A Feminist Critique of Feminist Social Science.* New York: St. Martin's Press.

Feree, Myra Marx (1979). "Employment without Liberation: Cuban Women in the U.S." *Social Science Quarterly* 60 (June), 35–50.

——— (1980). "Working-Class Feminism: A Consideration of the Consequences of Employment." *Sociological Quarterly* 21 (Spring), 173–84.

Finlay, Barbara Agresti (1981). "Sex Differences in Correlates of Abortion Attitudes among College Students." *Journal of Marriage and the Family* 43 (August), 571–82.

Fulenwider, Claire (1980). *Feminism in American Politics: A Study of Ideological Influence.* New York: Praeger.

Gilligan, Carol (1982). *In a Different Voice: Psychological Theory and Women's Development.* Cambridge: Harvard.

Goot, Murray and Elizabeth Reid (1975). *Women and Voting Studies: Mindless Matrons or Sexist Scientism?* Beverly Hills: Sage.

Granberg, Donald and Beth Wellman Granberg (1981). "Pro-Life versus Pro-Choice: Another Look at the Abortion Controversy in the United States." *Sociology and Social Research* 65 (July), 424–33.

Greenstein, Fred I. (1961). "Sex-Related Political Differences in Childhood." *Journal of Politics* 23 (May), 353–71.

——— (1965). *Children and Politics.* New Haven: Yale.

——— (1975). "Benevolent Leader Revisited: Children's Images of Political Leaders in Three Democracies." *American Political Science Review* 69:1371–99.

Gurin, Patricia (1985). "Women's Gender Consciousness." *Public Opinion Quarterly* 49, 43–63.

——— and Aloen Townsend (1986). "Properties of Gender Identity and Their Implications for Gender Consciousness." *British Journal of Social Psychology* 25 (June), 139–48.

Haavio-Manila, Elena (1970). "Sex Roles in Politics." *Scandinavian Political Studies* 5:29–38.

Heiskanen, Veronica Stolte (1971). "Sex Roles, Social Class, and Political Consciousness." *Acta Sociologica* 14:83–95.

Helson, Ravenna, Valory Mitchell, and Geraldine Moane (1984). "Personality and Patterns of Adherence and Nonadherence to the Social Clock." *Journal of Personality and Social Psychology* (May), 1079–96.

Hershey, Marjorie (1977). "The Politics of Androgny? Sex Roles and Attitudes toward Women in Politics." *American Political Quarterly* 5 (July), 261–88.
——— and John Sullivan (1974). "Sex Role Attitudes, Identities and Political Ideology." *Sex Roles* 1:37–57.
Hess, Robert and Judith Torney (1967). *The Development of Political Attitudes in Children.* Garden City: Doubleday.
Hooks, Bell (1981). *Ain't I a Woman: Black Women and Feminism.* Boston: South End Press.
Hyman, Herbert (1950). *Political Socialization: A Study in the Psychology of Political Behavior.* New York: Free Press.
Iglitzin, Lynne (1974). "The Making of Apolitical Woman: Femininity and Sex-Stereotyping in Girls." In Jane Jaquette, ed., *Women in Politics,* 25–36. New York: Wiley.
Jaquette, Jane S. (1974). "Introduction: Women in American Politics." In Jane S. Jaquette, ed., *Women in Politics.* New York: Wiley.
Jaros, Dean, Harry Hirsch, and Frederick J. Fleron (1968). "The Malevolent Leader: Political Socialization in an American Subculture." *American Political Science Review* 62:564–75.
Jennings, M. Kent (1979). "A New Look at the Life Cycle and Political Participation." *American Journal of Political Science* 23 (November), 755–71.
——— and Barbara G. Farah (1980). "Ideology, Gender, and Political Action: A Cross-National Study Survey." *British Journal of Political Science* 10 (April), 219–40.
——— and Richard G. Niemi (1974). *Political Character in Adolescence.* Princeton: Princeton University Press.
Klein, Ethel (1984). *Gender Politics.* Cambridge: Harvard University Press.
Lane, Robert (1959). *Political Life.* New York: Free Press.
——— (1962). *Political Ideology.* New York: Free Press.
Langton, Kenneth P., ed. (1969). *Political Socialization.* New York: Oxford.
——— and M. Kent Jennings (1969). "Mothers versus Fathers in the Formation of Political Orientations." In Kenneth Langton, ed., *Political Socialization,* 52–83. New York: Oxford.
Laponce, Jean (1970). "Dieu: à droit ou à gauche?" *Canadian Journal of Political Science* 3 (July), 257–74.
Locksley, Anne (1982). "Social Class and Marital Attitudes and Behavior." *Journal of Marriage and the Family* 44 (May), 927–40.
———, Eugene Borgida, N. Brekke, and C. Hepburn (1980). "Sex Stereotypes and Social Judgment." *Journal of Personality and Social Psychology* 39:821–31.
———, C. Hepburn, and V. Ortiz (1982). "Social Stereotypes and Judgments of Individuals: An Instance of the Base-Rate Fallacy." *Journal of Experimental Social Psychology* 18:23–42.
McGlen, Nancy E. (1980). "The Impact of Parenthood on Political Participation." *Western Political Quarterly* 33 (September), 297–313.
Mackie, Marlene (1983). "The Domestication of Self: Gender Comparisons of Self-Imagery and Self-Esteem." *Social Psychology Quarterly* 46 (December), 343–50.
Matthaei, Julie (1982). *An Economic History of Women in America.* New York: Schocken.
Miller, Arthur, Patricia Gurin, Gerald Gurin, and Oksana Malanchuk (1981). "Group Consciousness and Political Participation." *American Journal of Political Science* 25, 494–511.
Morgan, Jan (1974). "Women and Political Socialization: Fact and Fantasy in Easton and Dennis and in Lane." *Politics* 9 (May), 50–55.
Orum, Anthony M., Roberta S. Cohen, Sherri Grasmuck, and Amy W. Orum (1974). "Sex, Socialization, and Politics." *American Sociological Review* 39 (April), 197–209.

Rohrbaugh, Joanna Bunker (1980). *Women: Psychology's Puzzle*. Brighton: Harvester.

Rubin, Gayle (1974). "The Traffic in Women: Notes on the Political Economy of Sex. In Rayna Reiter, ed., *Toward an Anthropology of Women*, 157–210. New York: Monthly Review Press.

Sapiro, Virginia (1981–82). "If U.S. Senator Baker Were a Woman: An Experimental Study of Candidate Images." *Political Psychology* 3 (Spring–Summer), 61–83.

Sapiro, Virginia (1982). "Public Costs of Private Commitments or Private Costs of Public Commitments: Family Roles versus Political Ambition." *American Journal of Political Science* 26 (May), 265–79.

Sapiro, Virginia (1983). *The Political Integration of Women: Roles, Socialization, and Politics*. Urbana: University of Illinois Press.

Sapiro, Virginia (1986). "The Effects of Gender Segregation of Work on Political Orientations and Behavior." Paper prepared for the Annual Meeting of the International Society for Political Psychology, Amsterdam.

Sigel, Roberta S. and Nancy L. Welchel (1986). "Minority Consciousness and Sense of Group Power among Women." Paper prepared for the Annual Meeting of the Midwest Political Science Association, Chicago.

Stevens, Olive (1982). *Children Talking Politics: Political Learning in Childhood*. Oxford: Martin Robertson.

Stout-Wiegand, Nancy and Roger B. Trent (1983). "Sex Differences in Attitudes toward New Energy Developments." *Rural Sociology* 48 (Winter), 637–46.

Weinberg, Martin S. and Colin J. Williams (1980). "Sexual Embourgeoisment? Social Class and Sexual Activity, 1938–70." *American Sociological Review* 45 (February), 33–48.

Welch, Susan (1977). "Women as Political Animals? A Test of Some Explanations for Male-Female Political Participation Differences." *American Journal of Political Science* 21 (November), 711–30.

REFLECTIONS ON BLACK WOMEN WRITERS

REVISING THE LITERARY CANON

Nellie McKay

There is no doubt that black women as writers have made drastic inroads into the American literary consciousness since the beginning of the 1970s, and the film success of Alice Walker's *The Color Purple* has indeed placed the entire group within a new dimension in the national consciousness. Aside from its merits (or demerits) as book and/or movie, *The Color Purple* is important for what its popularity means in terms of the recognition it compels for the works of black women. Thousands, perhaps millions, of people who had not, until now, ever heard the name of Alice Walker, and countless others who had, but who were able to ignore her (although she has been publishing fiction and poetry since the late 1960s), have seen and will see the film—learn her name, and respond to her work, whether they acknowledge its richness, or see it as a misrepresentation of the black experience. Above the din of the controversy that *The Color Purple* has sparked inside and outside of the black community, many will discover something new about the experiences of black women in America. For what black women as writers have consistently provided for themselves and others has been a rendering of the black woman's place in the world in which she lives, as she shapes and defines that from her own impulses and actions.

Before *The Color Purple* the only comparable achievement for a black woman writer was made by Lorraine Hansberry's *A Raisin in the Sun*, which was first staged in 1959. This play, for which Hansberry won the New York Drama Critics Circle Award of "Best Play of the Year," over Tennessee Williams's *Sweet Bird of Youth*, Archibald MacLeish's *JB*, and Eugene O'Neill's *A Touch of the Poet*, made her not only the youngest American, the first woman, and the first black person to achieve that honor, but also the first black woman to have her work produced on Broadway. *A Raisin in the*

Sun, seen by millions of Americans on stage, screen, and television, has been translated into more than thirty languages and produced on all continents of the globe. It foreshadowed the emergence of a new movement in black theater, a new place in letters for black women writers, and opened one artistic door onto the large stage of the Civil Rights Movement of the 1960s and 1970s.

A Raisin in the Sun is not autobiographical. Lorraine Hansberry came from a black middle-class family which had long overcome the problems faced by the characters in her play. But if Hansberry was economically removed from the dilemma of the Youngers, the family she writes about, she was nevertheless emotionally attached to the issues she explored through them, issues that remained at the core of the lives of the majority of black people in America in the 1950s. The experiences of her dramaturgical family were part of the collective three-hundred-year-old consciousness of what it meant to be born black in America. In giving several of the key roles in her play to women, she had also followed in the footsteps of her less well-known earlier sisters who had sought to write out of their black female awareness and point of view on that reality.

At the center of *Raisin* is that most memorable Mama: Lena Younger, whose grandeur takes vengeance for all the black mammies previously presented in American literature. For black women in American literature, from the beginning, having been depicted as either sexually loose and therefore tempters of men, or obedient and subservient mammies, loving and tender to the white children they raised and forever faithful to the owners they served. Lena Younger defies more than two hundred years of such stereotyping of black women, and turns black female strength, too often maligned by everyone else, into the means by which her son Walter shapes his emerging manhood. Lorraine Hansberry was not the first black woman who gave us such a positive image of black women, but she was the first in her own time whose voice reached as wide an audience as hers did. Her achievement opened a wider way for the black women writers who came after her.

What is significant in the Lena Younger image in *Raisin* for the purposes of this paper is that she is the central force that holds her family together, that she has no ambivalences regarding the inherent human worth and dignity of herself and those whom she loves, and that speaking from inside of her own experiences, she demonstrates that the black struggle to transcend dwarfs the victimization that would otherwise have destroyed black people a long time ago. And while Mama Younger stands as the force at the center of her family, there are also the other women in that drama whose roles are fully as important as her own: daughter Beneatha, who wants to be a doctor so that she will be able to heal sick and broken black bodies, but whose sophisticated cynicism meets with the stern rebuke of her mother; and Ruth, Walter's wife, whose concerns for the welfare and well-being of her children precipitates a family controversy over abortion that belies the notion that poor and/or black people produce babies without consideration for what happens after they arrive. Years later, when Ruth will tell Travis and his siblings stories about their grandmother, or when Beneatha recalls her young adulthood and the conflicts she had with her mother, the scripts to those narratives will bear no resemblances to the majority of those concerning black mothers and/or women that appear in the literature written by black men or white men or women.

Since the success of *A Raisin in the Sun* the names of an impressive number of black women writers have become fairly well known to large numbers of Americans, and at the same time new and different images of black women have emerged from their pens. But while it is accurate to give credit to Hansberry's success as foreshadowing the contemporary wider recognition of black women writers and critics, the momentum it signalled had its beginnings more than two hundred years earlier. The history of the creative efforts of black women in America began with the beginnings of literacy, in 1746 with Lucy Terry's "Bars Fight," a poem about an Indian raid on the white settlement of Deerfield, Massachusetts, and continued with Phillis Wheatley's *Poems on Various Subjects, Religious and Moral* in 1773. Terry's and Wheatley's extant works confirm that black women in the eighteenth century had literary voices which they made bold to use, while black women of the nineteenth century, building on what preceded them, authenticated their voices by speaking to local and national issues that had direct impact on the lives of black people. From Sojourner Truth, abolitionist and feminist, who could neither read nor write but whose words were recorded by others, to Jarena Lee, evangelist, who documented the hundreds of miles she logged across the country preaching and teaching and saving souls, to Maria Stewart, the first woman in the country to make a profession of the public lecture circuit, and Anna Julia Cooper and Frances Watkins Harper, whose feminist, antiracist writings are as contemporary as today, we know that these women spoke loud and clear in celebration of the positive characteristics of human life, and in strong criticism of racial and gender oppression. This history assures us that black women have not ever been artistically or critically silent, even though for most of the past their voices went largely ignored by those who did not wish to hear them. In their own voices, black women have always confirmed and authenticated the complexity of the black American female experience, and in so doing have debunked the negative stereotypes that others created of them while denying them audience for their words. Now, finally admitted to a larger hearing than they ever previously enjoyed, both past and present black female literary voices combine to alter the historical nature of the discourse and to play a prominent role in revising the canon from which they were long excluded.

There is no need here to again recite the history of the stereotyping of black women in American literature by others than themselves. That has been adequately done by several critics.[1] It is important, however, to note that the efforts to reverse the negative images of black women in literature began as early as these women began to find an opportunity to write: with the slave narratives, fiction, poetry, and nonfiction prose of the nineteenth century. The spoken words of women like Sojourner Truth, and the writings of other women like Stewart, Cooper, and Watkins-Harper, among others, were primary in the struggle against slavery and the abuses of women, especially of black women. Their boldness and assertiveness define these women as a highly intelligent, morally outraged group in a struggle against white injustice to blacks and male dominance of women.

In the earliest known novel by a black woman, *Our Nig or Sketches from the Life of a Free Black* (1859), by Harriet Wilson, the abused heroine, Frado, is a hardworking, honest child of mixed racial parentage who is caught in a web of white hatred and cruelty. Frado is neither an immoral woman nor a mammy, the most frequent of the stereotypes of black women in that time, and Wilson uses her characterization of the helpless child to emphasize the unfairness of a social structure that permitted individuals to treat black people in a less-than-human fashion. In writing this novel, Wilson, of whom not a great deal is known, was the flesh-and-blood example of the rebel against the treatment she outlined in her book. As such, she provided another concrete example of black women's estimation of their self-worth. For one thing, she explicitly wrote her narrative as a means of earning money to take care of herself and her ailing son. Wilson, who lived in Boston and other areas of New England, and who sets her work in that geographical location, took advantage of the tradition of the sentimental female novel, which at that time enjoyed enormous popularity. The form of her book—the epigraphs, style, and structure of the narrative—shows that she was well aware of many of the conventions of novel writing at the time, and that she considered them valuable to plead the case, not of the poor white heroine who eventually achieves a good marriage and a happy home, as they did in the white female novels, but of an abused black child and woman who was unable to realize the goals of white protagonists. Wilson, deserted by her husband, was sufficiently self-assured to imagine that writing held the possibilities of a vocation for her.

But the slave narrative, not fiction, was the mode that dominated the earliest Afro-American attempts at literature, which through its existence revised the nature of the American "Self." Until recently, most of the attention to this body of work has focused on the writings of men, with *The Narrative of Frederick Douglass, An American Slave, Written by Himself* receiving the majority of the plaudits. It is now recognized that the female slave narrative deserves attention for its own sake—for its unique contributions to the genre. The narrative of Harriet Jacobs, in particular, *Incidents in the Life of a Slave Girl*, published in 1861 under the name of Linda Brent, is a stunning literary success, equal in every way to the preeminent male slave narrative. Jacobs, a South Carolina slave who became a fugitive at age twenty-seven, told a story that brilliantly deconstructs the meaning of the female slave experience in relationship to that of her male counterpart and the white world around her. The literary prowess she displayed in her careful delineation of the sexual harassment she suffered from her owner, her masterly circumvention of his intentions toward her, her patience and determination to free herself and her children, and her understanding of the differences between psychological and physical freedom make her tale a female classic. As an early narrative by a black woman, one of the most significant contributions that *Incidents* makes to the history is its identification of the existence of and effectiveness of a woman's community in which black and white, slave and free women sometimes joined forces to thwart the brutal plans of masters against helpless slave women. In Harriet Wilson's *Our Nig*, the cruel stepmother of the fairy-tale convention is replaced by the cruel mistress and her equally cruel daughter, while the men in the story, sympathetic to Frado, are ineffective against the wickedness of the female members of their family. On the contrary, Jacobs, who hides in the crawl-space of her grandmother's house for seven years, in real life, is assisted in this effort by a number of women until she can safely escape. Similarly, other black women's slave narratives pay tribute to the roles that women play as models and inspiration in their struggle to rise above oppression. The "sisterhood" of black women and the peculiarity of relations between black and white women that appears in later black women's literature were already well documented in the black female slave narrative tradition.

If the slave narrative as a genre revised the concept of the American self, then, as a separate body of work, the narratives written by slave women are especially important for their revisionist elements in relationship to the narratives of ex-slave men and the American female experience in the autobiographical accounts of white women. We are indebted to Frances Foster's study, " 'In Respect to Females. . .': Differences in the Portrayals of Women by Male and Female Narrators," for alerting us to the implications of gender in slave narratives a few years ago.[2] Of necessity, the experiences of white women in the age of the "cult of true womanhood" were very separate from those of black slave women, but slave men and women also had different perceptions of their common condition. In the narratives of ex-slave men, for instance, slave women appear completely helpless and fully exploited. Much of this is identified as the result of their sexual vulnerability, and the women are pictured as victims without recourse to means of protecting or of defending themselves. Images of these women on auction blocks, stripped to their waists, their children having been sold away from them—all because of the licentiousness of their masters—are among those that abound in the literature. In Douglass's narrative for instance, he is painstaking in his descriptions of the beatings slave women were often given. His accounts of the sounds of the whips against their flesh and the flow of the blood from their backs are graphic. On the other hand, in telling their own stories, ex-slave women did not concentrate on the sexual exploitation they suffered. They did not deny it, but they made it clear that there were other elements in their lives which were important to them as well. In short, they saw themselves as more than victims of rape and seduction. As Foster points out, when they wrote, they not only wanted to witness to the atrocities of slavery, but also to celebrate their hard-won escapes. Their stories show them to be strong, courageous, dignified, and spirited in spite of the world in which they were forced to live. They depicted themselves as complex human beings with a desire to engage in discourse that took the breadth of their experiences into consideration. In writing, they were no longer secondary characters in someone else's script, but heroines in their own creations. As noted earlier, these black women writers focused less on individual performance and more on the positive roles that engaged women. They allotted time to the value of family relationships, not only to beatings and mutilations by slave masters. As they related their stories, ex-slave women took control of their narratives in much the same way as they took control of the circumstances that enabled them to survive and escape captivity.

Jacobs's narrative provides a good example of this mode. While she tells us of her dilemma with her master, the focus of *Incidents* is largely on her attempts to become free and to free her children. She demonstrates that she had power over her master while she was concealed in her grandmother's house, and she used this power to lead him to believe that she had left the state. She further tells us of her success in finding employment after her escape, and of the happy union she had with her children in the North. Her self-confidence was never destroyed by the abuses of slavery, and her self-esteem remained strong through the difficulties of her escape. Taking up where Foster left off, other critics have noted, from textual evidence in *Incidents*, how well Jacobs understood the meaning of freedom in her dealings with northern whites, especially in her contacts with women. Associated with both the feminist and abolitionist movements, she analyzed her situation and wrote perceptively of the racism of white feminists. Like Wilson, she made use of the sentimental tradition in women's fiction, but skillfully subverted that tradition for her own purposes. It is interesting that both Wilson and Jacobs rejected the convention of marriage and the happy ending of popular white female fiction. There are several less fully developed ex-slave women narratives, but all are equally confirming in their assertion of the positive identity of their authors. Among them we have Elizabeth Keckley, a seamstress who later made a successful living by tending the wardrobes of presidential first ladies in Washington; Susie King Taylor, a woman of many talents, from laundress to schoolteacher; and Amanda Berry Smith, a preacher. All wrote, not only to expose the evils that had been done to them, but also to demonstrate their abilities to gain physical and psychological liberty by transcending those evils.

The poetry, fiction, and nonfiction prose of black women to come out of the latter part of the nineteenth century wage open warfare against racism and gender oppression, on one hand, and on the other, encourage and castigate blacks in an effort to promote the "uplift" of the race. As other critics have often noted, the novels by black men and women with the mulatto heroine were often an appeal to whites for the elimination of atrocities, based on racial prejudices, against blacks, especially in the face of the evidences of the extent of blood co-mingling between the races. Barbara Christian has done an excellent exploration of the range of the intentions of Frances Watkins Harper, for instance, who was responsible for the publication of some eleven volumes of poetry, religious in tone and mainly directed toward the less fortunate, in her effort to "make songs for the people," who spoke out and wrote overtly scathing essays against white racism and sexism. She wrote a novel as well, *Iola LeRoy, Shadows Uplifted* (1892), with a mulatta heroine who revises this type of protagonist as s/he appears in novels such as William Wells Brown's *Clotel; or The President's Daughter* (1853). Unlike the tragic character whom Brown and others portray, Harper's heroine, given a chance to escape from her race, chooses to marry an Afro-American and dedicate her life to helping unfortunate black people. Anna Julia Cooper, who wrote no fiction, used didactic prose in *A Voice from the South: By a Black Women of the South*, not only to admonish white Americans for their injustices against other Americans, but to celebrate the achievements of black women and to sternly reproach the shortcomings of black men, particularly when those failings diminished the value of what black women strove to achieve.

A much neglected black female voice that spans the period between the end of the nineteenth century and the activities of the Harlem Renaissance of the 1920s is that of Alice Dunbar Nelson, who for a short time was married to the famous Paul Laurence Dunbar. Her importance to the history of Afro-American letters continues to be eclipsed by his. But the recent publication of Dunbar Nelson's diary, *Give Us Each Day, The Diary of Alice Dunbar-Nelson*, edited by Gloria Hull, has added an important work to the corpus of black women's writings. While twentieth-century black women's autobiographies have often proved to be frustrating documents because of their lack of openness, and the tendency of the authors to avoid private disclosures, this diary reveals the side of Dunbar Nelson that would otherwise remain unknown to the world. Dunbar Nelson, who was born in 1875 and died in 1935, like many of the writers of that era, was middle-class, educated, and highly sophisticated, a journalist as well as short-story writer, dramatist, and poet. In the ease with which she handled more than one literary form, she belongs to a group that includes women like Georgia Johnson and Angelina Grimké, both poets and dramatists, whose pens made known that black women were not only involved with the practical problems of education and economics for black people, but also with the creation of art and literature. Most of these women earned a living by teaching, the only respectable profession that was open to them, but one that was also in line with their ideas of service to others. Especially as dramatists, Dunbar Nelson, Johnson, and Grimké addressed many of the social problems facing the black community, and agitated for changes to alter them. Racism of all kinds, including lynching, were topics of their plays, and these women went as far as to take up the issue of poor women and the need for birth control education in the struggle against poverty and ignorance.

On the opposite side of the coin of achievement, from Dunbar Nelson's diary we learn some details of how women of her standing coped with many of the problems that confronted them in their private lives, away from the long days and busy schedules which make their histories as impressive as they are. Space does not permit an accounting of the financial difficulties which she faced for almost all of her life, or the strength and creativity she put into protecting her public image from the chaos of her private world. Suffice it to say that she worried a great deal over an accumulation of debts; that a fear of bouncing checks is one of the themes in the book; and that she was a woman who could pawn her jewelry to pay her water bill, and go immediately from that second task to address a meeting of wives of professional white men, dressed like a "certified check." From the diary too, there is further confirmation of the strength of the women's community which female slave narrators introduced into the literature. Not only did Dunbar Nelson live in a family in which women were pre-eminent, regardless of the men who entered their lives at different times, but her world outside of her family was peopled by women like Mary McLeod Bethune and Nannie Burroughs, famous educators, in addition to the Club Women and the writers and artists of her time.

Dunbar Nelson and the women who appear in her diary are complex figures who do not fit the stereotypes of black women of their day in the literature of others. They were exciting and strong, but they were also very human in the ways in which they responded to experience. They worked, laughed, loved, cried, and survived because they were tough-minded and respected themselves and others. They transgressed the boundaries of the expectations of women in that day, and created themselves in their own images. In respect to what she discloses of their private lives, Dunbar Nelson's diary is extremely important in the process of the revision of the literary images of ambitious upwardly mobile black women of the early part of the century.

The 1920s were the years in which black culture flourished as it has not done before in America, and the center of the activity was in Harlem, New York City. Following on the heels of the large black migration from a rural to an urban environment that began early in the century, and an increase in the West Indian and African populations in the country, the artistic and scholarly communities, as a group, set themselves to the task of defining the black experience in as positive a way as they could. It is now common knowledge that Jessie Fauset, black woman poet and novelist, in her role as W. E. B. DuBois's assistant at the *Crisis* (one of the most important journals of the time), was instrumental in bringing all of the important writers of the period into public view. In addition, Fauset was the only member of the group to publish three novels between the early 1920s and early 1930s. She, along with Nella Larsen, author of two novels in the late 1920s, have received less attention as writers than their male counterparts because of a perception that their works belong to the genteel tradition of the novel of manners. That condition is moving toward rapid change, however, as contemporary black women critics re-evaluate the writings of women before the 1960s; as cooperative publishers make out-of-print texts available for classroom use; and teachers and professors in Women's Studies and Afro-American and other literature courses make use of them.

Not all the women who came of age in the 1920s or who were associated with the Harlem Renaissance emerged then or did their best work in that period. Dorothy West, novelist, short fiction writer, and journalist, and Pauli Murray, family chronicler, poet, and civil rights activist were young women attracted to the verve of the cultural movement, but whose work appeared later in the 1930s and 1940s. The most illustrious of the women in the later-blooming group to have had an association with the Renaissance was Zora Neale Hurston. In the early 1970s, her work was re-discovered and it did more than any single writer's work to mobilize the energy of contemporary black women critics. Hurston arrived in New York from Florida by way of Baltimore and Washington, D.C., in 1925, after having won a prize for short fiction published in *Opportunity* magazine. Before her mature work in the 1930s and 1940s she continued to write short stories, earned herself a degree in anthropology from Columbia University, did fieldwork in the South and the West Indies, and was a colorful figure among the Harlem literati. In her time she received only minor praise for her work, and long before her death in 1960 she was forgotten by most of the literary world and derided by those who remembered her. In the early 1970s, her now-acclaimed novel, *Their Eyes Were Watching God* (1937), retrieved her name from oblivion and set the wheels rolling for the new black feminist criticism of the 1970s and 1980s. In relationship to black literature until then, this novel turned aside from the literature of protest against racism and racial discrimination to explore the inner dynamics of black culture, and to introduce, as heroine, the ordinary, uneducated black woman in search of a self-defined identity. Taking place almost entirely within the black community, *Their Eyes* explores primal relations between black men and women as they had never been done before. Here are rural people without concern for "social uplift," but whose lives are rich with a heritage that has fostered black survival for generations. Janie, her central character, is the first black feminist heroine in the fictional canon. At the same time, the folklore in all of her books makes Hurston's work an important source of information far beyond the boundaries of literature. Unfortunately, her other works have often been adjudged "lesser" than *Their Eyes*, even by her most ardent supporters. This too is a judgment that may well be revised in the near future, as at least one other novel of hers, *Moses, Man of the Mountain* (1939), a black folk rendition of the biblical myth, has finally begun to attract critical attention. Her autobiography, *Dust Tracks on a Road*, is a problematical text from the point of view of its concealments and evasions. But again, new studies in black women's autobiographies suggest that such concealments are a prominent convention in the tradition. As black women's autobiography stands, Hurston may not be the exception most people now think she is. However, had she written nothing of importance other than *Their Eyes Were Watching God*, her place in history would still be fully assured. She did indeed change the nature of the black female heroine in American literature.

From the end of the nineteenth century through the conclusion of the 1940s, the women mentioned above were among those who produced works that were representative of the kinds of writings that black women were engaged in for the first part of the century. Although, except for rare exceptions, they never received the public recognition they deserved, they wrote. They were ambitious, versatile in what they could do, and very productive. As nineteenth-century black women writers had done before them, they continued to explore racism and gender oppression in their writings, especially in fiction and autobiography. Because they were working within the black tradition of protest against white racism, they handled this issue more overtly than they tended to do with gender oppression, especially as that existed within the black community. Since most of these writers were members of the intellectual middle class as well, they also gave a good deal of attention to the "progress" of black people as a whole, an idea that tended to place white middle-class values in a position of superiority in relationship to values inherent in Afro-American culture. In the autobiographical literature of the period the emphasis was on the level of achievement women had made in education and economic independence, although many narratives focused on the ways in which these women worked to "elevate" young women and children, mainly by rescuing them from lives of poverty and immorality and leading them to paths of industry and morality. Hurston, as noted above, unlike many of the writers in her time, deviated from popular black trends and looked backwards to the black folk culture for the materials of her art. As a result, she often incurred the anger of her peers, who felt that her stance in applauding the inner vitality of that culture and her lack of attention to the deprivations of racism worked at cross purposes to their goals. They felt that her position undermined their efforts to force social change since it diluted their efforts to present a united front in confronting the white world.

Between 1940 and the beginning of the 1960s there was a good deal of creative activity on the part of black women writers. In 1949 Gwendolyn Brooks received the Pulitzer Prize for poetry, and became the first black American to be so honored. Brooks, whose work began appearing in 1945, continues to be a poet with enormous energy. Her excursions away from poetry produced a novel, *Maud Martha*, in 1953, and an autobiographical narrative that resembles a prose poem, *Report From Part One*, in 1972. Brooks's work, until 1970, though highly stylized, turned to face the plight of urban blacks in her home city of Chicago. Life on the segregated South Side, with its many disadvantages, was the subject of her prize-winning poetry. Her poetry did for blacks in this urban ghetto what Langston Hughes had earlier done for their counterparts in Harlem. In her novel she examined the inner thoughts of a young woman who is not pretty by conventional standards, or dynamic, or specially gifted, but who has the confidence in herself to seek her happiness. Since 1970, Brooks's work has taken on a decided black militant posture.

A number of other writers made important contributions to the literature of black women during these decades. Particularly deserving of special mention are Margaret Alexander Walker, another prize-winning novelist and poet; Adrienne Kennedy, playwright; Alice Childress, playwright and fiction writer; and Ann Petry, journalist, short-story writer, and author of three novels. After some years of neglect, Petry is experiencing a return to acclaim with the 1985 re-publication of her most well-known work, *The Street*, originally issued in 1943. In this novel, written in the naturalistic mode, the heroine, Lutie Johnson, bright, beautiful, ambitious, hard-working, and a single mother, is defeated by the hostile environment of the ghetto, represented by a Harlem street. In choosing to use the conventions that she did, Petry creates a character who, unlike most black women's heroines, is alienated from all the support systems available to poor black people: the church, extended family, and a network of friends. Other works of the period emphasize the distressing results of racism on black life, but most demonstrate that survival is possible when their protagonists make use of black support institutions. Especially missing in this novel is the community of women that had for so long been a mainstay in the conventions of black women's fiction.

The 1950s ended on a note of great promise for black American women writers, and in spite of the politics of white racism and of gender, and the sexism of many black men, the rising tide of the Civil Rights Movement was helpful to many of these writers. While Lorraine Hansberry's play received the most outstanding acclaim of all in 1959, there were other women who came to public view with less fanfare, but who were of no less importance to the tradition. One such was Paule Marshall, whose novel, *Brown Girl, Brownstones*, was the first black narrative to probe the sensibilities of an American-born adolescent girl of West Indian parents. Marshall, since then, has built her literary career around the interconnections blacks of West Indian heritage feel with white western civilization in the United States. For although most of the Islands were colonized by different European countries, African residuals remained stronger in them than among American blacks, largely because the populations in the islands contained a majority of African descendants. In her second novel, *The Chosen Place, The Timeless People*, published a decade after *Brown Girl*, Marshall's heroine is a West Indian woman who, after several years of living in England, returns to her island home to battle the ills of imperialism there. In *Praise Song For the Widow*, her 1983 work, she examines the recovery of "roots" by a middle-aged West Indian American woman on a journey back to her West Indian past. This is a theme that Marshall, a first-generation American with a West Indian background, seems to find fruitful to pursue. Between her novels she has produced a number of short stories as well, most of them with some "island" flavor.

Writers like Gwendolyn Brooks, Margaret Walker, Alice Childress, Paule Marshall, and Ann Petry continue to be productive in the 1980s. Within the last three decades, however, a remarkable number of new writers have joined their company, many of whom have produced an astonishing volume of writings. Those of us who have been privileged to follow the careers of writers Toni Morrison, whose first novel was *The Bluest Eye* (1970), Alice Walker, since her novel *The Third Life of Grange Copeland* (1970), and Maya Angelou, whose first volume of autobiography was called *I Know Why the Caged Bird Sings* (1970), are aware of how large the output has been in a short time. All of these women have produced multiple volumes of fiction, poetry, autobiography, and essays. Even the newest writers to emerge, like Ntozake Shange and Gloria Naylor, who did not publish until the beginning of the 1980s, have been prolific.

The literature of black women of the 1960s, 1970s, and 1980s follows in the tradition of the earlier times, but is also very different from what went before. Previously, in the slave narrative tradition and the fiction, autobiography, and drama, black women worked hard to debunk the negative stereotypes that other writers had imposed on them. In some instances what they produced were counterstereotypes that depicted black women as strong, and always overcoming hardships. The writers of the present generation see no need to perpetuate only those images, and are now exploring all aspects of black women's experiences—their weaknesses and failings, as well as their strengths and ability to transcend race and gender oppression. Writing from inside of their own experiences, and the knowledge of the experiences of black women for more than three hundred years in America, they examine the innate humanity of the characters they portray—characters who embody qualities that make them neither flawless heroines, immoral individuals, or helpless victims. A good example of this reconciliation of human traits shows up in Toni Morrison's first novel, in which a young black girl, driven insane in her quest for the white western ideal of female beauty—blue eyes—is balanced by the second black girl who understood and rejected the self-destructiveness inherent in a black woman's identifying with such an ideal. In like manner, the conflicts between black men and women that Alice Walker exposes in *Grange Copeland* and other novels are more than an accounting of how brutal some black men can be to their women, but rather a search for the roots of that brutality as a means toward reconciliation between the embattled sexes. Morrison, Walker, and dozens of other new black women writers are "prophets for a new day," in which black American women writers are demanding honor in their own country.

The hallmark of contemporary black women's writings is the impulse toward an honest, complicated, and varied expression of the meaning of the black woman's experiences in America. There is little effort to conceal the pain, and just as little to create the ideal, but a great deal to reveal how black women incorporate the negative and positive aspects of self and external reality into an identity that enables them to meet the challenges of the world in which they must live. Not all black women are strong and enduring, yet a core of resistance to emotional and physical oppression, and a will to discover the path to survival and beyond resides even in those works in which these women do not transcend. As I noted earlier, a long history of black women and the art-of-words exists, and the literature of black America, in its oral and written contexts, has been within the province of its women from the beginning of the American experience. The work of the writers has been ongoing, and has included every branch of the literary family. From the perceived utility of the slave narrative of ante-bellum days to the more highly crafted and sophisticated forms of the present time, black women have told their own stories both as a way of self-confirmation and a means of correcting the erroneous white and male record of their inner reality. Black women writers project a dynamic "I" into the canon, one that makes more complete the reality of the multi-faceted American experience.

NOTES

1. For a detailed but concise history of this stereotyping see Barbara Christian, *Black Women Novelists* (Westwood: Greenwood Press, 1980), 3–34.
2. Frances Foster, " 'In Respect to Females . . .': Differences in the Portrayals of Women by Male and Female Narrators," *Black American Literature Forum* 15, no. 2 (Summer 1981), 66–70.

SELECTED BIBLIOGRAPHY—BLACK WOMEN'S FICTION

Bambara, Toni Cade. *Gorilla, My Love*. New York: Vintage, 1972.
———. *The Salt Eaters*. New York: Vintage, 1980.
———. *The Sea Birds Are Still Alive*. New York: Vintage, 1977.
Brooks, Gwendolyn. *Maud Martha*. New York: Popular Library, 1953.
Butler, Octavia. *Clay's Ark*. New York: St. Martin's Press, 1984.
———. *Kindred*. New York: Simon & Schuster, 1979.
———. *Mind of My Mind*. New York: Doubleday, 1977.
———. *Patternmaster*. New York: Doubleday, 1976.
———. *Survivor*. New York: Doubleday, 1978.
———. *Wild Seed*. New York: Doubleday, 1980.
Chase-Ribound, Barbara. *Sally Hemings*. New York: Viking Press, 1979.
Childress, Alice. *Like One of the Family: Conversations from a Domestic's Life*. Brooklyn: Independence, 1956.
———. *A Short Walk*. New York: Coward, McCann & Geoghegan, 1979.
Cliff, Michele. *Abeng*. New York: The Crossing Press, 1984.
Fauset, Jessie Redmond. *The Chinaberry Tree*. New York: Frederick A. Stokes Co., 1931.

————. *Comedy, American Style.* New York: Frederick A. Stokes Co., 1932.

————. *Plum Bun.* New York: Frederick A. Stokes Co., 1927.

————. *There is Confusion.* New York: Boni & Liveright, 1924.

Guy, Rosa. *Bird at My Window.* Philadelphia: Lippincott, 1966.

————. *A Measure of Time.* New York: Holt, Rinehart, & Winston, 1983.

————. *Ruby.* New York: Viking Press, 1976.

Harper, Frances E. W. *Iola Leroy, or Shadows Uplifted.* Philadelphia: Garrigues Brothers, 1892.

Hopkins, Pauline Elizabeth. *Contending Forces: A Romance Illustrative of Negro Life, North and South.* Boston: Colored Co-Operative Publishing Co., 1900.

Hunter, Kristin. *God Bless the Child.* New York: Scribner's, 1964. Reprint, New York: Bantam, 1970.

————. *The Lakestown Rebellion.* New York: Scribner's, 1978.

————. *The Landlord.* New York: Scribner's, 1966. Reprint, New York: Avon, 1970.

————. *The Survivors.* New York: Scribner's, 1975.

Hurston, Zora Neale. *Jonah's Gourd Vine.* Philadelphia: Lippincott, 1934.

————. *Moses, Man of the Mountain.* Philadelphia: Lippincott, 1939.

————. *Mules and Men.* Philadelphia: J. P. Lippincott, 1935.

————. *Seraph on the Suwanee.* New York: Scribner's Sons, 1948.

————. *Tell My Horse.* 1938. Reprint, Berkeley: Turtle Island, 1981.

————. *Their Eyes Were Watching God.* Philadelphia: Lippincott, 1937.

Jones, Gayl. *Corregidora.* New York: Random House, 1975.

————. *Eva's Man.* New York: Random House, 1976.

————. *White Rat.* New York: Random House, 1977.

Kincaid, Jamaica. *Annie John.* New York: Farrar, Straus & Giroux, 1985.

————. *At the Bottom of the River.* New York: Farrar, Straus & Giroux, 1978.

Larsen, Nella. *Passing.* New York: A. Knopf, 1929.

————. *Quicksand.* New York: A. Knopf, 1928.

Lee, Andrea. *Sarah Phillips.* New York: Random House, 1984.

Marshall, Paule. *Brown Girl, Brownstones.* New York: Random House, 1959.

————. *The Chosen Place, The Timeless People.* New York: Harcourt Brace Jovanovich, 1969.

————. *Praise Song For the Widow.* New York: Putnam, 1983.

Meriwether, Louise M. *Daddy Was a Number Runner.* Englewood Cliffs, N.J.: Prentice-Hall, 1970. New York: Pyramid, 1971.

Morrison, Toni. *The Bluest Eye.* New York: Holt, Rinehart, Winston, 1970. Reprint, New York: Pocket Books, 1972.

————. *Song of Solomon.* New York: Knopf, 1977.

————. *Sula.* New York: Knopf, 1973.

————. *Tar Baby.* New York: Knopf, 1981.

Naylor, Gloria. *Linden Hills.* New York: Ticknor & Fields, 1985.

————. *The Women of Brewster Place.* Penguin Books, 1982.

Petry, Ann. *Country Place.* Boston: Houghton Mifflin Co., 1947.

————. *The Narrows.* Boston: Houghton Mifflin Co., 1953.

————. *The Street.* Boston: Houghton Mifflin Co., 1946.

Shange, Ntozake. *Betsy Brown.* New York: St. Martin's Press, 1985.

————. *Sassafrass, Cypress and Indigo.* New York: St. Martin's Press, 1982.

Shockley, Ann Allen. *The Black and the White of It.* Florida: Naiad Press, 1980.

————. *Loving Her.* New York: Avon, 1974.

————. *Say Jesus and Come to Me.* Avon, 1982.

Sutherland, Ellease. *Let the Lion Eat Straw.* New York: New American Library, 1979.

Walker, Alice. *The Color Purple.* New York: Harcourt Brace Jovanovich, 1982.

————. *In Love and Trouble.* New York: Harcourt Brace Jovanovich, 1973.

————. *Meridian.* New York: Harcourt Brace Jovanovich, 1976.

————. *The Third Life of Grange Copeland*. New York: Harcourt Brace Jovanovich, 1970.

————. *You Can't Keep a Good Woman Down*. New York: Harcourt Brace Jovanovich, 1981.

Walker, Margaret. *Jubilee*. Boston: Houghton Mifflin, 1966. Reprint, New York: Bantam, 1975.

West, Dorothy. *The Living Is Easy*. Boston: Houghton Mifflin Co., 1948.

Wilson, Harriet H. *Our Nig; or, Sketches from the Life of a Free Black in a Two-Story White House, North, Showing that Slavery's Shadows Fall Even There*. Boston: George C. Rand & Avery, 1859; 2nd edition, New York: Vintage Books, 1983.

Wright, Sarah. *This Child's Gonna Live*. New York: Delacorte, 1969. New York: Dell, 1971.

Paradigmatic Implications

RE-VIEWING THE IMPACT OF WOMEN'S STUDIES ON SOCIOLOGY

Jessie Bernard

Questions

Over twenty years ago I asked: "What, if any, is the effect on learning of the sex of the transmitter of human knowledge?" And what, I asked further, is the effect, if any, "of the sex of the innovator on the acceptance of ideas?" (Bernard, 1964, vii). I did not attempt to answer those questions.[1] No one had, so far as I knew, as yet researched them. But David Riesman was stimulated by the questions to wonder:

> whether, if women had a larger influence on . . . [scientific] work, other sorts of discoveries might not be made, other "laws" emphasized, and altered patterns of scientific and academic organization preferred or discovered. . . . It could be argued that it took a particular set of sex-role attitudes as well as specific religious and cultural values for Western science and technology to develop initially, although to continue the work, one might speculate as to whether a different pattern of attitudes might not be productive. (Bernard, 1964, xix-xx)

Right on! feminists began to say. To paraphrase Hamlet, "There are more things in heaven and earth, gentlemen, than are dreamt of in your sociology." These "things" were not merely things to dream about but realities to be confronted by way of women's studies.[2] And women researchers and scholars were soon to take them out of the dream world and render them visible. They were, in fact, to participte in what can only be called the Feminist Enlightenment.

Skipping lightly over that first great Enlightenment, the one in Eden, we may legitimately say that the current Enlightenment in the female world has come some two centuries after the great eighteenth-century Enlightenment in the male world. The fact that the history of the male world has differed from that of the female world has meant that periodization has not

always been synchronic for the two. Jane Tibbetts Schulenberg has, for
example, pointed out some of the divergences. She found that whereas in
the early Middle Ages the divergences were minimal, in late medieval
times they were pronounced (1979, 27). A silent revolution had occurred.
By the twelfth to fifteenth centuries women had dropped out of history or
were veneered over by chivalry. Schulenberg found that what was a Renaissance in the male world was far from that in the female world. It is not
surprising, therefore, to find that the Enlightenment in the male world
occurred in a different century from that in which it occurred in the female
world.

The Feminist Enlightenment began in the nineteen sixties and seventies
when it was occurring to a great many young women scholars that what
they had been learning did not reflect their own experience, that their
image of themselves was one created by the male world, that they were
looking at themselves and their history as defined by that world. That the
very weapon of the battle against ignorance—science—was shaped to answer the questions asked by the male world. They turned to academia for
help. And the academy—with varying degrees of alacrity—responded in
the form of Women's Studies. By the early seventies women were being
told that they had come a long way.

By that time the questions I had raised in 1964 and the answers suggested by Riesman had ceased to be minor issues in the social science and
behavioral disciplines. In the early seventies I, along with many others, was
challenging the sexist bias in sociology and asking if the feminist attempt to
re-orient the paradigms of the sociological canon could succeed. In 1973,
when Indiana University introduced its Women's Studies Program, feminists were asking for more than mere inclusion. What was being called for
was recognition of the important paradigm shift women's studies was
introducing.[3] And now, in the eighties, we are being asked to re-view the
impact of women's studies on the several disciplines, in my case, sociology.
How, in brief, have the 1964 questions been answered? What has been the
effect on the sex—gender—of the innovator and transmitter on the acceptance of ideas?

Some Answers

In terms of sheer numbers, the answer overall is quite positive. Catherine
R. Stimpson tells us that whereas in 1969 there had been only 16 women's
studies course syllabi, by 1982 there were some 20,000 courses and 450
certificate- or degree-granting programs in the United States (1983, 1).
Virginia J. Cyrus, national coordinator of the National Women's Studies

Association, reported in 1984 that 150 schools were giving bachelor's degrees in women's studies, 50 were giving master's degrees, and about a dozen, the doctorate. There were, in addition, no fewer than 30 centers for research about women.

As a result of all this activity, teaching resources had increased enormously. A great torrent of books, monographs, articles, papers, talks, discussions, and conference reports and proceedings had issued from the computers and the presses and had been supplying data and at least tentative paradigms for interpreting them. Khrushchev was once quoted as saying that in time the USSR would bury us. He later explained that he had not meant bury us beneath the rubble of bombs but beneath their superior productivity.[4] It is to be hoped that in time women's studies will have produced such a volume of work as to overwhelm, if not bury, research that persists in excluding consideration of the female world.[5]

It is not only numbers that have increased; attitudes also have become more positive. In 1969, Florence Howe tells us, "women's studies were a joke on campuses, where they had even been heard of" (1983, 1). This is no longer true. At least the most conspicuous forms of sexism are no longer de rigueur. Few students graduate without having at least heard of gender-based structural components of societies.

Another great plus of work done in women's studies has been the expansion of vision; it has helped us see more. In the eighties that is apparent to scholars in a variety of disciplines. As Walter Goodman, in an article on women's studies in the *New York Times Magazine,* wrote: "Young women . . . are coming in and dealing with subjects that men wouldn't think of." According to Goodman, Carl Degler, a historian, "credits the movement with drawing attention to new areas of investigation, along with encouraging new ways of thinking about old subjects," and Elizabeth K. Minnich, a philosopher, argues that the presence of women in her discipline has the effect of making it more productive and less abstract. Women, she believes, are "more interested in using the tools of philosophy to clarify issues of genuine human concern than to address esoteric problems of interest only to a small group of professional philosophers" (Goodman, 1984, 51).

A final plus has been the expansion of women's studies beyond the parochialism of the past; women's studies have more and more included women from all over the globe, not merely as objects of Western research but as researchers themselves. Women from all over the world who are interested in women's studies are participating in conferences where they meet one another, exchange experiences, teach one another about their worlds, and learn about the worlds of others. Not always lovingly but certainly effectively.

Still, the gains have not been unequivocal. True, there are women's studies courses and programs, but some women have wondered if they are not being sequestered and "ghettoized," much to the relief of the fogies, old or young, glad to be rid of the necessity to deal with the issues they raised. And some have feared that even when women's studies achieve recognition, it is limited in scope and that the significance of the new research, its ramifications throughout all the disciplines, is not being perceived, let alone appreciated.[6] So much, then, for overall trends. "The first flush of growth is ended, and women's studies has entered a testing time that will determine the place it will eventually occupy in America's colleges" (Goodman, 1984, 49).

I will limit my evaluation of the impact of feminist research to the sociology of knowledge, specifically the sociology of science. Although its impact on academic organization and policy or on the profession itself is not my major concern, I might note in passing that "only a handful of colleges have granted women's studies full-fledged departmental status, which means a budget, tenured positions, and a degree of control by the department's own faculty. . . . Ninety percent of the courses that fit somewhere into women's studies continue[d] to be taught by faculty members attached to traditional departments" (Goodman, 1984, 40). Still, when the American Sociological Association was confronted with evidence of discrimination against women in academia it responded by setting up the proper organizational machinery for dealing with it, an action which, of course, was by no means the same as implementing its recommendations. But at least it gave formal recognition to feminist charges of discrimination in academia.[7]

Infertile Discipline?

Catherine Stimpson, among the most knowledgeable students of women's studies, finds that sociology has contributed comparatively less innovative thinking to feminist scholarship and research than have other disciplines (1982). In 1985 Judith Stacey and Barrie Thorne were making the same charge. Is sociology too data-bound? Less free-wheeling and permissive than, let us say, the humanities? I look—most tentatively—rather, to the history of the discipline in the United States, especially to the damage done to it by the identity crisis it endured in the first two or three decades of this century and the concomitant struggle for academic acceptance and respectability it engaged in, a struggle that led it to dissociate itself as an academic discipline from feminist thinking and the activism of women, which was considered status-reducing at that time.

A Sociological Identity Crisis

In the first quarter of this century sociologists were having a hard time establishing the scientific identity of their discipline, their own turf as an independent area of knowledge. Like other social science disciplines it had emerged from "Social Science"—a strongly reformistic hodgepodge discipline of the nineteenth century (Bernard and Bernard, 1942), and it was having to compete with other outgrowths of that discipline for academic space (Bernard, 1926). It had an academic history somewhat similar to that of women's studies half a century later. It too had to challenge the knowledge establishment in order to achieve recognition. It too was looked down upon, charged with do-goodism, accused of lacking focus or rigor. It too was the ugly duckling among the more prestigious disciplines, considered a mere catch-all for all the "anomalies of fact"—Kuhn's term—recognized in the paradigms of the standard established disciplines. But it too found the reigning paradigms in the other social-science disciplines inadequate for dealing with what was actually happening in the modern world.

There was a long battle during the early years of the century over the appropriate contents of courses in sociology. One consistent trend was the decline in, or transformation of, any subject matter that could be called "practical" or "applied" or "political." Among the most prestigious universities this trend reflected an effort to distinguish sociology from its roots in Social Science. Sociologists wanted to dissociate their departments also from the popular conception of sociology as the study of social problems or, even worse, as something to do with socialism (Bernard, 1929). They sought also to achieve an identity uncontaminated by quacks who called themselves sociologists. The rapid growth of the study of sociology had created a great shortage of teachers. In such an academic market:

> Second-rate and half-trained men have in consequence filled important positions. As a result of the demand for men, sociology has tended to be a sort of happy hunting ground for well-meaning sentimentalists, plausible charlatans, and other worthy persons unwilling or unable to weather the rigorous discipline of real scholarship. (Lundberg, 1929, 417)

The elite wanted nothing to do with these sentimentalists:

> Unquestionably one of the principal obstacles which sociologists have to overcome is the widespread confusion of the subject with various *Weltverbesserung* cults. The sociologist is constantly besieged with reformers of every kind, who blandly claim him as a fellow-crusader. If he succeeds in eluding the socialist, the labor cohorts, and the single taxers, he is likely to be adopted by the eugenists, the clergy, or other religious enthusiasts. Most powerful of all are the onslaughts of the social worker who has gone wrong—

lost his soul in theorizing or, still worse, sold it to the baleful "interests". (418)

Although it had seemed in 1909 that sociology was making headway against the "Social-Science," reformistic strain in its ancestry (Bernard, 1929, 28),[8] at least a rearguard action was still being fought by it in the 1920s.

The relevance of these points is that in such low-status, practical or applied or reformistic or social-problem aspects of the subject women tended to be more highly represented than they were in the more prestigious theoretical aspects. The academic warriors were not defending themselves against women so much as against the stigma of do-goodism associated with their Social-Science roots, which in the prestigious institutions militated against coveted academic respectability.

With such a history of struggle for recognition of their special and unique contributions, one might have supposed that sociologists would be the most enthusiastic welcomers into the canon of women's studies, which was having the same kind of struggle. Actually, the same arguments were used against women's studies as had been used against sociology itself.

"Women's Studies" Then and Now

Perhaps we may some day have a dissertation tracing the place women have occupied in the evolving sociological curricula of colleges and universities, documenting their contribution as innovators as well as transmitters of knowledge.

Courses about, by, and for women have a long academic history. Two kinds were especially important, and both, like sociology itself as well as the other social sciences, had roots in the nineteenth-century discipline "Social Science." One was the home economics tradition and one the social-service tradition (Bernard, 1964, 242–50). Though almost diametrically opposite in orientation, both had what later came to be called, contemptuously, a "do-good" character. A comparison between the women who created these two outstanding professions is thought-provoking. Both groups were outstanding in background—science in the case of home economics, law and political science in social service—but the home economists were not only nonfeminist (Bernard, 1981, 401–402) but in some cases even antifeminist, whereas those in the social-service tradition were strongly feminist, in the then contemporary sense of women's rights, and activist.

The home economists had developed in the Land Grant colleges primarily, though not exclusively,[9] to serve the farmer's wife as the county agent served the farmer. The social-service branch developed largely in urban settings and dedicated its energies primarily though not exclusively to urban women. The pioneer home economists were outstanding scientists with degrees in science from top universities (MIT in the case of Ellen Swallow Richards), but they were not feminist in orientation.[10] The social-service branch was headed by similarly outstanding women. Sophonisba Breckinridge, for example, was a lawyer with two doctorates, one in political science and one in jurisprudence. The impact of each of these two streams of "women's studies" on sociology was different (understandably, in view of their differing perspectives), but academic sociology's treatment of the two was similar, leading as it did in both cases to their exclusion from the hallowed halls of academic sociology.

Case-in-Point: The Women in the Department of Sociology at the University of Chicago

The story of how the sociological establishment created "patterns of exclusion and participation" of women in the American Sociological Society (later Association) and edged women's studies, in its then-conceptualized form, out of the University of Chicago at a time when it was the pacesetter of the profession has been traced by Mary Jo Deegan (1978, 14–24). The chair of that bellwether department, Albion W. Small, was not wholly consistent in his thinking. He recognized that there were some women scholars whose training and qualifications were the equal of men's but he felt this was a transitory situation, even dysfunctional; women's place was in the home. He felt that inculcating competitve attitudes in women was like injecting poison, to be administered only as medicine (Deegan, 15). Still, he also believed that equal pay for equal work was only a matter of simple justice.

He hired women to teach household administration, sanitary science, social settlements, and statistics (15), his version presumably of proper women's studies. Among those he hired were a constellation of extraordinarily brilliant women associated at one time or another with Hull House: Jane Addams, Anna Garlin Spencer, Lucy Salmon, Emily Green Balch, Lillian Wald, Anne Talbot, Grace Abbott, Edith Abbott, Sophonisba Breckinridge, Julia Lathrop. These women were laying the groundwork, theoretical and practical, for the welfare state of the 1930s.

These women viewed themselves as sociologists, "but they were barred from the institutional affiliations that would legitimize their claims. In addition to this structural discrimination, the women also adhered to a different vision of sociology than that practiced today" (15). Their courses, though not modern women's studies, dealt with subjects legitimate for sociology departments including, for example, the legal and economic position of women, the breakdown of families under urban pressures, factory legislation dealing with women, women and labor unions, women in industry. Several of them were associated with the research being done at Hull House. That work had proved stimulating to the early giants at the University, including W. I. Thomas and R. E. Park.[11] But, as Deegan has shown, the women were shunted out of the Department of Sociology into Household Administration, which soon became part of the School of Social Service Administration under the leadership of Edith Abbott, one of these "unlicensed" sociologists. Their courses were never restored (Deegan, 1978, 19). Small's discipline was thus purged of what he thought of as non-sociological women's stuff and saved from having to bestow academic recognition on it.

There were doubtless numerous reasons why the sociology department at the University of Chicago was so persistent and insistent on separating itself from the courses of such distinguished women, reasons related to the identity crisis sociology was going through. It had to prove itself just as value-free, just as macho, non-emotional, and impersonal as the physical and biological sciences or, even, the other social sciences were. It was demeaning to be reform-oriented as these activist women were.[12] The courses of these women were obstacles to recognition of the academic credentials of sociology. In their own place they were, of course, tolerable. As a matter of fact, outstanding. But their place was not in sociology departments.[13]

Not that there were not serious theoretical issues involved in this purging of the women. The whole issue of "value-free" sociology, for example. What was sociology all about, anyway? It was, of course, impossible to banish do-goodism in one form or another from the discipline altogether. The issue kept coming up.[14] It insinuated itself under a number of guises. "Social Problems" might turn into "Social Disorganization," but it could not so easily expunge its values. The issue led later to the splitting off of the Society for the Study of Social Problems. Evaluation research, policy research, and clinical sociology have become respectable terms. So the battle the department at Chicago was fighting was not simply over a gender issue. And it did, finally, learn how to "sociologize" its applied, practical, reformistic roots to render them academically respectable.[15]

Much of this is by now ancient history. Six decades later women's studies had been re-conceptualized. It still included a rich legacy of subject matter created by home economists and social workers. But it had changed drastically; it had become feminist in a new style. Until now most of the research by and about women had been under the guidance of male-created paradigms which led to questions, methods, findings, and interpretations as defined by men. Women's studies has now become feminist scholarship.

Transformation

Catherine R. Stimpson has traced this transformation:

> Since 1969, feminist scholarship has sought to reconceptualize reality to generate a large body of new ideas in a sweeping enterprise. Out of this endeavor have come four overarching theories that have helped us reconceptualize the world. They may seem self-evident today, but in 1969 it was a different story.
>
> 1. The study of women is important. Women are a group, a class, even a caste. To study women is to illuminate "sex/gender systems" or "sex/gender arrangements". . . .
>
> 2. Such a thing as "sexism" exists. Sexism is institutionalized discrimination against women. It applies to structures that make women secondary, marginal, second-class, and comparatively powerless.
>
> 3. The world may be conceptualized as two subworlds, male and female. . . .
>
> 4. There is a need to understand sexual difference (if possible)—its nature, cause, and meaning. At the risk of oversimplification: "minimalists" believe that history, economics, and culture mostly create sex differences, while "maximalists" believe that sex differences are profound, a-historical. (1983, 1–2)

1. *"The study of women is important."* It should be said that early in the century an eloquent statement of the importance of including women and their potential contribution to the sociological profession and canon had been made by the first president of the American Sociological Society [later Association], Lester Frank Ward (1843–1913). His name has all but disappeared from the literature of the discipline, despite his biographer's belief that his work was "a prelude to the feminist movement which his writings initiated in America" and that its "attack with the aid of all the sciences upon the universal fallacy of woman's place in the sun, opened the road to her emancipation" (Chugerman, 1939, 378). Chugerman himself, as Ward's biographer, invalidates this enthusiastic encomium. Ward's work did not initiate the feminist movement nor did it open the road to women's emancipation. Indeed, "what his sex theory needed most was just a hearing" (379). Instead, Ward's view was vehemently attacked and denied. "Only a small band of disciples who founded the suffragette movement accepted the theory, but to this day [1939] it is looked upon askance by all respectable and conservative folk" (379).[16]

Although Ward's theories about women were not widely accepted, it is worthwhile to glance briefly at them. He contrasted the prevailing andro-centric view of male superiority with a gynecocentric view of the natural superiority of women, emphasizing the deprivation society suffered by not using half of the world's talents:

> One great factor . . . has been omitted by nearly all who have discussed these questions [the quantity and quality of the talent resources of the world]. This factor is nothing less than exactly one half of the human race, viz., womankind. Galton's point of view is of course exclusively andro-centric. . . . DeCandolle devotes nearly two of the 576 pages of his book to "Women and Scientific Progress," but no woman had ever been admitted to any of the great academies of which he treats. Jacoby's list may contain the names of some women. It would be profitless to search for them. M. Odin is the only one who has seen that the true cause of the small literary fecundity of women has been their almost complete lack of opportunity. He shows that where they have really enjoyed any opportunity they have done their share. . . . The universal prevalence of the androcentric world view, shared by men and women alike, acts as a wet blanket on all the genial fire of the female sex. Let this be once removed and woman's true relation to society be generally perceived, and all this will be changed. (Ward, 1906, 231–32)

He goes on to make the same point Riesman was to make more than six decades later. Liberating women would do more than double talent re-sources; it would lead to greater creativity, "for women will strike out according to their natural inclinations and cultivate fields that men would never have cultivated" (232), fields undreamt of in a male-defined heaven or earth.[17] Ward was eloquent not only about women's potential contribution to sociology but also about their potential contribution to civilization itself. His position might have seemed sexist in that it seemed to be based on demands on women. But he was also a staunch supporter of the political as well as the intellectual rights of women, anticipating an essentially an-drogynous equality. Sociology, then, in the early years of the century had at least one great proponent of women's studies. But sociology did not follow his lead.[18] It lost his orientation as the century progressed and it was not until the seventies that the discipline began to reclaim that early heritage.

2. *"Such a thing as 'sexism' exists."* "The scholars who played an outstand-ing role in the founding of sociology were *sexists* to a man," the Schwen-dingers tell us (1974, 290, emphasis in original). They base their conclusion on their analysis of the theoretical work of the early leaders. The discussion here rests on a humbler base, a brief glance at the history of sociology textbooks. And the kind of sexism referred to is the sexism of invisibility. Except in textbooks on marriage and the family (the main entree of women into the sociological curriculum), little space was devoted to women or the world they lived in. And even in marriage and family textbooks the per-spective on women fluctuated; it was not always unbiased.

The year 1920 seems to have been the end of an era in these books. Women had achieved the vote; that, it was assumed, would end the women's movement. Any remaining issues would soon disappear. Feminism per se ceased to be a topic for discussion;[19] when the women's movement did appear, it was dealt with primarily as history. A 1934 text devoted little more than a page to the subject, noting that although discrimination against women still persisted, there were now ways of dealing with it such as the League of Women Voters and the National Women's Party (Groves, 1934). But almost a decade later, J. K. Folsom was seeing an ominous change in general attitudes toward women:

> During the 1930s there were many subtle ideological influences working against the democratic trend in the relation between the sexes. The idea was widely expressed that women have gone far enough toward equality and some have held that the situation is now unfair to men. (1943, 622)

And he asked why it was always "the women who are 'on the carpet'?"

A decade later Ray E. Baber, despite strong disclaimers, was bearing down hard on a negative note. "It is only fair to say that the discontent of many women is largely of their own making. One reason why some women are not contented with their work at home is that they are not doing it well" (1953, 389). And: "after reading the hot debates of women writers on the proper role of women, one is tempted to make at least one generalization—that modern women want to keep their cake and eat it too" (377). He cites the "petulant complaint" of a feminist leader and quotes a "class-conscious tirade" of another (379). And so on. Be reasonable, ladies. You've come a long way. What more do you expect? Equality?! Forget it. "It is doubtful whether absolute equality . . . can be attained" (377) and anyway, it's doubtful if most women want it.

In 1961, William Kephart was more generous. Unquestionably women were entitled to the same rights as those men were entitled to. Still there was, after all, a limit of the number of anti-family changes, including economic freedom, that a society could permit and still remain stable. He did not know the final solution but one thing that could be done was to improve the status of the homemaker (241). In 1963, at the beginning of the current feminist renaissance, Ruth Cavan noted that women had achieved numerous rights in the recent past but in the process many feminists had become embittered, hostile in their attitudes toward men as persons. Bitter sex antagonism characterized the relationship between men and women. To the extent that this antagonism was carried over into marriage it tended to pit husband and wife against each other and to create opposition rather than cooperation (1963, 516). Conversely, Talcott Parsons noted, apparently with approval, that segregation of sex roles—the male's being occupational and the female's, domestic—was functionally important because it shielded spouses from competition with each other (1959, 265).

This, in brief, was the none-too-sympathetic tradition women's studies had to buck in sociology as the sixties began. Women had become too uppity. As long as women had known their academic place as defined by men and had remained as invisible as possible, sociology had been able to find an inconspicuous corner for them, often in the study of the family if not elsewhere.

3. *"The world may be conceptualized as two subworlds, male and female."* The concept of "women's sphere" was an old nineteenth-century "control myth," to borrow a term from Jean Lipman-Blumen (1984). It referred to a world of sweetness and light in which women performed their supporting roles with tenderness and love (Bernard, 1981, passim). Sociology had relatively little to say about that world. It assumed that the research, analyses, and interpretations sociologists provided applied to both the male and the female worlds. The ideas that there were unique issues in the female world, that a discipline purporting to encompass all of society could not legitimately base itself on only its male component, that there was, as a matter of fact, anything of significance besides that component did not seem to occur to even the most thoughtful sociologists.

It has not been until relatively recently that any of the social science disciplines have come to recognize the inadequacy of many of their para- digms for female experience.[20] Only little by little is it dawning on the more perceptive male sociologists that their approach to the study of society has serious flaws, that they have been overlooking a large part of it. Now one of them suggests that "a project on how women have been left out of so- ciology (that it's the study of male social life) makes a lot of sense. More and more is coming to light on this" (personal letter).

4. *"There is a need to understand sexual difference. . . ."* Despite a long research tradition, Stimpson's fourth point still calls for clarification. W. I. Thomas, one of the early giants in sociology, had done his dissertation on metabolic differences between the sexes and early in the century wrote *Sex and Society* (1907). "Although he viewed the behavioral differences between the sexes as a function of both internal (organic) and external (sociocultural) conditions, he followed the practice of his time by giving some primacy to the organic factors" (Volkhart, 1968, 16:2). The traditional textbooks in sociology did not make a great deal of sex differences; the great "nature- nurture" issue was more likely to focus on race and ethnicity. For the most part the differences that were dealt with were male-defined and evaluated by male criteria, with the effect, if not the intention, of picturing females as inferior so that they seemed to be ersatz men and, by inference, not suitable for certain kinds of activities.

Leona Tyler has traced several shifts in emphasis in the research on sex differences; feminists had considerable impact on it. "At the beginning, the feminist movement generated interest in the question of whether the *intelligence* of women was or was not equal to that of men. What most investigators hoped to find was scientific evidence for the [*intellectual*] equality of the sexes" (1968, 7:207).[21] Later, attention was turned to measures of masculinity and feminity and, still later, to societal roles and how children are socialized into them (208). Women's studies has tended to select different characteristics to research and to evaluate differences according to different criteria, noting that differences did not necessarily mean inferiority except perhaps on male turf in male games.

Especially relevant is the distinction increasingly being made between sex and gender, the first referring primarily to genetic characteristics and the second, to characteristics built on genetic differences (Bernard, 1971). There are, thus, two kinds of differences between males and females, one being categorical, a matter of either-or (with rare anomalous exceptions), and the other distributional, a matter of more-or-less, with varying degrees of overlap. Women's studies notes that there is a tendency to reduce distributional differences to categorical ones by reporting them in terms of averages, thus underplaying the degree of overlap in the two distributions. Instead of reporting results as "men are *yyy*" and "women are *xxx*", the suggestion is that they should be reported as "more men than women are *yyy*" and "more women than men are *xxx*." This makes room for the women who are more *yyy* than the average man and the men who are more *xxx* than the average woman.

Stimpson had made a distinction between students who were "minimalists" and those who were "maximalists," the first tending to underplay sexual differences because they had been used as evidence of female inferiority and the others to emphasize them, arguing "Vive la différence!" Judith Lorber has analyzed the strategic pros and cons of each position (1981), concluding that although "feminism's goal is logically a gender-free minimalist society . . . in the immediate future, some organizations, coalitions, and networks will have to be all or predominantly female maximalist in order to build up . . . power" (64).[22] A considerable body of psychological research, primarily on student populations, had shown eight differences to be unsupported; four, fairly well established; and seven, ambiguous or questionable (Maccoby and Jacklin, 1974). In 1986 Lorber pointed out that achieving equity between the sexes called for a minimalizing policy, a "dismantling of Noah's ark" which was organized on a gender basis. She specified how such a policy could be implemented for the achievement of a social order without a gender base. Her analysis carries minimalization "to the max." She concedes that such an order would call for careful monitoring for there are too many people, female as well as male, who shout "long live the differences." As yet these concerns of women's studies have not had serious impact on sociology. There is a considerable amount of resistance to minimalization.

Resistance

Despite the figures cited at the beginning of this chapter, "considerable numbers of academics continue to view the whole idea [of women's studies] with suspicion, disdain, or indifference. To them, women's studies presents a low order of scholarly endeavor—'safe,' 'biassed,' 'smacking of a party line and a further 'politicization' of the university" (Goodman, 1984, 39).[23] It was surprising how many reasons faculties could find for rejecting or resisting women's studies. The simplest was to ignore it as trendy, a passing fad that would soon, mercifully, fade away. Or cavalierly to read it out of the canon. Or to deny its premises. Or to denigrate it as too narrow in scope. Or see no need for it; sociology did include women and their world; sex had always been one of its major variables; it did take full account of sexual differences; that was all that was needed. So there was no problem of invisibility. There was neither need nor room for women's studies in sociology departments. It wasn't sociology anyway. It was too political.[24]

Two arguments used against the subject were that it was not truly a discipline and that even if it were, its methodology was suspect. "Does it constitute, at least potentially, an academic discipline with a unique methodology?" (Goodman, 50). And Dean Richard P. Taub of the University of Chicago answered the question with a categorical negative: "Women's studies is not a discipline" (40). A sociologist who requested that his name not be used concluded that "there is no logic in intellectual life for singling out any group as a separate discipline" (40). Then, perhaps a sub-discipline? as, for example, *educational* psychology? *labor* economics? *cultural* anthropology? *female* sociology?

Equally challenging has been the question of methodology. Researchers in the field of women's studies have argued for intuition and experience as well as the standard traditional methods of research (50).[25] But "scholars who prize objectivity are put off by some of the research methods being advanced by theoreticians of the women's studies movement" (50). They question the reliability of such research.

Less likely to be verbalized was the argument that women's studies was irrelevant to male concerns or, if relevant, shrill and foolish. W. J. Goode has stated the irrelevant perspective precisely:

> [T]o most men what is happening seems to be "out there" and has little direct effect on their own roles. To them the women's movement is a dialogue mainly among women, conferences of women about women, a mixture of just or exaggerated complaints and shrill and foolish demands to which men need not even respond except now and then [1982, 131]. . . . Men are often simply less motivated to observe carefully many aspects of women's behavior and activity because women's behavior does not usually affect what men propose to do. (137)

The world of knowledge has been a male world, a world created by and for men and dedicated to the problems that challenged them, seeking answers to questions that they wanted answers to. Their peers and competitors were men. The processes that operated in that male world to distribute rewards and penalties were geared to a male ethos. The knowledge that was pertinent to them was therefore about their—male—world. The relevance of women was in another realm of discourse. All the male world needed to know about females was how they related to men, not how their own world operated, not as autonomous human beings. In the male world, the knowledge garnered by women's studies was not only irrelevant but also trivial, tangential, off-beat, unimportant, with little theoretical power. Nothing much, therefore, was lost by omitting it.

Such parochial resistance to Women's Studies may be mollified if not reversed with the publication of a new professional journal, *Gender and Society*, which will make it harder and harder to ignore this rich vein of scholarship.

Once in a while relics of the old status-demeaning point of view surface, as when a one-time president of the American Sociological Association stated that men who studied the family—the one area most permissible for women—were "queer" (Davis, 1949, 393). The study of women was low-status stuff. Extending the curriculum to include more about women would be demeaning to the discipline. "Breaking and entering" such a male-oriented intellectual structure was obviously not going to be easy.

Aside from an unsympathetic tradition there were other, more personal explanations possible for foot-dragging, including sheer inertia. A teacher of social problems, let us say, who has accumulated a great pile of notes on the Marxist theory of poverty is not cheerfully going to substitute a pile of notes on the feminization of poverty. Nor is he cheerfully going to discard extensive notes on male criminology to add materials on wife abuse, child abuse, battered women, rape, sexual harassment. Nor are professors in the burgeoning field of medical sociology going to be eager to curtail the voluminous body of data on the profession from the physicians' perspective to make room for women's studies research that focuses on the female patient and medical mismanagement of her body or that traces the changes in the very practice of medicine—unnecessary removal of the uterus, radical mastectomies, over-tranquilization—that feminist research has highlighted. And students of marriage, family, and motherhood are not going to be happy about having to rework their notes at least every term if not every few weeks as women's studies research output grows. And professors of work are not going to be eager to add "work of the heart" (Hochschild, 1984) to their syllabi. In all these courses the teachers may finally resort to the easiest—and wrong—way to deal with the problem: they will "add women and stir." Or attach a separate section to their syllabus.

There may also be resentment involved in explaining the slow pace of incorporating women's studies in the sociological canon. Aside from the fact that, as Sally Slocum notes, "when women in colleges and universities are questioning the fundamental tenets of academic fields ranging from history and philosophy to the natural sciences," there is certain to be resentment among tenders of these fundamental tenets. "To suggest that disciplines need to be corrected—either in their ideas or methodology—is to challenge professors' sense that they understand the assumptions underlying their disciplines" (in Edward B. Fiske, 1981). In the interests of the discipline it may be a challenge worth meeting but the challenged honchoes are not likely to see it that way. Their prestige is on the line.

A paradigm shift, further, is bound to be painful for some members of a scientific community. The paradigm shift called for in acceptance of women's studies is analogous, though of course not identical, to the one Galileo introduced to his resisting peers. Sociology has been a discipline that has surveyed the society it studied from what its creators conceived of as its center, as the pre-Galileo astronomers had viewed the solar system. Of course the earth was, obviously, the center. Of course, as everyone could see, the sun and stars moved around it. There was no way to view the universe except from the earth's point of view. And it was clear that the heavens were oriented toward it. In a similar, though not identical way, sociologists have viewed their society from the part of it they experience. They have looked at non-males as, in effect, their satellites. As members of a men-only club might look through the window at those non-eligibles out there. It could be as shocking to be told that there were other ways of looking at a society as to be told that the earth revolved around the sun, not the other way round.

The last explanation for ignore-ance, non-acceptance, rejection, or denigration of women's studies is even subtler than the others. It has to do with a crisis of conscience. In his analysis of this situation, Robert Merton, with his usual gift for neologisms, has given us two much-needed additions to our vocabulary, namely, "social sadism" and "sociological euphemisms."[26]

Social Sadism and Sociological Euphemisms

Merton introduces a quotation from Kenneth Clark's *Dark Ghetto* (1965):

> More privileged individuals may understandably need to shield them-
> selves from the inevitable conflict and pain which would result from accept-
> ance of the fact that they *are* accessories to profound injustice. The tendency
> to discuss disturbing social issues such as gender discrimination, segrega-
> tion, and economic exploitation in detached, legal, political, socio-economic,
> or psychological terms as if these persistent problems did not involve the
> suffering of actual human beings is so contrary to empirical evidence that it
> must be interpreted as a protective device. (75)

The terms used by researchers are sociological euphemisms, says Merton,
designed to protect those who use them from recognition of the suffering
they are causing, from their "social sadism."

> Social sadism is more than a metaphor. The term refers to social structures
> which are so organized as to systematically inflict pain, humiliation, suffer-
> ing, and deep frustration upon particular groups and strata. This need have
> nothing at all to do with the psychic propensities of individuals to find
> pleasure in cruelty. It is an objective, socially organized, and recurrent set of
> situations that has these cruel consequences, however diverse its historical
> sources and whatever the social processes that maintain it.
>
> This type of sadistic social structure is readily overlooked by a perspective
> that can be described as that of the sociological euphemism. This term does
> not refer to the obvious cases in which ideological support of the structure is
> simply couched in sociological language. Rather, it refers to the kind of
> conceptual apparatus that, once adopted, requires us to ignore such intense
> human experiences as pain, suffering, humiliation, and so on. In this con-
> text, analytically useful concepts such as social stratification, social exchange,
> reward system, dysfunction, symbolic interaction, etc., are altogether bland
> in the fairly precise sense of being unperturbing, suave, and soothing in
> effect. To say this is not to imply that the conceptual repertoire of sociology
> (or of any other social science) must be purged of such impersonal concepts
> and filled with sentiment-laden substitutes. But it should be noted that
> analytically useful as these impersonal concepts are for certain problems,
> they also serve to exclude from the attention of the social scientist the intense
> feelings of pain and suffering that are the experience of some people caught
> up in the social patterns under examination. By screening out these pro-
> foundly human experiences, they become sociological euphemisms. (1972,
> 38)

The euphemisms jettison a great deal of content; they make no provision
for assessing the individual costs or gains. It is, then, just a short step to
assume that:

the aspects of psychosocial reality which these concepts help us to understand are the only ones worth trying to understand. The ground is then
prepared for the next seemingly small but altogether conclusive step. The
social scientist sometimes comes to act as though the aspects of the reality
which are neglected in his analytical apparatus do not even exist. By that
route, even the most conscientious of social scientists are often led to transform their concepts and models into scientific euphemisms. (39)

The euphemistic scientist has thus erased a whole area of reality.

Women's studies for some time now has been unmasking these euphemisms, calling attention to the covered-up reality, seeking to replace them
and thus restore the missing parts. Women's studies calls, in effect, for re-
introduction of the blacked-out suffering.[27] There are battered wives, there
are abused children which such terms as "domestic violence" are too bland
to cover. Women's studies has also been showing sociologists that their
own definitions of research problems, their own presentations of results,
are subjective in the sense that they have rendered invisible a considerable
part of the situations they have dealt with. In brief, sociology has kept the
female world all but invisible because to recognize it in all its dimensions
would be unpleasant if not actually painful. They would then have to see
themselves as part of the oppression of the underdog. They would have
met the enemy and learned that it was them.

Overall, then, a re-viewing of the impact of women's studies on sociology
shows that it is not as weak as it was a decade ago but neither is it as strong
as we might have hoped it to be today. The half-filled glass, though not
empty, is far from full. Still, I have no doubts about the outcome. In time,
as Thomas Kuhn has pointed out, the paradigms and models—in the
present context, of women's studies research and scholarship—will over-
take, if not replace, the conventional ones of the received sociological
canon. The timing of this succession will depend on many trends in our
society, including the availability of jobs for those training in our discipline.[28] So I do not anticipate a specific time, a specific moment, when all
the most prestigious sociologists will suddenly experience the "click" or a
Pauline epiphany.

I believe, nevertheless, that most sociologists want their discipline to be
as good as it can be and that they are willing to incorporate into the canon
whatever is valuable. Interestingly, it is Robert Merton, one of the most
venerated of the sociologists of science today, who makes that case. In the
peroration to the paper quoted above he says: "Insiders and Outsiders in
the domain of knowledge, unite! You have nothing to lose but your claims.
You have a world of understanding to win" (44). Researchers and scholars
in women's studies stand ready to answer his call. It might happen one day
when the brightest doctoral candidate in the department asks if he can do

his dissertation on a feminist-oriented topic and his mentor realizes that his usual down-putting, discouraging remarks—about how bad it would be for his career if he did write on a feminist-oriented topic—fall on uncomprehending, if not incredulous, ears.[29] And that he is going to have to run fast to keep up with the oncoming generation.

NOTES

1. I did, however, illustrate how contributions by women were discriminated against by journal editors in the case of a young German woman. "There was a young girl of nineteen in a small town of north Germany with a strong bent for research, but when her brother went to the University of Goettingen she, according to the customs of her country, remained at home. Agnes Pockels had observed the streaming of currents when salts were put into solution and, by attaching a float to a balance, had found that salts increased the pull of the surface of the fluid. In other words, she had discovered surface tension. This was in 1881. She did not know whether anyone else had ever observed this phenomenon, but, through her brother, she brought her work to the attention of the Professor of Physics at Goettingen. It was, however, new and he failed to grasp its significance. For ten years she went on studying the properties of solutions quite alone in her own home. Then the renowned English physicist, Lord Rayleigh, began to publish on this subject, and so she wrote to him about her work. With a fine sense of honour he sent a translation of her letter to the English journal, *Nature*, asking that it be published. He wrote that the first part of her letter covered nearly the same ground as his own recent work and that with very 'homely appliances' she had arrived at valuable results. . . . Then for a few years he arranged for the publication of all of her work in English, until the Germany of another era (1898) was proud to accept her discoveries for publication in her own language" (Sabin, 1935, 69). This "gatekeeping" effect on women's studies is the theme of a special issue of *Women's Studies International Forum*, 6, no. 5, 1983.

2. I am going to use the term "women's studies" as a singular noun, as a convenient term for all the feminist research and scholarship triggered by the current feminist movement. It may include the work of male authors, of course, if the orientation is a feminist one. Or not include female authors if the orientation of their work is non- or antifeminist in perspective.

3. Indiana University was the first institution to introduce a whole course devoted exclusively to sociology (Bernard, 1929, 12).

4. As Japan, allegedly, now "buries" us in some areas of production.

5. We are far from achieving this goal as yet. In publishers' catalogs the number of books dealing with women is impressive but far from impressive outside of women's studies lists. Many MSS. do not therefore reach the readership that would appreciate having them. A growing number of small feminist presses offer channels for the publication of feminist work not acceptable to mainstream publishers.

6. It was disappointing to this author that as late as 1979 an entire issue of the *British Journal of Sociology* dealing with stratification ignored gender. Again, an enormous grant had been given for a study of women and underachievement which was based on a sample of employers (79).

7. The impact of women's studies on government policy, on legislation, on court decisions, on popular culture, on the temper of the times, on public attitudes has been important. A considerable body of literature has grown up dealing with it. No doubt some scholar will soon give us a compendium of these impacts.

8. In 1902 "social reform" was by far the most widely accepted subject in

sociology departments. In 1907–1908 "social problems" was the third most common out of 337; in 1910 "practical" courses (including problems, charity, philanthropy, criminology) were third or fourth out of 145. In the *American Journal of Sociology*, articles on "social pathology" peaked in the first decade of the century. Among research projects engaged in by sociologists in 1927, those dealing with applied topics were sixth out of 17 subjects among 259 sociologists (Bernard, 1929).

9. Some of them were interested in urban service also, such as nutritional education and public kitchens.

10. Ellen Swallow Richards, with a doctorate from MIT, was proudly non-feministic: "Perhaps the fact that I am not a Radical or a believer in the all powerful ballot for women to right her wrongs and that I do not scorn womanly duties, but claim it as a privilege to clean up and sort of supervise the room and sew things, etc., is winning me stronger allies than anything else. Even Professor A. accords me his sanction when I sew his papers. . . . Last night Professor B. found me useful to mend his suspenders. . . . So they can't say *study* spoils me for anything else" (Carolyn Louisa Hunt, 1958, 1–2).

11. R. E. Park in particular used the so-called Hull House maps (Deegan and Burger, 1981).

12. Breckinridge, for example, who was a strong activist in women's movements and an officer in the National American Woman Suffrage Association, insisted on the importance of economic equality as well as the suffrage. "She consistently supported women's trade unions, and as a lawyer she helped draft bills regulating the wages and hours of women's employment. With Jane Addams, she was partly responsible for the progressive party's endorsement of these issues in 1912" (Lasch, 1971).

13. The women who taught these courses to generations of students were powerful influences in the federal government during the early years of the century, activists as well as academicians.

14. The recipients of the "goodism" came in time to include corporations, businesses, and government agencies.

15. Much of the thinking behind the poverty programs of the 1960s was based on sociological research analyses.

16. But not by Charlotte Perkins Gilman, a currently resuscitated feminist heroine who felt all women should honor Ward for his gynecocentric theory. "Nothing more important to women has ever been given to the world" (Chugerman, 379). She dedicated her own book, *The Man-Made World* (1911) to Ward as follows: "To Lester F. Ward, sociologist and humanitarian, one of the world's great men; a creative thinker to whose wide knowledge and power of vision we are indebted for a new grasp of the nature and processes of society, and to whom all women are especially bound in honour and gratitude for his gynaecocentric theory of life, than which nothing more important to humanity has been advanced since the theory of evolution, and nothing more important to women has ever been given to the world" (Chugerman, 379).

17. Ward was not wholly consistent in his position with respect to women. In one place he speaks of the "vast, complementary forces which woman alone can yield," but also of a kind of androgyny: "If women were the recognized social equals of men, we should see a very different state of society from that which now exists. . . . men and women wearing nearly or quite the same kind of dress. . . . performing substantially the same duties . . . past-times, recreations and pleasures. If the equality of the sexes were recognized, we should see both sexes educated alike . . . both accorded the same rights, not only in political affairs. Under the head of rights may be ranged all the sexual inequalities, still higher rights" (1903, I:657, 650–55). His statement of "the right to themselves, the right of controlling their own persons, the possession of their own bodies" (655) sounds eerily contemporary. Compare with Lorber's "dismantling Noah's ark," below.

18. It cannot be said that Ward and his feminist perspective were sunk without a trace. In 1905 his work became the basis for a popular textbook by James Q. Dealey but even this was not enough to confer wide popularity on Ward's work. It came, in fact, to seem old-fashioned. His name continued to show up from time to time, mainly in footnotes or, if given more mention, it was usually to be refuted. It is doubtful if any graduate student today knows what Ward's gynecoentrism was all about. The reasons for his near obliteration from the sociological canon may not be irrelevant today as women's studies knocks more insistently on the establishment door.

19. The family textbook I studied as an undergraduate—Willystine Goodsell—in the early 1920s had been written in 1915 and re-issued from time to time for over a decade. It presented the radical feminist points of view then current but was careful to counterpose refutations.

20. Among the best-known examples of the "anomalies of fact"—to use Thomas Kuhn's expression—that have called for paradigm shifts in psychology are those of McClelland, in his study of achievement motivation, and Kohlberg, in his study of moral development. McClelland had found that the inclusion of women among his subjects so cluttered up his findings that he had to exclude them from his sample. Matina Horner helped to explain the anomalies by her researh showing that fear of success had to be factored into any study of achievement motivation in women. Follow-up research found that it was not fear of success that limited achievement for women but fear of success in competition with men. In their own world they were not at all fearful of success. Kohlberg also found anomalies in his study of moral development. Here, again, women as subjects muddied the findings; they acted as though they were morally "retarded," rarely if ever achieving the highest level of moral development. When Carol Gilligan looked at the moral development of women she found a quite different ethos guiding their moral decisions.

21. Rosalind Rosenberg has traced the part women psychologists played in overcoming inherited nineteenth-century concepts of the nature of female mentality (1982).

22. Ruth Dixon (1980) arrived at the same conclusion on the basis of U.S. experience in development. And so have I (1987).

23. In reply to this objection raised by a university against establishing women's studies, I once wrote: "I understand and applaud your effort to maintain breadth and scope in the courses your University offers . . . and I support such a policy. May I therefore assure you that women's studies easily meet the specifications of breadth and scope in a large number of universities both here and abroad. The very nature of history has been influenced by the work of both men and women scholars who have given us new insights into our past, often ignored in the past. Economists are enlarging their perspective in the light of the research done in women's studies. The political structure of our society is being re-viewed by political scientists under the influence of suffrage and other political movements as researched and analyzed by modern scholars. My own discipline is expanding its boundaries, more and more incorporating materials once ignored and finding that they greatly enrich its store of knowledge. . ." (Sept. 22, 1982).

24. In reply to this objection I reminded one chair that Washington was filled with Ivy League faculty members "being political."

25. The issue of methodology was not limited to gender preferences. As early as 1921 a major sociology textbook was noting that "the best studies of family life at present are in fiction, not in . . . sociological literature" (Park and Burgess, 216). The so-called case method flourished for a long time. The 1920s introduced the new measurement techniques developed by psychologists and taken over by sociologists as well as new statistical methods taken over from economists and biostatisticians. A great cult of objectivity arose. Still, there remained a so-called "qualitative" approach to methodology, the "communal," which contrasted with the

"agentic," the first preferred by women researchers, the second, by men (Carlson, 1972, 17–32).

26. This may be a good year to review Merton's concept of the sociological euphemism. When a missile is a Peacemaker and tax increases are revenue enhancers, why shouldn't a deserted or abandoned woman be a displaced homemaker? When, because we are dealing with very large numbers, a politician calls insignificant a difference that means that thousands of children or old people are going hungry, cold, or homeless, the pain is wiped out. We can turn our eyes away.

27. There is already a Woman's New World Dictionary, published by Know, Inc., and in 1985 Routledge and Kegan Paul published A Feminist Dictionary. Among the words that have been needed: misandrism, "hatred of men." The term may also mean refusal to suppress evidence of one's experience with men, or a woman's defense against fear and pain, or an acceptable attitude in a sexist world (Smith, 1983).

28. In a restricted market there is a tendency for young scholars to stick to safe and narrow topics. And Alice Rossi reminds us that sooner or later the American Sociological Association will have to face the fact that our profession has "crested" in terms of numerical size (1983, 3). Fewer young scholars will wish to take the risk of choosing new areas of research. Still, how many books, articles, conferences, colloquia, seminars can we continue to devote to Weber? even Durkheim? How many times can we restore Parsons and tear him down again? The great masters were, in effect, writing about the great sociological "news" of their time. The great sociological "news" today is the breakdown of one great system and the creation of another. Women's studies is reporting that "news."

29. One English major said "she had switched to women's studies after her English professor had rebuffed as 'inappropriate' her efforts to discuss the status of women in the work of Virginia Woolf" (Goodman, 56). Another young woman was not so brave. She gave up her project on women's friendships when she was chided for choosing such a trivial subject.

REFERENCES

Baber, Roy E. 1939 (1953). Marriage and the Family. New York: McGraw-Hill.

Bernard, Jessie. 1929. "The History and Prospects of Sociology in the United States." In Trends in American Sociology. Edited by George A. Lundberg, Read Bain, and Nels Anderson. New York: Harper.

———. 1964. Academic Women. University Park: Pennsylvania State University Press.

———. 1971. Women and the Public Interest. Chicago: Aldine.

———. 1981. The Female World. New York: Free Press.

———. 1987. The Female World from a Global Perspective. Bloomington: Indiana University Press.

———. See L. L. Bernard.

Bernard, L. L. and Jessie Bernard. 1942. Origins of American Sociology. New York: Thomas Y. Crowell.

Burger, John S. See Mary Jo Deegan.

Burgess, E. W. See Robert E. Park.

Carlson, Rae. 1972. "Understanding Women: Implications for Personality Theory and Research." Journal of Social Issues 28:17–32.

Cavan, Ruth Shonle. 1963. The American Family. New York: Thomas Y. Crowell.

Chugerman, Samuel. 1939. Lester F. Ward, The American Aristotle. Durham, N.C.: Duke University Press, 1965.

Clark, Kenneth. 1965. Dark Ghetto. New York: Harper & Row.

Davis, Kingsley. 1949. *Human Society.* New York: Macmillan.

Deegan, Mary Jo. 1978. "Women and Sociology: 1890–1930." *Journal of History of Sociology* 1(no. 1):11–34.

———. 1981. "Early Women Sociologists and the American Sociological Society: The Patterns of Exclusion and Participation." *American Sociologist* 16:14–24.

——— and John S. Burger. 1981. "W. I. Thomas and Social Reform: His Work and Writings." *Journal of History of the Behavioral Sciences* 17:114–25.

Degler, Carl. 1982. *At Odds.* New York: Oxford University Press.

Dixon, Ruth B. 1980. *Assessing the Impact of Development Projects on Women.* Washington, D.C.: Office of Women in Development.

Fiske, Edward B. 1981. "Women's Research Challenges Long-Held Beliefs." *Washington Post*, Nov. 23.

Folsom, Joseph Kirk. 1943. *The Family and Democratic Society.* New York: Wiley.

Gilligan, Carol. 1982. *In a Different Voice.* Cambridge: Harvard University Press.

Gilman, Charlotte Perkins. 1911. *The Man-Made World, or Our Androcentric Culture.* New York: Charlton.

Goode, William J. 1982. "Why Men Resist." In *Rethinking the Family, Some Feminist Questions.* Edited by Barrie Thorne with Marilyn Yalom. New York: Longman.

Goodman, Walter. 1984. "Women's Studies: The Debate Continues." *New York Times Magazine*, April 22.

Goodsell, Willystine. 1914. *A History of the Family.* New York: Macmillan.

Groves, Ernest R. 1934. *The American Family.* New York: Lippincott.

Hochschild, Arlie Russell. 1983. *The Managed Heart, Commercialization of Human Feeling.* Berkeley: University of California Press.

Howe, Florence. 1983. "Women and Higher Education: A Case Study of Feminist Research." *Comment* 14 (May).

Hunt, Carolyn Louisa. 1958. *The Life of Ellen S. Richards.* Washington, D.C.: American Home Economics Association.

Jacklin, Carol Nagy. See Eleanor Emmons Maccoby.

Kephart, William. 1961. *The Family, Society and the Individual.* Boston: Houghton-Mifflin.

Kuhn, Thomas. 1970. *The Structure of Scientific Revolutions.* Chicago: University of Chicago Press.

Lasch, Christopher. 1971. "Sophonisba Breckinridge." In *Notable American Women 1607–1950, A Biographical Dictionary.* Edited by Edward T. James. Cambridge: Harvard University Press.

Lipman-Blumen, Jean. 1984. *Gender Roles and Power.* Englewood Cliffs, N.J.: Prentice-Hall.

Lorber, Judith. 1981. "Minimalist & Maximalist Feminism," *Quarterly Journal of Ideology* 5 (no. 3, Fall):61–66.

———. 1986. "Dismantling Noah's Ark." *Sex Roles* 14 (nos. 11/12):567–80.

Lundberg, George A. 1929. "The Logic of Sociology and Social Research." In *Trends in American Sociology.* Edited by George A. Lundberg, Read Bain, and Nels Anderson. New York: Harper.

Maccoby, Eleanor Emmons and Carol Nagy Jacklin. 1974. *The Psychology of Sex Differences.* Stanford: Stanford University Press.

Merton, Robert K. 1972. "Insiders and Outsiders: A Chapter in the Sociology of Knowledge." *American Journal of Sociology* 78:9–47.

Minnich, Elizabeth K. 1983. "Equity and Beyond." *Comment* 14 (May).

Park, Robert E. and E. W. Burgess. 1921. *Introduction to the Science of Sociology.* Chicago: University of Chicago Press.

Parsons, Talcott. 1959. "The Social Structure of the Family." In *The Family: Its Function and Destiny.* Edited by Ruth Nanda Anshen. New York: Harper.

Pope, Christie. 1983. Personal letter, Dec. 13.

Riesman, David. 1964. Introduction to *Academic Women* by Jessie Bernard.

Rosenberg, Rosalind. 1982. *Beyond Separate Spheres, Intellectual Roots of Modern Feminism.* New Haven: Yale University Press.

Rossi, Alice. 1983. "Size of Profession May Have Crested." *Footnotes* 11 (Dec.).

Schulenburg, Jane Tibbetts. 1979. "Clio's European Daughters: Myopic Modes of Perception." In *The Prism of Sex.* Edited by Julia A. Sherman and Evelyn Torton Beck. Madison, Wis.: University of Wisconsin Press.

Schwendinger, Herman and Julia R. Schwendinger. 1974. *The Sociologists of the Chair. A Radical Analysis of North American Sociology 1883–1922.* New York: Basic Books.

Smith, Barbara. 1983. "We Need a Better Vocabulary." *New Directions for Women* 15 (Sept.–Oct.).

Stacey, Judith and Barrie Thorne. 1985. "The Missing Feminist Revolution in Sociology." *Social Problems* 32:301–16.

Stimpson, Catherine R. 1982. Paper presented at American Sociological Association meetings, San Francisco.

———. 1983. "Our Search and Research: The Study of Women Since 1969." *Comment* 14 (May).

Thorne, Barrie. See Judith Stacey.

Tyler, Leona. 1968. "Sex Differences." *International Encyclopedia of the Social Sciences.* New York: Macmillan.

Volkhart, E. H. 1968. "W. I. Thomas." *International Encyclopedia of the Social Sciences.* New York: Macmillan.

Ward, Lester Frank. 1906. *Applied Sociology, A Treatise on the Conscious Improvement of Society by Society.* Boston: Ginn & Company.

———. 1883. *Dynamic Sociology.* New York: Appleton.

WOMEN, MEN, THEORIES, AND LITERATURE

Carolyn G. Heilbrun

Let me begin with a confession, since it is the quickest way to annunciate a problem alive to most of us who teach English. In addition to being a professor of English literature at Columbia University, I write what is known as popular literature. Personally, I find this nomenclature disheartening: if there is a professional Association of Popular Culture (and, indeed, there is one), does that mean that most of us are, in the work to which we have devoted our lives, engaged in unpopular culture? The *CEA Critic*, a publication of the College English Association, ran an article that asked forthrightly, "Masterpieces or Garbage"?[1] The implication, as we need no deconstructionist to tell us, is that our choice is between teaching masterpieces, which no one reads except under duress, or teaching garbage, an enterprise drearily self-explanatory. It is, however, as both a teacher of masterpieces and a producer of "garbage" that I tell the following anecdote.

An evening class in popular culture—to be more exact, in the detective novel—somewhere on the West Coast (exactly where I do not know, for reasons that will soon become clear) held its final session and voted on its favorite novel. They determined (this is clearly one of the advantages of popular culture) that they would call up the author of their favorite work. Amazed as I was to hear from them, I was even more amazed to discover that their classroom boasted a telephone connected for long-distance dialing. (I have been a full professor for nearly a decade, but Columbia allows me only local calls.) They called as my husband and I were, in our decorous way, retiring at midnight. I am not certain whether the authors of popular culture are expected to stay up all night as a regular thing or whether the class had rather lost track of the nation's time zones. In fact, so astonished was I that I should have believed I had dreamed the whole thing had my husband not been there. We have been married a long time, but we do not yet dream the same dreams.

Since I am a literary type, two quotations immediately came to mind

when I had hung up. The first is from a speech J. Hillis Miller delivered in
1979 at an ADE seminar:

> I believe in the established canon of English and American literature and in
> the validity of the concept of privileged texts. I think it is more important to
> read Spenser, Shakespeare, or Milton than to read Borges in translation, or
> even, to say the truth, to read Virginia Woolf.[2]

What he would think of reading Heilbrun I hardly dare contemplate.

The second quotation is from popular culture, Salinger's *Catcher in the
Rye*, to be exact. The young hero explains:

> I read a lot of classical books, like *The Return of the Native* and all, and I like
> them. . . . What really knocks me out is a book that, when you're all done
> reading it, you wish the author that wrote it was a terrific friend of yours and
> you could call him up on the phone whenever you felt like it. That doesn't
> happen much though.   (p. 25)

Torn as I am between my devotion, as teacher, to masterpieces and my
pleasure at the vitality of a popular-culture class that telephones an author,
I do not think the choice before us, if we wish to bring excitement back to
the classroom, is so violent a one as opting for "garbage." Inhibited by
more than time zones, we may be unable as well as unwilling to telephone
our favorite authors; yet we can, I believe, restore excitement to the classroom if we bring to bear on "masterpieces" the insights of critics who, in
Stanley Fish's words, "challenge the assumptions within which ordinary
practices go on."[3] I shall argue, moreover, that feminist criticism—whether
practiced by women or, as is increasingly the case, by men—is probably the
most powerful challenge to ordinary practice now at hand.

Let me begin with a book by Robert Kiely, professor of English at
Harvard. He is discussing three stories: "The Dead," by Joyce; "The
Shadow in the Rose Garden," by Lawrence; and "The Legacy," by Woolf. In
each story, Kiely tells us, "an apparently happy and ordinary marriage
undergoes a sudden and violent rupture." He continues:

> The story of marriage becomes an entirely different matter for the modern
> writer when he begins to treat it as a plot with two authors. . . . Plot defined
> as the anticipated design of a single imagination seems no more appropriate
> than marriage defined in a similarly rigid and single-minded fashion. The
> husbands in the three stories are "obtuse" narrators of marriage plots over
> which they ultimately discover they have only limited control. The story has
> been lived simultaneously by wives with chapters in mind that the husbands
> have not even begun to imagine. The crisis occurs when "texts" of the two
> marriage plots are brought together. There is no *corpus delicti*, no naked

intruder under the marriage bed to be thrashed or chased trouserless out of the window. The confrontation is a verbal one, a clash not of events but of languages that have derived from differing situations and fail to merge.[4]

I need hardly point out to you that the idea of two "texts" in marriage sounds like the latest in feminist criticism or psychology. And so it is. Some years ago Jessie Bernard revealed that, if you talk to both partners in a marriage, instead of only the one who knows she is in trouble, you discover that there is not one marriage but two: his and hers. They do not agree even on what we have fondly thought to be facts: where money is spent, how often they make love, how often they converse, and about what (*The Future of Marriage* [New York: World, 1972]). Kiely may not have heard of Jessie Bernard and all her works; he is writing of three authors of masterpieces he has loved and read and taught since his graduate school days. Yet he is asking the same critical questions currently being raised with such exciting effect by feminist writers and teachers.

Let us now turn to another contemporary critic, Tony Tanner, in *Adultery in the Novel* (Baltimore: Johns Hopkins University Press, 1979). In the passage I want to consider, Tanner begins by quoting the New Testament story of the woman taken in adultery. He continues:

> The scribes and Pharisees (society in this context) set up a situation in which the woman is brought forward as a classified object to be looked at and talked about; they have depersonalized her (a woman taken in adultery) and reified her (she is "set" in the midst). Christ refuses to look and, initially, refuses to talk. That is, he refuses to participate in this purely specular attitude to the woman and to discuss her as a category. By doing this he restores the full existential reality to the situation that society seeks to deny. By treating the woman as spectacle and category, the representatives of society attempt to alienate her from her own being and to separate themselves from her by adopting the role of being the community from which the woman by her offense has isolated herself. Christ refuses to participate in their discourse, and when he does speak it is to them directly. This has two effects. It thrusts them back into their own interiority (they are "convicted by their own conscience"), and it dissolves the group identity within which they have concealed themselves.
>
> In this way Christ disperses the social stare that petrifies the wrongdoer, just as he uncongeals the legal language that seeks to imprison her in a category. . . . This is a subtler act than driving out the moneylenders, for this time Christ has banished the whole language and attitude of social "accusation" from the temple. He then speaks to the woman directly, as an individual. . . . What Christ has done is enforce a reconsideration of the context in which the woman's act should be considered.   (pp. 21–22)

We may all of us, once the shock of perceiving Jesus as a feminist critic is past, agree that such a discussion is interesting and provocative, at least to those among us whom it does not make profoundly angry. But we are in trouble when this deconstruction of the canon—this placing of the woman, without punishment, outside her assigned place, this connecting of her sin with male sin—leaves the realm of discussion and enters the realm of discourse. By "discourse" I mean those exchanges within which power is actually exerted (as when Foucault states in *The Order of Things* that "every educational system is a political means of maintaining or modifying the appropriation of discourses, with the knowledge and power they bring with them.")[5] So a member of the MLA writes to Joel Conarroe, its executive director, expressing his views on a recent convention at which he was disturbed by an alleged "feminist takeover." These observations, Conarroe comments, "struck me as wondrous strange. Because feminists, after decades of not feeling welcome at the party, have set up a lively table near the middle of the room, are they suddenly dominating? Taking over? . . . That several meetings are devoted to [feminism] is surely not a sign of a takeover but an indication that this area is where energy, as well as research projects, can be found at this particular time" (*MLA Newsletter*, Spring 1980, p. 2).

My point is easily taken. With such discourse we may be in trouble, but we have also brought excitement back into the classroom, and not, let me add, by discussing detective novels or science fiction. Indeed, the struggle between the more theoretical critics and the old-style humanists like the man who wrote to Joel Conarroe has reached, for an academic contest, the status of the world series. But let Geoffrey Hartman describe the situation:

> In the past few years . . . a new battlefront has emerged. Critics, whether journalists or academics, send their wit and vocabularies charging against "deconstruction," "structuralism," "revisionism," and other foreign-sounding heresies. The sudden blaze of attention as when a war first breaks out, has even reached America's favorite parlor game, "The Dick Cavett Show," which devoted two of its recent sessions to literary criticism. . . . Now people are fighting about criticism . . . as if there were a politics of that subject too. One critic, Gerald Graff, has taken on the so-called Yale school no fewer than four times . . . ; an Australian critic emblazons his essay in *The London Review of Books* with the title "The Deconstruction Gang"; Alfred Kazin [in *The New Republic*] deplores "the triumph of deconstructionism" . . . while William Pritchard, in *Hudson Review*, talks of a "hermeneutical mafia" that contaminates good English prose. . . . In England literary theory has become the focus of a heated public debate. "Structuralism and Dry Rot" was the headline of an attack in *The Observer*.[6]

Hartman goes on to comment on the whole situation, but I want to extract only one further sentence from his argument: "Marxism, struc-

turalism, psychoanalysis, deconstruction—all regard language as a powerful and complex social force that limits or even undermines the autonomy
of the individual." The word "feminism" is notable by its absence. Yet not
even Hartman would deny that language has been a powerful social force,
male, that undermines the autonomy of the individual, female. He just
feels awkward with aspects of feminist criticism that lead to what he has
called, in another connection, "the gendrification of literature" ("Shake-
speare Gendrified," *New York Times Book Review,* 22 March 1981, pp. 11, 18–
19).

If we retreat for a moment from Geoffrey Hartman to structuralism, we
find ourselves with the linguistic model of Lévi-Strauss, which accounts for
"social reality within the framework of a general theory of communication.
Kinships and marriage rules ensure the 'exchange' of women between
groups, as economic rules ensure the circulation of goods, and linguistic
rules that of messages."[7] What is the feminist response to this? I quote from
an article by Nancy K. Miller entitled "Emphasis Added: Plots and Plau-
sibilities in Women's Fiction," which appeared in *PMLA* (96, 1 [Jan. 1981],
3). Women writers, she tells us, are writers whose texts manifest themselves as fantasies within another economy:

> In this economy, egoistic desires would assert themselves paratactically
> alongside erotic ones. The repressed content, I think, would be, not erotic
> impulses, but an impulse to power: a fantasy of power that would revise the
> social grammar in which women are never defined as subjects; a fantasy of
> power that disdains a sexual exchange in which women can participate only
> as objects of circulation.

What we discover is that women who have been the objects circulated
wish now to become themselves subjects, themselves enabled to use circulation rather than be circulated. Let me put this another way, since Nancy
Miller, with whom I teach (more about that in a moment), is a semiotician
with an extended vocabulary, and I am a humanist generally given to
standard if not basic English. As human beings we all make fictions of our
lives, those of us who write books, or read them, and those who tell only
ourselves the stories of the lives we shall lead. But that fiction has already
been inscribed for women; they are to be married, to be circulated, to
mediate between the man and his desire for a son, between male groups.
In most French novels, for example, women's destiny encompasses two
possible destinations, which Nancy Miller has called the euphoric and the
dysphoric; that is, marriage or death.[8] The erotic destiny is all there is.

In England male novelists, almost from the beginning, began to imagine
fictions of women as opposed to the stories of male adventures: so in-

scribed, might the fictions of women yet reveal more exciting texts than the male fictions offered? Samuel Richardson thought so, as did many of his famous followers of both sexes. The English novel, having discovered female fictions, seldom deserted them: from Thackeray to Wilkie Collins, to Meredith and Gissing, through Henry James, Hardy, and Lawrence, to E. M. Forster and Angus Wilson, English male writers, as I have mentioned elsewhere, found the female destiny more challenging than the male. Not only women writers—Nancy Miller is writing of French literature, where only women writers indulged in "a fantasy in another economy"—but men also began to write of women who erupted out of the economy of female circulation. Those of us who study modern British literature need not pause to validate feminist criticism. We have only to recognize what we have been doing.

I have recently taught two courses with Nancy Miller, a product of Columbia's Department of French and Romance Philology. As its austere title suggests, that department is the place of linguistic metacritics at their most esoteric. Miller, trained by the master, Michael Riffaterre, has brought all those high skills and intelligence to feminist criticism. I, trained in the school of Lionel Trilling to the strains of moral realism, still echo to what Forster called "the fag end of Victorian liberalism." Into this Trilling universe I have had to learn to inject the techniques of decoding that would enable me to understand how these liberal ideas, which I still honor, established themselves. In the (to me, at least) extraordinary dialogue that took place in the seminars between Miller and me and between me and our students, the dazzling Riffaterrian skills and the Trillingesque moral choices illuminated one another. Each of us—close, perhaps, to the fag ends of our specialties—became literally, and literarily, inspired to new and exciting work. Our excitement was increased by the knowledge that the economy of male domination, when deconstructed, when submitted to poststructuralist decodings by the most dazzling practitioners, reveals woman as the vital key. Poststructuralism, indeed, has taken over the feminine as one of its major metaphors, going beyond the impasse between feminism and structuralism, challenging what Derrida has called "credulous man who, in support of his testimony, offers truth and his phallus as his own proper credentials."[9]

My recommendation for returning excitement to the classroom is, admittedly, a radical one. I am suggesting that feminism, in the intellectual as well as the political sphere, is at the very heart of a profound revolution. Those who oppose feminism are in danger, furthermore, of imitating those creationists—from Darwin's time and our own—who question the validity of evolution. Like the creationists, the opponents of feminist criticism argue as protectors of a common body of "culture" as they have known it and as it shelters them.[10]

I have come to believe that we who teach literature can learn a great deal from Darwin and from the revolutionary effect of his work. As a commentator on Darwin explains:

[the] world of 1857 was the only world a sane man, scientist or otherwise, could desire. As far as the biologists were concerned, it was a dependable world, the classical world, still, of fixed definitions. "To Aristotle," Herbert J. Muller writes, "definition was not merely a verbal process or a useful tool of thought, it was the essence of knowledge. It was the cognitive grasp of the eternal essences of Nature, a fixed, necessary form of knowing because an expression of the fixed, necessary form of Being." Into that satisfied and satisfying universe, the quiet, kindly, unassuming Charles Darwin had dropped a bomb.[11]

I believe that many of us in the humanities are today engaged in challenging a world view. We are dropping a bomb into the stable world of literary masterpieces. In the words of Thomas Kuhn, Darwin changed the paradigm under which science operated, and "when paradigms change, the world itself changes with them." Kuhn has described the change that lies before us:

Led by a new paradigm, scientists adopt new instruments and look in new places. Even more important, during revolutions scientists see new and different things when looking with familiar instruments in places they have looked before. It is rather as if the professional community had been suddenly transported to another planet where familiar objects are seen in a different light and are joined by unfamiliar ones as well. . . . In so far as their only recourse to that world is through what they see and do, we may want to say that after a revolution scientists are responding to a different world.[12]

Like Darwin, literary critics today are searching the earth for evidence of a "script" wholly unlike that written for us by the sacred literature. You will have noticed that, well over a century after Darwin, his discoveries and our right to teach them are being questioned. As Darwin himself wrote:

Although I am fully convinced of the truths given in [*The Origin of Species*], I by no means expect to convince experienced naturalists whose minds are stocked with a multitude of facts all viewed, during a long course of years, from a point of view directly opposite to mine. . . . But I look with confidence to the future,—to young and rising naturalists, who will be able to view both sides of the question with impartiality. (quoted by Kuhn, p. 151)

Max Planck would echo him years later: "a new scientific truth does not triumph by convincing its opponents and making them see the light, but rather because its opponents eventually die, and a new generation grows up that is familiar with it." (quoted by Kuhn, p. 151)

The excitement, I believe, lies in making that new generation familiar with our discoveries; in realizing that we have the chance both to read masterpieces—not, I hope, as narrowly defined as Hillis Miller wishes, but masterpieces nonetheless—and yet bring to the classroom the sense of wanting to call up the author. What Darwin can teach us is that, without acting or feeling like revolutionaries determined to overthrow the establishment, we can propose a new view of the world. Moreover, if we cease to think of the canon as creationists think of the Bible, that is to say, as a text that must be not only "privileged" but isolated and reified, we may even allow some popular and "emerging" literatures into our most conservative classrooms. We shall do so, not because we must turn to popular works as the only literature people are willing to read, but because the masterpieces have become so newly vital that they will continue to dazzle beside works more easily encountered.

NOTES

1. Donald E. Morse, "Masterpieces or Garbage: Martin Tropp and Science Fiction," in *CEA Critic*, 43, No. 3 (March 1981), p. 14.

2. J. Hillis Miller, "The Function of Rhetorical Study at the Present Time," in *The State of the Discipline, 1970s–1980s*. A Special Issue of the *ADE Bulletin*, No. 62 (Sept.–Nov. 1979), p. 12. I have taken the quotation, however, from Sandra Gilbert, "What Do Feminist Critics Want? or, A Postcard from the Volcano," *ADE Bulletin*, No. 66 (Winter 1980), pp. 16–23. This excellent article, essential to an understanding of the state of feminist criticism, is recommended to all who have not yet read it.

3. Quoted in Annette Kolodny, "Not-So-Gentle Persuasion: A Theoretical Imperative of Feminist Literary Criticism," Conference on Feminist Literary Criticism, National Humanities Center, Research Triangle Park, N.C., 27 March 1981, p. 7. The quotation is from Stanley Fish, *Is There a Text in This Class?* (Cambridge: Harvard University Press, 1980). See also Annette Kolodny, "A Map for Rereading; or, Gender and the Interpretation of Literary Texts," *New Literary History*, 9 (1980), 451–550.

4. Robert Kiely, *Beyond Egotism: The Fiction of James Joyce, Virginia Woolf, and D. H. Lawrence* (Cambridge: Harvard University Press, 1980), pp. 87, 89.

5. Quoted in Alan Sheridan, *Michel Foucault: The Will to Truth* (London: Tavistock, 1980), p. 127.

6. Geoffrey H. Hartman, "How Creative Should Literary Criticism Be?" *New York Times Book Review*, 5 April 1981, pp. 11, 24, 26.

7. Josue V. Harari, "Critical Factions/Critical Fictions," in *Textual Strategies: Perspectives in Post-Structuralist Criticism*, ed. Josue V. Harari (Ithaca: Cornell University Press, 1979), p. 19.

8. See Nancy K. Miller, *The Heroine's Text* (New York: Columbia University Press, 1980).

9. Jacques Derrida, "Becoming Woman," trans. Barbara Harlow, *Semiotext(e)*, 3, No. 1 (1978); quoted in Miller, "Emphasis Added," p. 47.

10. See the proposed Family Protection Act, as well as articles on opposition to "secular humanism," *New York Times*, 17 May 1981, Sec. A, p. 1; and Marvin Perry, "Banning a Textbook," *New York Times*, 31 May 1981, Sec. E, p. 19.

11. Philip Appleman, "Darwin: On Changing the Mind," in *Darwin*, ed. Philip Appleman (New York: Norton, 1970), p. 634.

12. Thomas S. Kuhn, *The Structure of Scientific Revolutions*, 2nd ed. (Chicago: University of Chicago Press, 1970), p. 111.

About the Authors

Barbara R. Bergmann is Professor of Economics at the University of Maryland. Former chair of the American Economic Association's Committee on the Status of Women, she has recently published *The Economic Emergence of Women*.

Jessie Bernard, now living in Washington, has written numerous articles and over a dozen books in sociology, the most recent of which is *The Female World from a Global Perspective*. An award was named in her honor by the American Sociological Association for her contributions to the field.

Ruth Bleier is Professor of Neurophysiology at the University of Wisconsin Medical School and is past director of the Women's Studies Program at Wisconsin. In addition to numerous scientific publications, she is also the author of *Science and Gender: A Critique of Biology and Its Theories on Women*.

Carol P. Christ, Visiting Lecturer at Harvard Divinity School, is Professor of Women's Studies and Religious Studies at San Jose State University. Co-chair of the Women and Religion Section of the American Academy of Religion, she co-edited *Womanspirit Rising* and has written *Diving Deep and Surfacing* and *Laughter of Aphrodite*.

Carol Gilligan is Associate Professor of Education, Graduate School of Education, Harvard, and is best known for *In a Different Voice: Psychological Theory and Women's Development*.

Carolyn G. Heilbrun, Professor of English at Columbia and past president of the Modern Language Association, is a feminist literary critic and author of numerous works, including *Toward a Recognition of Androgyny*, as well as the Amanda Cross mystery series.

Carol Nagy Jacklin, Professor of Psychology and Professor of the Program for the Study of Men and Women in Society at the University of Southern California, has written extensively on the psychology of sex differences, including the pathbreaking study with Eleanor Maccoby entitled *The Psychology of Sex Differences*.

Louise Lamphere, Professor of Anthropology at the University of New Mexico, has written extensively on the role of women from a cross-cultural perspective. She is best known for the collection she co-edited with Michelle Rosaldo, entitled *Women, Culture and Society.* Her recent research on urban working-class women appears in *From Working Daughters to Working Mothers: Immigrant Women in a New England Industrial Community.*

Nellie McKay, Associate Professor of American and Afro-American Literature at the University of Wisconsin-Madison, teaches and publishes on black writers. Her book on Jean Toomer appeared in 1984, and she is currently working on a study of black women's autobiographies and an edited collection of essays on Toni Morrison.

Virginia Sapiro, Professor of Political Science at the University of Wisconsin-Madison, is author of *The Political Integration of Women* and *Women in American Society.* She is Chair of the Women's Studies Program and served as the founding president of the American Political Science Association Organized Section on Women and Politics.

Joan Wallach Scott, Professor of Social Science, Institute for Advanced Study, has published widely in the field of women's history, including *Women, Work, and Family* (co-authored with Louise A. Tilly).